W9-CKJ-366

THE BIG BACKYARD BUILDING BOOK

—being the best of both:

THE BACKYARD BUILDING BOOK and
THE BACKYARD BUILDING BOOK II

in one busy blockbuster.

James E. Churchill

Illustrations by James E. Churchill II

Stackpole Books

Part One is Dedicated to Jolain and Trapper Jim, who have kept me building since they were born.

Part Two is dedicated to Beulah and Adolph, whom I owe more than I can ever repay.

THE BIG BACKYARD BUILDING BOOK
Copyright © 1983 by Stackpole Books

Published by
STACKPOLE BOOKS
Cameron and Kelker Streets
P.O. Box 1831
Harrisburg, Pa. 17105

TH 148 . C 627   1983   690'.89   8 3 – 6 1 2

Printed in the U.S.A.

CONTENTS

INTRODUCTION

Every homeowner wants to add to the comforts of his home and improve his property at the same time, but all too often today's sky-high building costs frustrate this ambition. The cost problem can be licked, however, and this book tells you how.

Do your kids need a place to play around the house without making a shambles of the furniture or risking their lives in the street? Then make your backyard a playground by building a Kentuck Kamp Fort, a Forest Ranger Fire Tower, an Observatory and Photography Darkroom, or a Mississippi River Barge.

Planning on having outdoor barbecues this summer but don't have an outdoor fireplace yet? No need to hire a mason to build one. The book not only tells how to install a barbecue pit in the backyard but also gives complete instructions for building a picnic table and benches to help you enjoy all that mouth-watering outdoor cooking.

Want to provide your overnight or weekend guests with luxurious accommodations at low cost? Then build them a geodesic dome, modified yurt, or screenhouse for them to stay in and an outdoor sauna bath to help them relax. And to keep guests comfortable in winter (and for your own hideaway), there is a more solid and elegant solar-heated guest house.

But people aren't the only guests you can accommodate. A wonderful variety of birdhouses will accommodate some of the most desirable guests in a backyard. There is even an apartment house for purple martins. Of course birds have to eat, so there are feeders you can easily make as well as baths to keep the feathered guests happy.

Man's best friend is not forgotten; he rates some elegant establishments, even the first — to my knowledge — doghouse with active solar heat.

Who wouldn't like to grow and enjoy his own

vegetables the year round? It's easy when you follow the instructions for building a greenhouse. You can choose the type of greenhouse best suited to your level of building skill, from a simple window greenhouse you can attach to the side of your home to an A-frame greenhouse to a full-size, conventional greenhouse.

Thinking of starting your own cottage industry, one that will bring in badly needed supplementary income in these days of inflationary prices? The possibilities offered here are enough to keep you busy. Besides selling the produce you grow in your own greenhouse, you can make furniture in your home workshop, lit by power provided by a wind generator in your handsome home-made windmill. The same chapter also tells how to fabricate a wind motor which will turn a water pump to keep a commercial fish pond open in winter or cool it in summer.

For each project described in this book the author has provided instructions sufficiently detailed to enable the homeowner with reasonable manual skills to complete it with maximum economy of time and effort. Hopefully, this publication will further the build-it-yourself trend so evident today among homeowners. City dwellers, suburbanites, and rural folks alike are finding that they save money and time and obtain a better structure if they do the work themselves.

A reader who builds all of the projects in this book should increase his estate by more than $50,000 at a cost to himself of from one-fourth to one-half that amount. This, of course, depends upon how shrewd a material buyer the reader is and where he lives. One good general tip on buying lumber is always to check more than one supplier since prices vary unbelievably.

The author does not intend to leave the reader without backup information. If at any time during the construction of any of the projects in this book a question is raised that cannot be answered by the book, just write him a letter and he will speedily make a report to you. Please enclose a stamped, addressed envelope. The author's address is:

James E. Churchill
Route #2, Box 160
Florence, Wisconsin 54121

With the help of this book you can proceed confidently in your program of home improvement, but do be careful of high places, sharp tools, and trying to do too much at one time.

PART I

The Best of **THE BACKYARD BUILDING BOOK**

Chapter 1

SIMPLE GUEST HOUSES

My brother who lives in sunny California has an overflow of house guests from the Midwest during the frigid months. In fact, he said one morning he stepped on three abdomens and a larynx getting to the bathroom. He weighs 226 pounds, and the resulting shrieks of pain convinced him that he had to find some place for his surplus guests to sleep besides the hallway. They enthusiastically agreed.

At almost the same time a cousin who lives near a Michigan ski resort had a similar problem. He said people wanted to stop over and talk to him during the skiing season that he hadn't heard from since school days and he's forty-five. However, he loves skiing and was glad to hear from all these people. Naturally, during the peak of the season his visitors cannot find a place to stay since all the commercial accommodations are sold out far in advance. They all wind up staying at good ol' Cousin Albert's place and four to twelve extra people in a two-bedroom house soon leads to strained relationships, even among good skiing companions.

Both confided these problems to me during a get-together last summer. We talked it over and a possible solution developed. Build a small house or cabin just for the guests, a guest cabin as it were.

Some obvious problems were immediately apparent here, mostly centering around finances, since these good people were still paying the mortgages on their own houses. Total costs for the building could not exceed $1000, they mentioned through tight lips. Since low-cost buildings are a favorite subject of mine, I immediately began to search out structures that would answer their desires. They both live in the suburbs and the buildings would have to be adaptable to the neighborhood; yet they wanted something distinctive.

It didn't take me too long to settle on two designs that would have possibilities, and by the time the Yule season came around I decided I would have to visit them and explain how to build these. In fact, maybe even do the actual building. Building experimental buildings when someone else pays the cost is

9

Fig. 5-1. Geodesic dome guest house.

fun. My brother opted for a geodesic dome, style 2V ³/₈, no doubt being entranced by the beautiful sketch I made of it on a shopping bag with a red crayon. With him settled into gathering the materials, I tucked my sketch of the design I selected for Cousin Albert under my arm and immediately sped to Michigan. He and his wife both went into a trance when I showed them the Mongolian yurt I drew on real writing paper with a real pencil and explained to them just how it would be constructed. Grandmother O'Connor who was staying with them was interested also. She said it looked just like an uppity outhouse. Nevertheless we proceeded.

Now, I explained to Cousin Albert that a genuine Mongolian yurt is made from small flat boards similar to the boards that we call furring strips and they cover it with material similar to felt. In fact, we perused a book called *Build A Yurt* and carefully studied the baby gate design that author Len Chorney used for

building the walls where he held furring strips together with bent nails and tied them together with cable. "Too flimsy," said Cousin Albert. "Definitely too flimsy," said his building inspector. I didn't necessarily agree but I went home and decided to try to find something else to build it with that wouldn't cost any more but would be more acceptable. In the meantime my brother called; he said bring the family, come out for a short vacation, and let's start building the dome. We left immediately.

GEODESIC DOME

The first step in building the 16-foot geodesic dome was to select a location where the finished building couldn't block his view of the valley below and wouldn't interfer with tilling his garden or use of the lawn for gatherings or games.

MATERIALS LIST FOR GEODESIC DOME

1. 36 8 × 8 × 16-inch concrete blocks
2. 10 4 × 4's, 8 feet long
3. 120 feet 2 × 6 material for floor joists
4. 200 square feet ⅝-inch exterior plywood for flooring
5. 10 12-inch 2 × 4's for base hubs
6. 8 4 × 8 sheets ⅜-inch plywood for skin
7. 2 4 × 8 sheets ¾-inch exterior plywood
8. 160 running feet of clear 2 × 4 lumber for struts
9. 40 square feet ¼-inch-thick clear plastic for windows
10. Paint and roofing material as needed

Staking Out the Perimeter

When we had the site selected, we drove a stake in the approximate center, pounded a six-penny common nail into the top of the stake, tied a string to the nail, made a knot in it at 8 feet, and walked slowly around the center stake driving other stakes every foot to outline the perimeter. It took fifty stakes to outline the perimeter and even then we had one space between stakes which was longer then the others. No matter, we said to each other, since we only want ten equally spaced points around the perimeter anyway. To find the ten points we simply took the string and stake and used it like the legs of a giant compass to find ten equally spaced marks on the circumference of the circle. We drove red-tipped stakes at these points which outlined the foundation when they were all in place. These stakes marked the exact points where the foundation blocks would be set (see Fig. 5-2).

Setting the Foundation Blocks

Next we dug down at these points to an 18-inch depth and placed three 8 × 16-inch cement blocks one on top of the other in the holes. We used a string

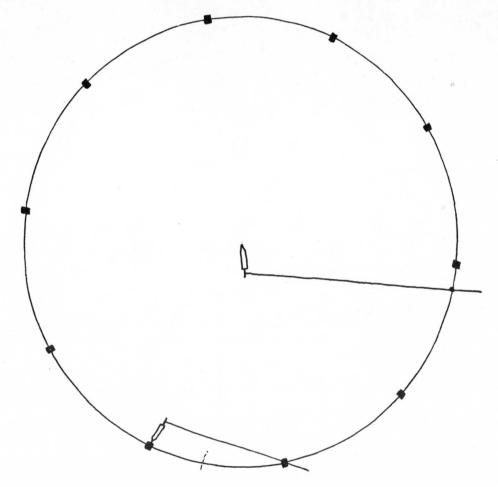

Fig. 5-2. Laying out the geodesic dome foundation.

and line level to make certain that the top surfaces of the top blocks were all even. Further, we went to the exact center of the foundation, which was the point where we had driven the original stake, and installed a double cement block foundation. Then we filled the cores of all blocks with cement. Finally, we set a $^3/_8$ × 8-inch bolt in the wet concrete in the center of each perimeter piling. When this was done, we went to the mountains trout fishing for two days while they were curing. When we got back the concrete was hardened and we could continue.

Flooring

The next step was to purchase ten 8-foot 2 × 6's which had been pressure-treated with a creosote base, decay-preventive preservative. Then $^1/_2$-inch diameter holes were drilled in the 2 × 6's, one hole in each piece so they could be placed over the bolts embedded in the concrete. These hole locations were found by laying the 2 × 6's alongside the bolts and projecting the bolt locations onto the planks with a pencil and square. With this done, the girders for the floor were in place. Next, 2 × 4's were nailed on 16-inch centers between the 2 × 6's (see Fig. 5-3). Then the flooring of $^5/_8$-inch-thick exterior grade plywood was nailed on top of the girders and joists. Here we got into a slight argument. I wanted my brother to use tongue-and-groove 2 × 6's instead of the plywood, placed in a hex pattern which would have made a beautiful floor. I did finally get Cousin Albert to use it in his yurt, but that's getting ahead of my story.

Hubs and Struts

Now that the floor was done, we sat on it and traded tall stories for most of the next day while we were planning how to form the hubs for the dome

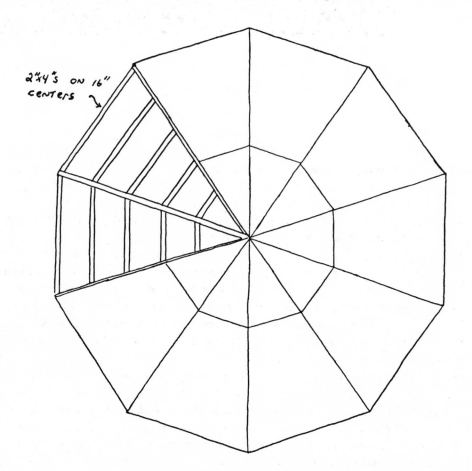

2"×4"s on 16" centers

Fig. 5-3.   Geodesic dome floor.

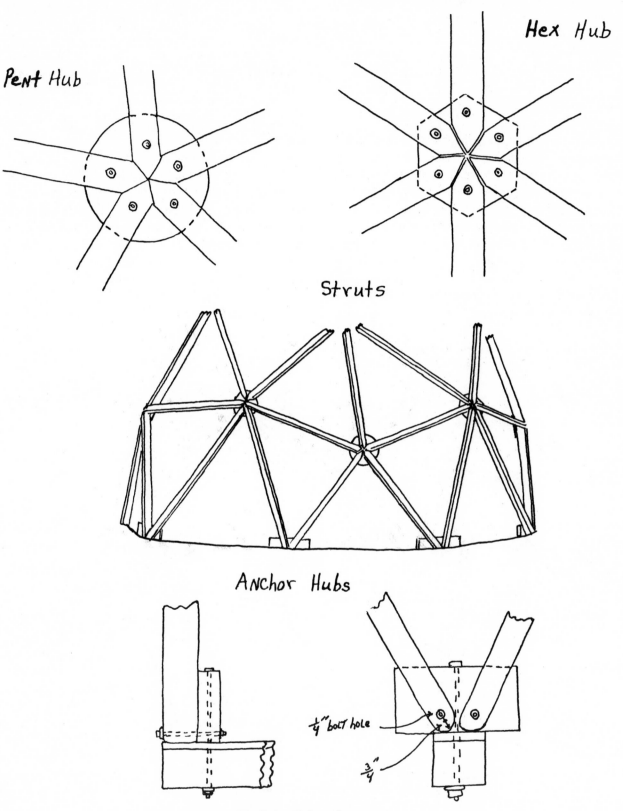

Pent Hub

Hex Hub

Struts

Anchor Hubs

¼" bolt hole

¾"

Fig. 5-4.   Hubs and struts.

framing. We finally decided to nail the base hubs to the floor and use that as a starting point. We ignored all the warnings in the various dome books about building a model first and started to work. When we were all done, I wasn't sure whether we gained or saved time that way but I suspect we gained time, since building a model is almost as hard as building the building.

The anchor hubs were made up first and nailed in position. It took ten anchor hubs. (An anchor hub is simply half of a hex hub.) We formed ours by sawing 2 × 6's into 1-foot lengths and then nailing them to the floor in ten separate evenly spaced locations 60½ inches apart, measuring on the circumference of the circle with a flexible steel tape. We didn't nail these very securely yet, since we decided they might have to be changed slightly after the struts were placed, which turned out to be the case. When all the anchor hubs were in position, we installed the first struts. They were made from 2 × 4's. It took ten 50½-inch 2 × 4's and ten 57½-inch 2 × 4's to complete the struts for the first row. They were fastened to the hubs with

¼-inch bolts, placed through the width of the strut and through the hub. This allowed them to be free to pivot. To hold them in position we just tightened the bolts so they gripped the struts. The correct angle was found by projecting half of a 4-inch circle on the hubs with a pattern. To make this pattern from cardboard draw a 4-inch circle on the cardboard. Then use the radius measurement to mark off six equally spaced circumference sections; lastly, cut the circle in half with a scissors. Naturally, a 4-inch plastic protractor would also fill the bill. Anyway, 4 inches from the center of the hub the centerlines of the struts should be separated 4 inches. At the center they should meet and rest on the floor. This requires that they be tapered at the end. Also note that one long and one short strut is fastened to each hub (see Fig. 5-4), but they alternate so that a short strut on one hub is adjacent to a short strut on the adjoining hub; likewise, the long struts are adjacent to each other on adjoining hubs. One way of thinking of this is to say each hub is either lefthand or righthand. In the correct positioning the lefthand hubs are all separated by righthand hubs.

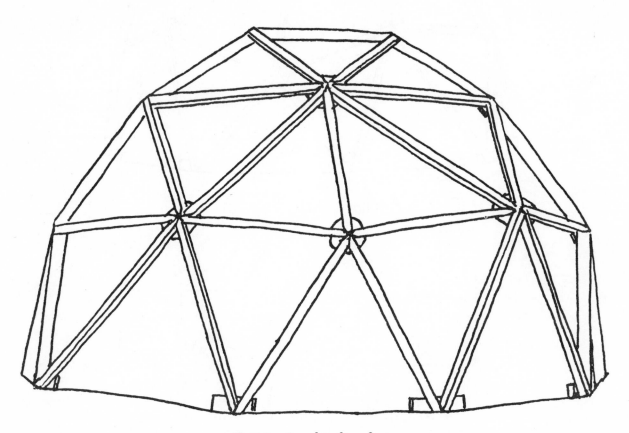

Fig. 5-5.   Complete dome frame.

When we had more or less correctly positioned all of these hubs and had the struts in place, we noticed that the upper ends of the struts all nearly touched each other. This was indeed fortunate since the next step was to install the first row of full hubs (see Fig. 5-3).

All of the remaining hubs are either full hex or pent hubs. This structure, we found, required six pent hubs and ten hex hubs. We talked it over and decided to make them from ¾-inch plywood and bolt the struts to the hubs with ¼-inch machine bolts. Accordingly, we purchased a sheet of ¾-inch exterior grade plywood, borrowed a compass, ruler, and pencil from one of my brother's daughters, and went to work. Since we needed ten pent hubs with 4-inch sides, we drew ten 4-inch diameter circles on the plywood and then, using the radius measurements of the 4-inch circle, we found six equally spaced points on the circumference of the circles and connected the lines with a straight edge. Presto. We had formed the outlines for ten hex hubs. We sawed them out with an electric saber saw and sanded the edges with a hand sander.

Next we drilled a ¼-inch hole, recessed 1 inch from the points of the hexagon. When these were done, we set them aside and made up the six pentagon hubs. After tearing our hair, wringing our hands, and threatening numerous times to junk the whole project, we finally found that a 4-inch diameter circle can be changed into an almost perfect pentagon by making marks 4¹¹/₁₆ inches apart on its circumference and connecting the lines. Deciding that there might be a slight error here, we decided not to saw pentagon shapes out at all. Instead, we just cut out 4-inch circles and made pencil marks to indicate where the struts would radiate from the center of the circle. This worked so well that we wondered in retrospect why we had gone to the trouble of sawing out the hexagon shapes for the hexagon hubs. However, after the skin was put on, the combination of hexagons and circles had a pleasing effect. In fact, one of the first things we noticed was that the struts formed a hexagon where they joined at the hexagon hubs and a pentagon where they joined at the pentagon hubs. This too was aesthetically pleasing.

When it came time to put the hubs in position on the first row of struts, we had some trouble figuring exactly where they should go. Finally we developed a method which went like this. All round (pent) hubs had short struts joined to every point, and all hex hubs had long struts going to the six o'clock and twelve o'clock positions. After that it was easy. However, for this to work out, each long and short strut must be positioned correctly on the base hubs.

Once we had the whole framework joined together, we went over it again, adjusting the struts until all the triangles were symmetrical. When they were all in place, we drove eight-penny finishing nails through the hubs into the struts. After that was done, we found we could easily chin ourselves on the frame without affecting it a bit (see Fig. 5-5).

The complete frame was a source of wonder to us and we sat around admiring it and sampling good California wine. The neighborhood children were attracted to it immediately and began climbing all over it. I noticed the champion climber of them all was a little girl who hardly looked strong enough to climb on the seat of a bicycle. No doubt a dome frame would make a welcome addition to a playground.

Covering the Frame

After a while we couldn't think of any more reasons for not proceeding; so we began thinking about the covering for the frame. Since ⅜-inch thickness exterior plywood was economical, easy to install, and readily available, we decided to use that. After studying the frame of our dome we decided we would have to cover each triangle separately since each triangle is at a slightly different attitude from every other. Simple enough, we agreed. We just measured each triangle, projected the dimensions on a sheet of plywood, and sawed them out. We also found each triangle was a slightly different size from every other; so each had to be carefully measured. Also, after the first one was made, we got the very bright idea of mortising the edges together, which eliminated the wide crack left at the top of right-angle edges. The angle we used for a mortise varied slightly, but was generally about 15 degrees. For windows we sawed out triangles of clear plastic and fitted them into the frame on opposite sides of the structure. My brother found out after he had used these windows for about a year that he couldn't keep the joints sealed; so he finally had a triangle window frame made up for it so that he could put a piece of glass in the frame.

When the frame was covered, we went over the entire skin, sealing all the seams between the joints with roofing tar. Then we were ready to start roofing.

Roofing

We had no illusions about this structure shedding rain as it was. Possibly it could have been fiberglassed to make a tight rainproof structure, but the price of this was rather forbidding. We also considered and discarded other sealing material such as asbestos roof covering, but in fact, couldn't come up with anything that was likely to beat commercial roofing.

Brother Gene finally found and used a type of asphalt shingle called Shangles. These shingles look like wood shakes but are easier to apply to the curvature of the dome than wooden shingles would be.

Installing the Door

Installing a door in a dome is simplicity in itself. You just take a piece of chalk and measure for the outline across the triangles. Make up a frame, brace the frame for the structure so it doesn't collapse when you cut out the struts, cut them out, put the frame in place, and nail them together. Before cutting, decide what sort of door you want. It, of course, has to be built out on the top so the frame will stand straight up.

When the frame was all put in place, we decided we should have just left one triangle for the door. This would have provided a unique door that retained the integrity of the frame.

When the dome was all done and we were standing back admiring it, the same little girl who was climbing on it before said, "How come you built an igloo, Mister? Huh, huh, what's the igloo for, Mister?"

A few days later the family and I left for Cousin Albert's to help him put up his yurt.

YURT

Cousin Albert, prudent soul that he is, had a model of a yurt from cardboard and was quite im-

pressed with it. He said that you should make a model of everything and he's probably right. Anyway, we laid out the foundation for his structure exactly the same way as we laid out the structure for the dome. That is, we selected the site and used a string and stake to draw around the perimeter of the circle. Then we staked it off. Things changed drastically then, however.

MATERIALS LIST FOR YURT

1. 12 10-foot poles, minimum 4-inch diameter, for foundation and side walls
2. 14 poles for floor joists, lengths to be measured in field
3. 140 square feet tongue-and-groove 2 × 6's for flooring
4. 140 square feet ⁵⁄₈-inch Celotex for insulation under floor
5. 128 running feet of 1 × 4 furring strips to reinforce the Celotex
6. 200 running feet of 1 × 4 furring strips for sheathing base
7. 12 sheets of ³⁄₈-inch plywood for sheathing
8. 96 running feet of 1 × 4 for batten strips
9. 2 windows and 1 door
10. 12 10-foot poles for rafters
11. 16 running feet of 2 × 6 for rafters reinforcement at the skylight
12. 200 square feet of roof sheathing, ⁵⁄₈-inch plywood or equivalent
13. Shingles to cover the roof
14. 18-inch diameter ¹⁄₄-inch acrylic plastic skylight
15. Lumber to partition the interior as desired
16. Interior furnishings, electric lines, plumbing, etc.

While we had been in California, Cousin Albert had been busy scheming. With his model as a guide he had developed a foundation frame combination based on wooden poles which are easily available in Michigan. After studying his sketch I wholeheartedly agreed with his ideas and we went to work.

Foundation and Side Wall Framing

The poles that we used for Cousin Albert's yurt had to be sunk in the ground 3 feet (see Fig. 5-6), extend 7 feet above the ground, and be no less than 4 inches in diameter on the small end. This, of course, took 10-foot poles that tapered very little. Fortunately, Cousin Albert had a country place with a stand of

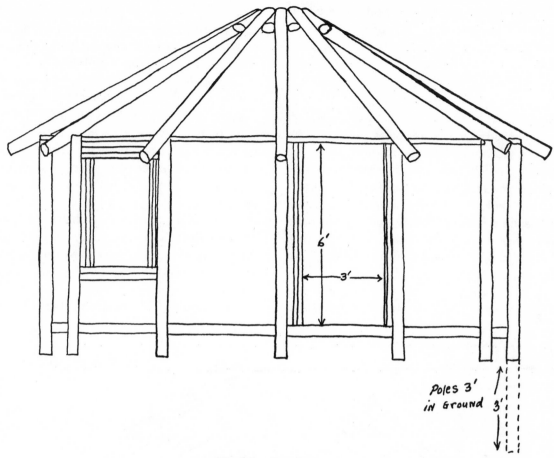

Poles 3'
in Ground 3'

Fig. 5-6. Yurt frame.

white cedar that could be utilized. We cut, peeled, let dry, and treated twelve of these poles before we started the actual building. The first 4 feet of the butt of the poles were treated with creosote; the remaining part with a commercial waterproof preservative. Probably if a person had to buy these poles, he would be better off to use something else belowground, such as concrete blocks. The postholes were back-filled with tamped concrete instead of dirt. We made sure each post was exactly straight up and down before the concrete hardened by laying a carpenter's level on two opposite sides of each pole. When the concrete did harden, we sawed all the posts off level at exactly 6 feet, 6 inches aboveground by using a chalk line and a line level to measure from one pattern post to all the rest. Once the correct level was found, we sawed each post off square by leveling and nailing a board on each side of the post and sawing directly above the boards.

Electricity and Plumbing

When this was all done we had the foundation and framing for the side walls complete. Next we had to bring the electricity and plumbing up to the floor. Working under the floor would be difficult since we left only a 6-inch crawl space.

We brought electricity to the yurt by tapping into the house entrance electrical box and bringing a new 30-amp, 110-volt circuit underground to our project. As an added precaution we installed a grounded fuse box in the yurt when we finished the wiring. The plumbing drains were connected to a 6-inch sewer pipe that was eventually connected to the house septic system above the septic tank. This, of course, posed no additional strain on the septic system since if the guests were in the main house they would be using practically the same amount of water which would end up in the same septic tank anyway. The water line was buried in the same trench with the electric line. When we had the work done which would have to be done under the floor, we proceeded to install the floor.

Floor

Since Albert had a woodlot that would yield an almost unlimited supply of free poles, we elected for economy's sake to use poles for the floor joists. The upper surfaces of the poles would be kept level by using a chain saw and chain saw guide to saw a flat surface on each pole. Another characteristic of our floor that made this possible was that we were going to use tongue-and-groove 2 × 6's for the finished flooring. Tongue-and-groove 2 × 6's can span 4 feet, so we would not have to place floor joists every 16 inches as is common. We used 4-inch minimum diameter peeled white cedar posts notched into the side wall

posts and nailed to them. We bridged from each side wall post to its opposite on the opposing wall, alternating the butts with the exception of the midcircumference posts, which were joined by poles placed at right angles to the rest (see Fig. 5-7). An additional row of short posts was placed at the centerline. As we installed each pair of poles we nailed 4 × 8 sheets of ⁵/₈-inch-thick Celotex across the bottom surface of the poles. This had to be done as we went along since we couldn't crawl under the yurt after it was done. The Celotex was reinforced with 1 × 4 lumber furring strips placed across it at 4-foot intervals. We placed sheets of aluminum foil vapor barrier on top of the Celotex between the poles but we added no filler. Albert reports that the dead air space this produced was a very good insulator and the floor is never cold for his skiing guests.

Prospective builders who might not have access

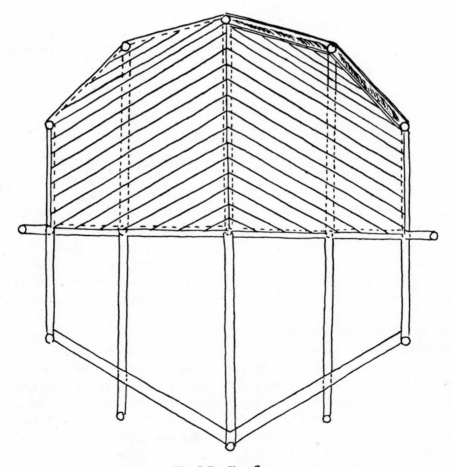

Fig. 5-7. Yurt floor.

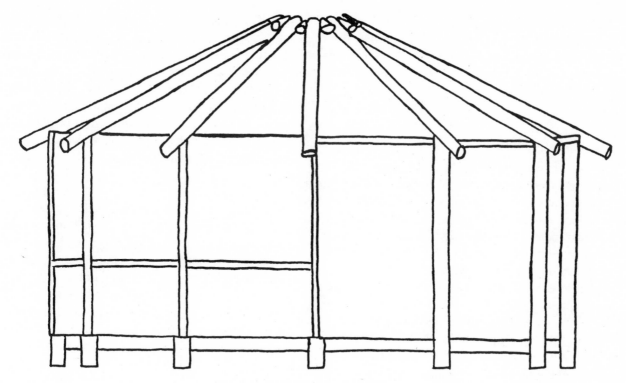

Fig. 5-8. Yurt frame with sheathing.

to poles can make their floor joists from 2 × 8's or 4 × 4's and utilize the same spacing if they use tongue-and-groove 2-inch lumber for the flooring.

The 2 × 6's were put down in a hexagon pattern starting from the outside. When they were all in place, we nailed them down, sanded the upper surface, filled all the nicks, sanded the surface again, and put on a coat of wood filler. It would be varnished with three coats of a good deck varnish at a later date.

Sheathing

When the floor was in place, we started thinking about the side walls. Since the poles we used for the side walls were not quite evenly dimensioned, we had a choice of shaving or sawing the outer surfaces of the poles so they would be symmetrical or nailing milled lumber furring strips to them. This process commonly called "furring out" was what we eventually used. It consisted of nailing a furring strip to the center of the pole so that the sheeting could be nailed to a flat surface.

We considered several types of sheathing before deciding on ³/₈-inch exterior grade plywood as the best for our purpose. Before we nailed the plywood to the poles, however, we lined the wall with 15-pound builder's felt, over-lapping the edges 3 inches, and stapling the felt to the poles after pulling it tight. See Figure 5-8.

Next we nailed on the sheathing, utilizing the horizontal method of nailing the sheets on with the full sheet on top. We used ³/₈-inch plywood since it is flexible enough to be bent around this radius. After the plywood was all nailed on, the joints were filled with caulking compound and 1 × 4 batten boards were nailed over the cracks. No additional siding was used; instead, the plywood and batten boards were painted with three coats of oil base cabin paint.

Windows

On the southwest and east walls windows were framed in with 2 × 4's. The windows we used had rough openings 2 feet 4 inches by 3 feet 6 inches. We used double-hung type windows with the sills, etc. already built for them. This saved considerable time but we were not fully satisfied with the appearance of these windows after the project was completed, and we felt we could have done better by installing fixed glass sandwiched between strips of 1 × 4 in the window frames and then depended upon the door and skylight for ventilation.

Framing the Door

We framed the door into the west wall. It measured 5 feet 11 inches by 36 inches and required a rough opening 72 by 38 inches. To frame the door into place, nail a 6-foot 2 × 6 to the inside surfaces of the two poles that the door would be located between. Across the tops of the 2 × 6's nail a 4-foot 2 × 6. Next measure the opening and place a third upright 2 × 6 to narrow the space to 37 inches. Use twenty-penny spikes to nail the 2 × 6's to the poles and sixteen-penny nails to nail the sections of 2 × 6 together. Now the opening for the door is framed. Usually it is advisable not to hang the door until all of the rest of the building, including bringing in the appliances, is complete. Knowing this, we left it out.

Installing the Roof Rafters

Once the above steps were completed, we had the building almost enclosed. The next step was to install the roof rafters. Again, since poles were easy to obtain, we decided to use poles for the rafters. Since we desired to have an opening in the center of the roof, which is conventional with the yurt, our poles did not need to reach clear to the center. In fact, after laying the angles out on paper we discovered that we wanted to have an 18-inch opening for the skylight and that we wanted the peak of the roof to be 10 feet from the floor. This would require the rafters to be 9 feet 7½ inches long. One foot of this length would be overhang in order to provide a wide eave, important to the overall appearance, and to prevent rain or snow from running down the side of the building from the roof.

Each rafter had to be custom-made, although we started with as near the same diameter poles as we could obtain. Using milled 2 × 4's, of course, would have been much simpler. The first step in making the roof was to find some way all the rafters could be held up on the unsupported ends until they would be nailed together. Since this roughly compared to making a temporary support for a ridgeboard in other structures, we made a stand from 2 × 4's which consisted of a 4-foot 2 × 4 nailed to one end of a 10-foot 2 × 4. This stand was taken in the door and set up in the center of the yurt. Then a rafter cut to the right length was used to find the correct height for the outside diameter of the skylight, which, of course, would be the end of the rafters. When this was found, the 10-foot upright 2 × 4 was sawed off to that length minus ⅜ inch. Next a section of ⅜-inch plywood measuring 20 inches square was nailed to the center of the 2 × 4. Then the rafters were laid in place and custom-notched for the top of each side pole. This was a two-man job; while one man held the rafter in place, the other marked the profile of the post on it. Then we took the rafter down again and used a small bow saw and sharp hatchet to cut out the notch. After the notch was as accurate as we could get it, we used a chalk line to snap a mark from the center of this notch to the center opposite end of the pole. This mark was then used as a guideline for beveling the end of the rafter. This bevel was set at a 30-degree angle since each rafter makes up 1/12 of the 18-inch diameter skylight. As the rafters were fabricated, they were laid in place and evenly spaced. Wedges were then custom-fitted and nailed into place between the rafters. The last rafter had to be custom-fitted since all the errors were apparent here. It was toenailed into each of its mating rafters and wedges. See Figure 5-9.

When all the rafters were securely in place, we removed the stand. Then in sheer exuberance I chinned myself in the skylight opening and, even though the ends were totally unsupported, they didn't even creak.

Roof Sheathing

We spent a few days thinking about what would make a good material for roof sheathing. We discarded the notion of using ⅜-inch exterior grade plywood since forming the sheets to the conical roof would be difficult and wasteful unless we first ripped the sheets into narrow strips. We had about decided to use 1-inch boards in whatever widths we could get them in, and, in fact, were talking to the owner of a small sawmill about buying some unplaned boards

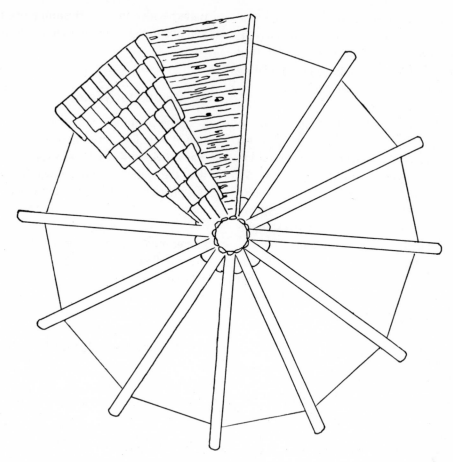

Fig. 5-9. Yurt roof.

from him when I happened to notice a huge pile of slabs he had lying there. Twenty minutes later we drove out with a pickup load of slabs, costing the magnificent sum of $1.00 and more than enough to cover the roof. When we got home we ripped the slabs into even widths with Cousin Albert's table saw, peeled the bark from them, and treated them on all sides with Penta. This would kill all the worms and fungus which were eating up the wood of the slabs. Then we laid them together as tight as we could get them and nailed them to the rafters. When it was done, we agreed that this was as good a roof sheeting as we could obtain even if we had paid out a lot of money.

Shingling

However, we still had to cover the roof to make it rainproof. Since it would seem a sacrilege to cover this slab roof with anything artificial, we decided to use wooden shake shingles. Further, Albert decided we could split them out ourselves from two huge old cedar trees that he had in his woodlot. I was slightly taken aback by this suggestion but decided to go along with him. After all, I could always leave if the going got too rough.

Splitting shingles turned out to be more fun than work even though it took us three days of more or less steady labor. First we cut down two of the biggest cedar trees he had and sawed the trunks into 2-foot lengths, being very careful to saw them straight. Then we shaved the bark from the outer surfaces of the trunks and, using our wedges, split them exactly in half. Next, we chopped out the heartwood by splitting across the grain. All that remained then was to split each one of the sections into sections that were 1 inch thick at the circumference and tapered more or less to a point at the center. We started out using a chisel to split the pieces and ended up with a froe made from a drawknife, which worked much easier. Our shingles weren't all even; in fact, some looked like boards but they almost all could be used by fitting one into the other. We also noticed one good thing about homemade shake shingles; no one can tell if and where you made a mistake roofing. We overlapped the shingles at least ½ of their length. If a shingle was too thick at the lead end and we couldn't fit it anywhere, we tapered it with the table saw. We nailed the shingles to each other and to the slab roof with zinc-coated eight-penny nails. Fortunately, we had nailed the slabs on across the roof so the shingles could be nailed on in the opposite direction.

Since cedar shingles age naturally to a soft gray color, we decided not to use any finish. Any other wood could be used for shingles also if it were treated with a good waterproof preservative.

How to Waterproof the Skylight

Making the skylight properly waterproof required a special procedure. Directly around the rim we built up a section with 2 × 2's. On top of this section we installed a 20-inch diameter, ¼-inch-thick acrylic plastic disc and held it in place with screen bead. All exposed wood was painted with a good waterproof preservative. Further, the area around the ¼-inch-thick acrylic plastic was sealed with caulking compound. Albert reports this skylight "has not shed a tear since we put her up."

Wiring

With our outside problems pretty well solved, we decided to finish the inside, concentrating on the electricity and plumbing first. Wiring the inside was very simple. We divided the entire house into two circuits, one for the outlets and one for the lamps. Both circuits were protected by a 15-amp circuit breaker back in the house. The overhead light in the living room was controlled by a wall switch near the door. The bathroom lamp was turned on and off with a pull chain. No lights were installed in the bedroom since it was anticipated that dresser lamps would be plugged into the wall receptacles (outlets). A receptacle was provided in each bedroom, one in the bathroom, and one in the living room to power a TV or radio.

Heat and Hot Water

The plumbing consisted of running a cold water line in from the master house plumbing. No hot water was provided since it was expected the guests would heat the water for shaving, washing, coffee, etc. on a hot plate. In winter when the wood stove was being used, a teakettle of water could be heated on that.

The stove was a logwood heater set up in the center near the bedroom walls (see Fig. 5-10). A freestanding fireplace also could be used with this setup if desired. At night a 110-volt electric heater equipped with a fan is used in very severe weather since this type of wood stove will not generally hold a good fire overnight.

The interior, including the ceiling, was insulated with 4 inches of foam insulation placed between the poles.

Custom-made Interior Siding

Since Albert wanted to maintain a rustic interior, we decided to nail furring strips vertically to the sides of the poles so that about ⅓ of the diameter of the poles would still be visible inside the rooms. Then we installed half-log siding that we made ourselves from aspen slabs.

Our custom-made aspen siding required considerable work. First we found a sawmill operator who was sawing aspen logs and visited him every day, carefully selecting slabs that were about 1½ inches thick and from 4 to 6 inches wide. We trucked these home and peeled the bark from them. Then we used Albert's table saw to saw out alternate 4- and 6-inch-wide siding boards. As fast as we had them sawed, we cut them into the proper lengths and nailed them in place between the interior logs. Then we immediately applied a thick coat of varnish so they would not darken, since untreated aspenwood tends to look dingy after aging. Making the siding turned out to be the most tedious job of all and I doubt that we were well repaid for our time, although it is certainly unique. Paneling or commercial exterior

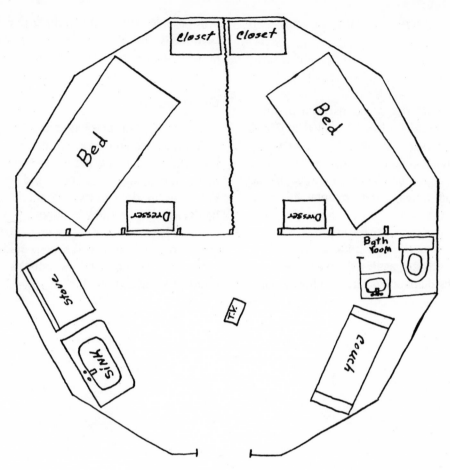

Fig. 5-10.   Floor plan for yurt.

Fig. 5-11.   Completed yurt.

siding would have been much faster and easier to use.

Inside Walls

We made the interior partitions from a single thickness of ³/₈-inch-thick plywood nailed to 2 × 4 studding. The studding was placed with its width parallel to the plywood and was exposed inside the bedroom. No swinging doors were installed in the partitions; instead, privacy was maintained by a burlap curtain which slid on an overhead wire. The panel behind the stove was made fireproof by building a 33 × 72-inch section of brick wall with the width of the bricks placed against the wall. The brick was fastened to the partition wall for stability by stapl-

ing loops of wire to the wall so that the loops fell between the brick joints, where they would be incorporated into the mortar of the joints.

Outside Entry Door

Cousin Albert purchased an exterior type of door called a garage entry door for the main entry door to his yurt. This pleased me no end since I thought he might want to saw down a tree and hew that out too. We hung the door in the 2 × 6 frame, installed the hardware, and the yurt was done.

We left the next day, slightly under the weather from too much of Albert's homemade wine at the christening but pleased nevertheless at the guest house I had helped build.

Chapter 2

GREENHOUSES AND HOTBEDS

Last January I visited a friend's greenhouse when the temperature was balanced precariously at the last plus number on the thermometer and an arctic wind swirled sheets of powdery snow across frigid fields. When he opened the door, tropical air enveloped me and I stepped forward into an oasis of tender green leaves and bright blossoms. It was like stepping from the Arctic Circle to a South Sea island in one step, and the warm, snug sensation this produced will remain in my mind as long as memories have meaning.

My friend raised flowers primarily for his own enjoyment but he sold some also. As a result, his greenhouse wasn't a liability financially. In fact, he said, if he chose he could make a good living raising plants for the various retail outlets. In the months that followed I looked further into the possibilities of a greenhouse and found that indeed there is hardly a cottage industry that has better potential for the green-thumber than raising house plants and food

plants in the greenhouse for the various retail and wholesale outlets.

Moreover, if you believe as I do that the world food supply has peaked and except for peculiar good years we are going to face continuing food shortages from now on, then the construction and use of a greenhouse takes of an urgent tone. Perhaps the day will come when every home will be built with an attached greenhouse as a matter of course, and raising vegetables and fruits the year around for the family food supply will be a required course at public schools.

A few years back all greenhouses were made of glass with metal or wood frames. They came in two general classifications: lean-to and freestanding. The lean-to greenhouse was the most economical to construct because it was built against a house or garage wall. Usually heat from the house was used to heat the lean-to greenhouse and, since it could be entered from the house at any time in any weather, it was the popular choice of hobby operators. Some disadvantages were that it could hardly be expanded when, as usually happens, more growing space was eventually desired and diseases, humidity, and cleanliness were hard to control.

Freestanding houses could be made to any size but they required a separate heat supply and expensive plumbing and wiring, and were far beyond the financial means of most homeowners, since they cost several thousands of dollars.

Fortunately most of these problems have now been met with the development of flexible fiberglass and clear plastics. Today anyone with a few simple tools can build a greenhouse with a wooden frame and cover it with plastic; depending on the size, it can cost less than a new suit.

Also, flexible fiberglass or plastic can be applied much tighter at the seams and is a far better insulator than glass. As a result, climate control is made easier. A further aid is the recent practice of installing a second layer of clear plastic on the inside of the greenhouse frame. This creates a dead air space which is a very effective insulator without sacrificing light transmission. In fact, window greenhouses made with double walls actually aid the home heating plant since they receive more solar heat then they lose, a process unlike the continuous rapid conduction of heat through glass that usually takes place when windows are installed.

WINDOW GREENHOUSE

Window greenhouses are easy to construct and the number of plants that can be raised in one is truly amazing.

A dear, old friend of ours, though born and raised in the country, was forced in his declining

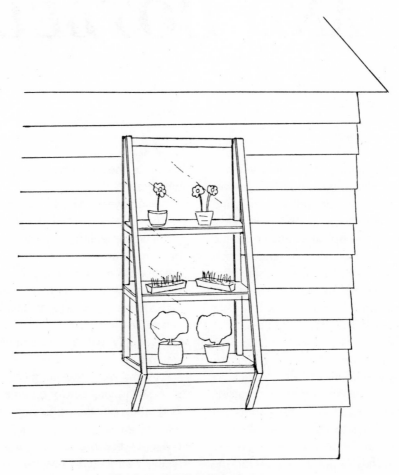

Fig. 2-1. Window greenhouse.

years to move into a large city. Restless and out of sorts without plants, he finally persuaded his landlord to let him install a window greenhouse on his south-facing, sixth-floor apartment window. In this growing space he managed to raise radishes, lettuce, and even two tomato plants. His crowning glory, though, was two miniature cornstalks which produced two ears of corn for his Christmas dinner.

The first year we went to live in the woods we arrived at our none-too-tight log cabin about the first of September. In Wisconsin that is the start of autumn. One of the first things we did was to enclose the three windows on the south side of the cabin with a fiber-glass and 2 x 4 platform. Before the ground froze we managed to get enough leafmold, peat moss, and loam together to fill two dozen large tin cans. This was our garden and we feasted all winter on greens and radishes which grew from these cans. Our only source of heat was a wood stove but we didn't lose one single plant, probably because we covered them on very cold nights with strips of an old wool mackinaw. Once we enclosed a screened porch with clear plastic and managed to raise dandelion and mustard greens all winter in it with hardly any additional heat.

Commercial models of window greenhouses are available, of course, but anyone can construct his own. Perhaps the first consideration will be what window or windows to use. They should face south, southeast, or southwest unless you intend to supply supplemental lighting. In that case any exposure will be all right.

Generally speaking, turning windows into a window greenhouse sacrifices the view from the location. Thus, if you have an unobstructed view of a snowcapped mountain or a nude beach, you may want to reconsider the location.

MATERIALS LIST FOR WINDOW GREENHOUSE

1. 2 8-foot 2 × 2's
2. 2 8½-foot 2 × 2's
3. 2 3-foot 2 × 2's
4. 2 2-foot 2 × 2's
5. 2 1-foot 2 × 2's
6. 9 4-foot 2 × 2's
7. 12 ¼ × 3½-inch cadmium-plated bolts
8. ½ pound six-penny nails
9. ½ × 48 × 36-inch hardboard shelf
10. ½ × 48 × 24-inch hardboard shelf
11. ½ × 48 × 12-inch hardboard shelf
12. 24 #6 × 1½-inch flathead wood screws
13. Paint and wood preservative
14. 12 ten-penny duplex head nails
15. 4 × 25-foot roll .037 translucent fiberglass
16. 100 feet ¾-inch screen bead
17. Box of brads
18. Roll of fiberglass wrapping insulation, 3 inches wide

The first step in construction is to procure the lumber. See the materials list for the amount and size. The 2 × 2's should be knot-free redwood or the equivalent. Saw out the desired sizes and then plane or sand a radius on all corners of all the framing members. This is to remove all corners and wood splinters so the covering won't be damaged. Next add two coats of a good preservative. Mix you own or procure a commercial mix. Let it dry overnight.

Next morning temporarily tack the structure together with 6D finishing nails. Now check Figure 2-2 carefully to see that all parts are in the right position and then drill ¼-inch holes through the members at the joints to install the ¼ × 3½-inch cadmium-plated carriage bolts, nuts, and washers, one at each joint. Next, place the ½-inch hardboard shelves in their proper position and use #6 × 1½-inch wood screws to fasten them in place. Countersink the heads.

The final step is to paint your creation with colors that harmonize with the exterior of the house. The interior surfaces can be painted to harmonize with the interior of the house, but make sure they are a pale color to reflect as much light as possible—white, of course, being the best of all.

The window greenhouse is fastened on the side of the house with duplex framing nails or wood screws. However, before it is installed, the insulation should be put in place. First place the window greenhouse in the desired position on the side of the house and make a pencil mark all around it. Set it aside and staple or tack strips of fiberglass insulation inside the pencil mark. The insulation sold for wrapping water pipes works well; of course, if scrap insulation is available, it can be utilized also.

Once the insulation is installed the window greenhouse is ready to be put in place, but before installing it remove the window's upper and lower sash. Generally they are held in place with slider strips and

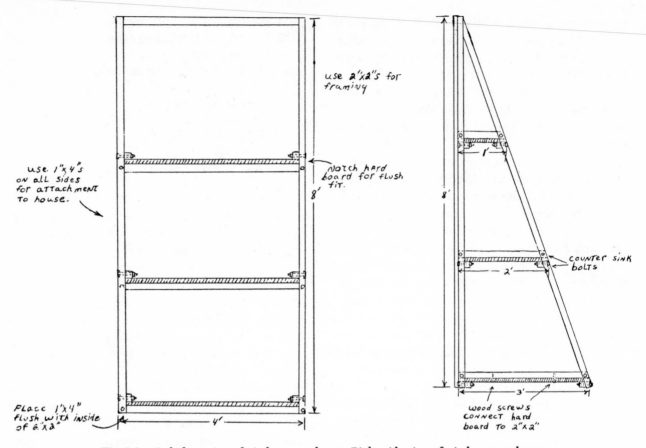

use 2"x2"'s for framing

use 1"x4"s on all sides for attachment to house.

notch hard board for flush fit.

8'

Place 1"x4" flush with inside of 6"x2"

4'

8'

1'

counter sink bolts

2'

3'

wood screws connect hard board to 2"x2"

Fig. 2-2.   *Left:* front view of window greenhouse. *Right:* side view of window greenhouse.

can be pried loose with a wide flat smooth pry bar. When the windows are removed, store them in a safe place where they can be stood up. Laying them down will almost certainly cause the panes to warp if they aren't supported some other way. Be sure to remember where you put them in case the cover of the greenhouse is damaged by a falling icicle or an inaccurately aimed football, and you have to reinstall the window.

After the window greenhouse is in position the plastic or fiberglass covering can be installed. Coverings range all the way from the very economical to expensive, with four-mill vinyl plastic probably being the cheapest material which will give satisfactory service. The recommended covering is translucent fiberglass in .037 thickness. It costs less than fifty cents a square foot at this writing. Rigid fiberglass panels are available also, and for a permanent installation consideration should be given to their use.

In cold climates a double wall covering should be installed. In this case the inside covering will ideally be four-mill vinyl plastic since it will last for a long time if used in conjunction with translucent fiberglass, which redirects the sunlight. Make sure screen brads or other wood strips are used over a double thickness of the covering where it is fastened. Also make sure the covering is pulled tight to prevent the wind from rippling it, which will eventually wear it out. With this done, the window greenhouse is ready to use.

Now, it is possible that you will have windows in your house that won't be compatible with this size and shape of window greenhouse—for example, a horizontal window. In that case carefully measure your window, draw up your own plans, and proceed, using the same materials recommended for this type of greenhouse. At any rate, when you have your window greenhouse done, you can start gardening.

It might be surprising to note that we have a total of twenty-four square feet of growing area within our window greenhouse, with each shelf placed to receive full sunlight. This means that we can grow at least two dozen house plants, 1 dozen tomato plants, or a considerable collection of other vegetables.

The first step is to find or purchase containers to raise your plants in. Clay flower pots are fine as are coffee cans, wooden boxes, or the trays made especially for this purpose and sold by garden supply stores.

The soil for raising vegetables can be home-mixed by combining one part garden mold, two parts leafmold, one part well-rotted cow manure, and one part clean, sharp sand. Mix the ingredients very well and keep moist.

Lettuce, radishes, tomatoes, onions, and carrots are some of the food plants that can be raised in this planting space. Soak all seeds overnight before planting them directly in the trays where they will eventually grow. Tomatoes can be started in peat pots if desired and finally transferred to 8-inch pots. It is recommended the first shelf be used for tomatoes, since they will have to be provided with about two square feet of growing space to fruit properly. Smaller plants such as radishes and lettuce can be planted between the tomato plants so the space will not be wasted. When the tomatoes blossom, they must be hand-pollinated or they will not set fruit, since there are no bees or other insects to do this naturally. Pollinating is usually done with a small artist's brush. Simply stroke each blossom containing pollen gently with the brush. This should transfer enough pollen between the blossoms for fertilization.

After the tomatoes are grown to the ripening stage the plants should be turned so each fruit receives as much sunlight as possible. Further, if the foliage is excessively heavy, it should be trimmed back or tied up so it doesn't shade the ripening fruits.

All garden plants should receive an application of a good complete liquid fertilizer every two or three weeks. Determine the frequency by the growth of the plants. When they slow down or stop growing, apply fertilizer. However, if they don't respond to fertilizer, discontinue its use. Water frequently enough to keep the soil moist.

Lettuce should be ready to eat in five weeks, radishes in three. So make successive plantings to keep a steady supply available. Some people raise tomato plants on a successive basis also so that one or two plants are bearing at any given time. Carrots have to have at least 6 inches of soil to bear usable roots. Use a small variety for best results (this is true for most vegetables).

Window greenhouses can be a source of never ending pleasure and interest to the plant lover. They can be made almost any shape that you desire to conform to the style of your house. Some people get so interested in "windowsill" gardening that they raise vegetables in one window, herbs in another, and flowers in still another. At the very least this is an economical way to see if you are compatible enough with indoor gardening to want to go to a hotbed or even to a larger, more expensive greenhouse.

HOTBED GARDENING

The next progressive step in winter gardening after the window greenhouse may be the hotbed. Now, a hotbed appears to be a form placed on the ground and covered with transparent material. There is actually much more to it.

First select a site where the drainage is very good. Directly on the top of a sand knoll is almost ideal but many locations are satisfactory. Stake out and excavate a rectangle about eight feet long and four feet wide to a depth of about two feet. Fill this rectangle with horse, cow, rabbit, or goat manure. If no manure is available, fill it with sawdust, wood chips, hay, green grass, or other organic matter that will decompose and generate some heat while it does. When the excavation is full, put on an old pair of boots and pack the manure so that there is about six inches of space between the manure and the top of the ground. On top of the manure place about 2 inches of moisture-absorbing sand.

To make our hotbed a reliably heated enclosure for raising plants requires the addition of an electric heating cable, or heating tape, which is placed on the sand. Use the type cable made especially for soil heating. This cable is manufactured with a built-in thermostat that keeps the temperature about 70 degrees for optimum plant growth. It will require a cable 160 feet long to protect the 32 square feet of growing area enclosed within this hotbed. Make sure it is placed so as to produce even heating and also make sure the thermostat is located near what will probably be the coldest corner. This type of cable

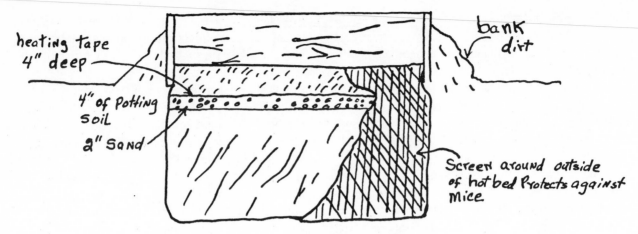

heating tape
4" deep

4" of potting
soil

2" sand

bank
dirt

Screen around outside
of hotbed Protects against
mice

Fig. 2-3. Cross section of hotbed.

shuts off automatically when the heat gets too high, and, depending on how much heat is generated by the decomposing organic matter, it might use very little energy. When the cable is in place, lay a screen or fine-mesh chicken wire over it and all around the perimeter of the hole. This prevents digging tools from damaging the cable and it also keeps rats and mice from setting up living quarters in your nice warm hotbed.

The final step is to finish filling the excavation with compost or garden soil made by the same formula as we used for vegetables in the window greenhouse. Fill the excavation about two inches over the top to allow for settling. Keep the connector plug of the soil heating cable from being buried, as it will be connected to the house current with an extension cord.

Now, with our "ground work" done we can install the frame. Procure and cut 1 × 12-in redwood or cedar boards to the lengths in Figure 2-4. Pine or fir can be used too if it is treated with a good preservative. Nail the boards at the corners with 2 × 2-inch cleats; use 10D plated nails. When the frame is completed place it over the excavation and level it up with bricks or similar material. Then stake it down on all four corners and shovel soil against the sides of the frame to form a bank to within an inch of the top. Now install two inches of foam insulation completely around the interior of the hotbed wooden frame. Two inches of foam is equivalent to six inches of fiberglass insulation for this purpose. Use white foam so it will

reflect light as much as possible. If you must use fiberglass, place the reflecting surface inside.

When the foregoing is all complete we can make the cover. It is generally expedient to make a double wall cover for the hotbed. Experiments have shown that up to twenty degrees lower temperature can be tolerated by plants in this hotbed if the cover is double wall plastic. Make the cover frame of 2 × 4 stock as shown in Figure 2-5. Put a cross brace of 2 × 4-inch or 2 × 2-inch in the center. Miter the corners at a 45-degree angle and fasten the joints with metal joint nails available in hardware stores and lumber yards. The plastic or fiberglass covering is stapled or nailed and then wrapped around the corners. Screen door hooks and eyes can be utilized for holding the cover in place. This is necessary to prevent a high wind from blowing it off. If desired, one side of the frame can be hinged. This will allow the cover to be raised slightly for ventilation, which should be provided about once a day, except in below zero weather. Don't raise the top at all in very cold weather as the plants are likely to be set back or made sterile by being chilled. On very cold nights, cover the hotbed with hay, old rugs, insulation, or other material to prevent heat loss.

This hotbed is effective for raising cool weather plants such as lettuce, endive, cabbage, broccoli, spinach, radishes, parsley, beets, and all types of pot greens, such as chicory. It is also very effective for starting warm weather plants such as tomatoes, peppers, cucumbers, squash, and melons. These plants

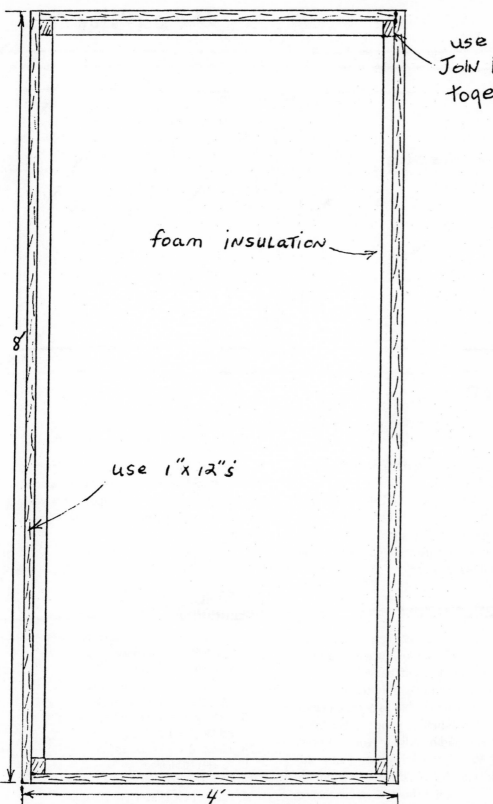

use cleats to
join boards
together

foam insulation

8'

use 1"x 12"s

4'

Fig. 2-4. Hotbed frame.

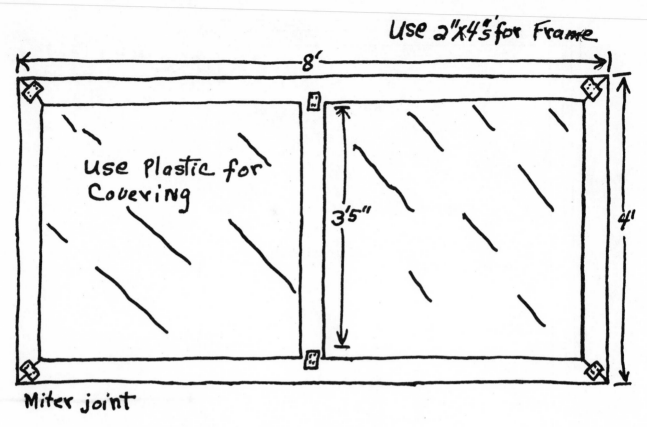

Use 2"x4's for Frame

8'

Use Plastic for Covering

3'5"

4'

Miter joint

Fig. 2-5. Hotbed cover.

can be hardened gradually as spring comes by reducing the intervals of heat. Finally, when the heat is not used any longer and the top can be left off the frame without damage, the started plants can be transplanted to your garden. Also, such plants can be started in this hotbed and then later set out in the greenhouse to continue growing.

A-FRAME GREENHOUSE

The A-frame greenhouse costs very little to build or operate, yet works well for growing early varieties of tomatoes, peppers, melons, and many other plants.

This type of greenhouse is almost the easiest structure to build that it is possible to design. Even if you have never built anything in your life, but know what a hammer, nails, and boards are, you can build this greenhouse. What's more, it has many advantages over conventional buildings. For instance, snow and rain will run off this structure so fast that no leakage or snow load problems are likely to be encountered. The location for this type greenhouse isn't

too critical either, since light will penetrate every corner because of its walls being perpendicular to the sun's angle. Another very important advantage is that no foundation is necessary since the weight is minimal.

MATERIALS LIST FOR A-FRAME GREENHOUSE

1. 20 $1/4$ ×6-inch carriage bolts, nuts, washers
2. 8 10-foot 2 × 4's or poles
3. 2 12-foot 1 × 10 boards
4. 15 4-foot 2 × 4's or 3-inch poles
5. 2 2-foot 2 × 4's or 3-inch poles
6. 1 24 × 60-inch door, hinges, lockset
7. 2 6-foot 2 × 4's
8. 1 3-foot 2 × 4 for door frame
9. 18 feet of door stop
10. 4 1 × 12 gussets for 2 × 4 A-frames
11. 3 rolls of 4 × 25-foot .037 fiberglass
12. 100 feet of 1 × 2 furring strips
13. 300 square feet of polyethylene for inside cover

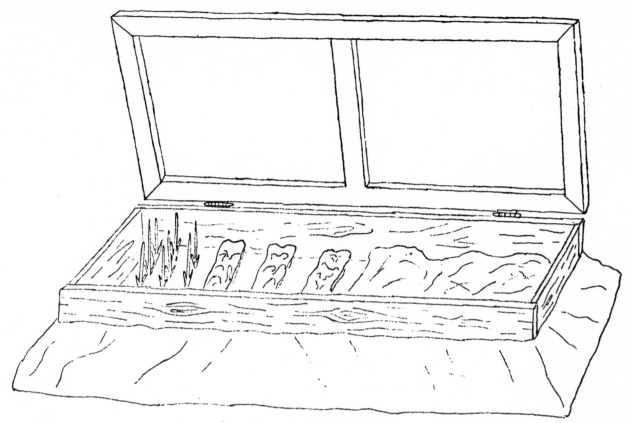

Fig. 2-6. Hotbed garden.

One of the first steps in building is to acquire poles for the rafters. Cedar is good as is redwood and treated fir or pine. Knot-free 2 × 4's also can be used if desired. The eight vertical rafters should be 10 feet long. Poles should be 4 inches in diameter on the small end, which of course, is always used at the top. They are notched at the top to overlap each other. The joints are held together with ¼ × 6-inch carriage bolts or nailed together with 20D spikes. If 2 × 4's are used, they can be mitered and fastened with joint nails.

Two feet under each joint a cross brace is installed. This also can be either a 2 × 4 or a pole, and it likewise is notched into the vertical rafters. The cross braces can be nailed with suitable spikes.

Horizontal rafters are also used. They can be spaced at 3-foot intervals and notched into the vertical rafters. Use nails or spikes to fasten them also. Try to keep them flush with the outside surface of the vertical rafters.

However, before fastening the side rafters make up all four frames for this 12-foot greenhouse. Note

that the front frame has the door frame installed. The two center frames do not have a cross member at the bottom while each end frame does. After the frames are made up, coat them with a good preservative and set them aside while you get the specialized floor ready for this greenhouse.

Much heat loss can be prevented and even some heat generated by the following method of designing the floor. First, lay out a trench one foot wide all around the perimeter of the prospective greenhouse site. The outside wall of the trench should form a rectangle six feet wide and eleven feet long. Remember to orient the greenhouse east to west if possible. Also try not to place it under a tree where falling limbs are likely to damage the covering. However, it is wise to take advantage of any natural or man-made wind breaks, since wind blowing directly on the greenhouse can cause noticeable heat losses. See the section Full-Size Conventional Frame Greenhouse later in this chapter for squaring up the structure properly with other buildings or a road.

When the trench is properly located, excavate it

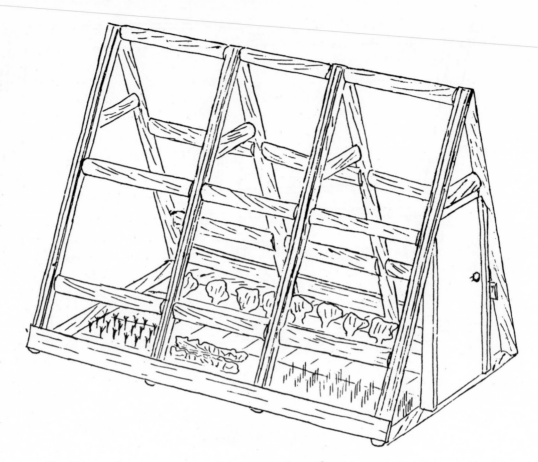

Fig. 2-7.   A-Frame greenhouse.

two feet deep and one foot wide. Keep the topsoil and subsoil separated in two piles if possible. Stake ½-inch mesh chicken wire all around the outer wall of the trench to keep out rats and mice. Then fill the trench with horse manure, or whatever organic material is available. The reason for this is twofold. First, the heat generated by the decomposing organic matter will help heat the greenhouse and, second, it will insulate the sides and thus prevent frost from creeping in at the sides. When the trench is full, tamp it down well and use topsoil from the execavation for covering the manure to a depth of six inches. It should be heaped to compensate for settling. If no organic material is available to place in a trench, bury a heating cable all around the perimeter of the inside of the greenhouse to keep out frost.

Immediately inside the first trench dig a second trench seven inches deep and one foot wide. This is the plant-growing space and it is the reason for all the

rest of the structure. After the soil is removed, place one 48-foot length of soil-heating cable in each trench, making sure it is placed according to the manufacturer's directives. Next, cover the cable with about 1 inch of sand and then place ½-inch mesh chicken wire over the cable to keep the digging tools of the gardener from damaging it.

Finally, when all of this is in place, add compost or a potting soil mixture to finish filling the excavation. It also should be slightly mounded to compensate for the settling which is bound to occur. In addition, a supply of potting soil should be kept available for additional filling.

The center two feet of this greenhouse should be leveled very well and then covered with flat, thick rocks painted black. Suitable rocks can be picked up in fields, along roads or in creekbeds. Paint them with a good grade of black enamel. If dark stones are available, no painting may be necessary. The coloring is to provide a surface that will absorb as much solar heat as possible. Thus, the stones will hold the heat and radiate it during the night or whenever the sun isn't shining. During long periods of sunless weather the reverse can sometimes occur; then the rocks can be covered to prevent a chilling effect. Naturally, the stones also provide a walkway to keep the greenhouse operator from coming in contact with the soil and plants. As you gain experience in operating this greenhouse, you may want to eliminate the center walk and use it for growing space. This is fine, especially in the warmer climates. Just place boards in strategic locations around the floor.

When heating cable is used, the soil must be kept moist or it will act as an insulator for the cable and little good will be realized from it. Naturally, since we are growing plants in the soil directly above it, the soil must be kept moist for the plants also.

When snow comes, it can be banked outside the

greenhouse to prevent frost from going down in the ground at the edges of the greenhouse.

Now, with floor and foundation all prepared, the frames can be put in place. It takes two people to set the frames up and nail the crosspieces to them. Each end of each frame should be placed on a flat rock or cement block to prevent it from sinking into the ground too far, which would slant the structure. A 1 × 12 board should be used all around the frame where the plastic contacts the ground.

Apply the fiberglass covering vertically over the frames. As it is being installed watch for protruding nails or wood splinters which could cause damage. Initially staple or tack the covering on the rafters. When it is all installed, nail 1 × 2 wooden strips over the seams on the rafters. Where possible, the covering should be doubled at the seams. Waste from the rolls can be utilized at the ends of the greenhouse.

Now, some supplementary heat should be

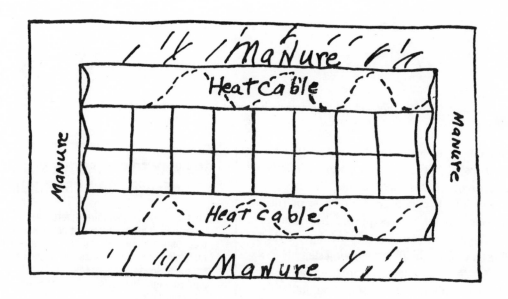

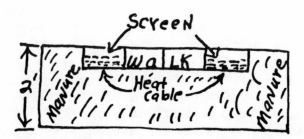

Fig. 2-8. Below-ground layout of A-frame greenhouse interior.

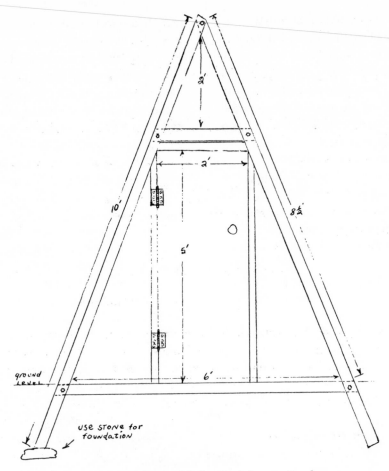

ground
level

use stone for
foundation

Fig. 2-9.   End frame with door in A-frame greenhouse.

available for this greenhouse for the coldest part of the winter. If the object is merely to prevent plants from freezing on the coldest nights a 5000 Btu. heater should do the job. It can be electric, gas, or oil. However, using the formula employed by heating contractors (see box), a 19,000 Btu. heater would have to be used to keep the plants growing steadily in the coldest climate at the coldest time of the year.

Heating a greenhouse is a fascinating subject. Over the hundreds of years that greenhouses have been in existence everything from hot springs to infrared heaters has been used. In the early days of American greenhouses many were heated with wood or coal. It was general practice to set up a space heater in the greenhouse with the pipe running the full length of the greenhouse to remove as much heat as possible from the smoke. This created problems with carbon monoxide and other gases circulating among the plants instead of fresh air. An improve-

ONE WAY TO FIGURE THE SIZE HEATER NEEDED FOR A GREENHOUSE

1. First find the temperature difference. This is the difference in degrees Fahrenheit between the lowest outside temperature and the temperature you want to maintain in the greenhouse. For instance, if you want to maintain an inside temperature of 60° and the coldest night temperature is −10°, the temperature difference is 70°.

2. Multiply the temperature difference by the number of square feet of exposed plastic or fiberglass. Include the roof, sides, and ends. Example: A 14 × 24-foot greenhouse has 744 square feet of area. Multiply the result of Step 1 (70) by 744. This will produce the figure 52,080.

3. If the greenhouse is covered with one layer, multiply the result of Step 2 (52,080) by 1.2. If the greenhouse is covered with a double layer, multiply the result of Step 2 by .8. Read the answer directly in Btu's. Example: 52,080 × .8 = 41,664.0 Btu's.

ment was to install the space heater outside the greenhouse in a shed of its own and run the smoke pipe the length of the greenhouse to a chimney located on the opposite end.

Wood and coal fires require frequent tending which sometimes involves getting up in the middle of the night, and there is the ever present danger that the fire will go out on the coldest night and let all the plants freeze. Many people have used wood or coal-heated greenhouses for years without a single accident, however, and a person operating on a limited budget could use a large wood stove; even make one from an old oil drum and burn waste wood, slabs, roots, coal, or whatever was available to heat his greenhouse at almost no cost. Accidents could be minimized by installing a warning device that would ring an alarm inside the house if the temperature fell too low. These devices will work with batteries if no AC electricity is available.

In our small A-frame greenhouse all sorts of combinations are possible. A wood stove could be used to heat it during very cold days and a portable kerosene heater set up to heat it at night in addition to the soil-heating cable. More expensive alternatives would be thermostatically controlled gas or electric heaters. In all cases some warning device should be used to signal dangerously low temperatures.

Equally important to heating the A-frame greenhouse is ventilating it. Since it is small and the door at one end proportionately large all that is generally necessary is to leave the door open for a few minutes each day, probably while the plants are being tended. A good indication of the condition of the air in the greenhouse is the odor. If it begins to smell musty, ventilation is needed. On spring or fall days some shading should be provided to prevent the plants from sunburning. A very good shading material to use with the A-frame greenhouse is cheesecloth

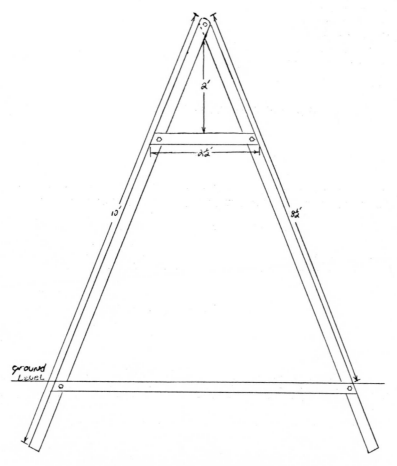

Fig. 2-10.   End frame without door in A-frame greenhouse.

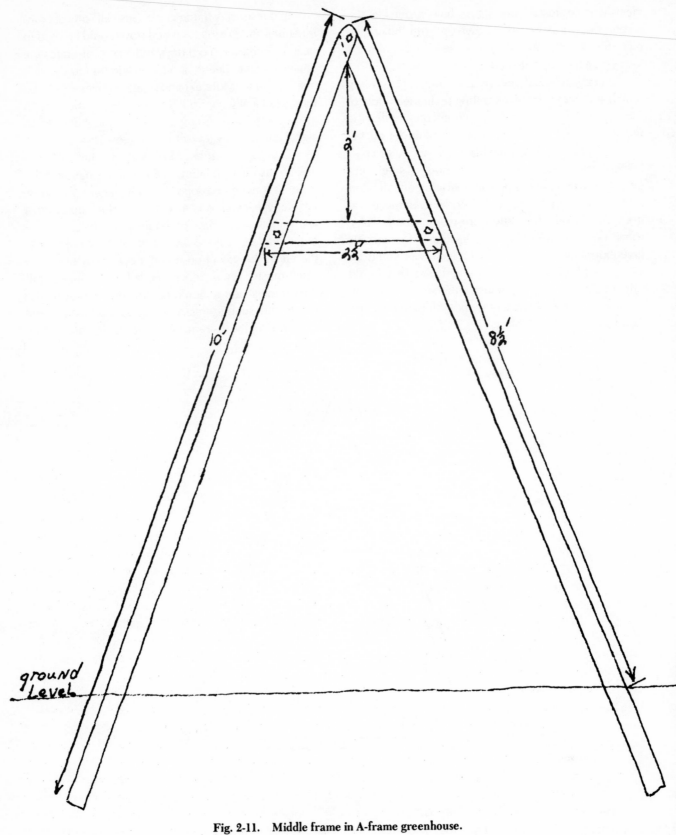

Fig. 2-11. Middle frame in A-frame greenhouse.

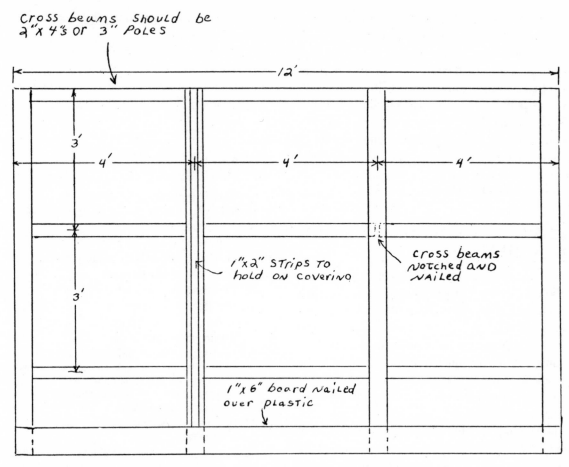

Fig. 2-12. Structural members of A-frame greenhouse.

stretched over stakes driven in the ground at each side of the plant rows inside the greenhouse. Cheesecloth allows enough light to promote plant growth while at the same time preventing an excess of heat and light which can cause sunburning.

Lest this discussion makes it seem as though it takes a great amount of time to tend this greenhouse let me point out that we average about five minutes a day in ours. Many times it only has to be looked after once a week, when it is watered.

Watering greenhouse vegetables should be done very carefully, especially in winter, so no moisture splashes on the leaves. This can cause mildew. It is better to use a perforated hose extending from a watering can to slowly soak the soil at the ground level.

EXCAVATED GREENHOUSE

The excavated greenhouse needs little or no supplementary heat since it uses the heat from the

ground as well as the heat from the sun to keep the frost away. The first step in building one is to excavate a basementlike structure of whatever size desired for the greenhouse. Drainage is of primary importance here or else you might wind up with a fishpond instead of a greenhouse since the excavation should be about six feet deep. Unless the side walls of the structure are very dry and firm, they should be shored up with cement blocks or treated timbers to keep the walls from caving in and to keep moisture out.

Sometimes old basements of houses that have burned down or been otherwise removed are good places to start a greenhouse of this type. Also on some farms and country places caves exist that face the south and are warm the year around. They, of course, are almost ideal.

Regardless of the excavation used, the top or entrance should be covered with clear plastic or glass to keep the cold out and the sunshine in. Vertical excavations should be covered with a peaked roof to shed snow and rain. Generally, some means of artificial ventilation will have to be provided in the warmer seasons with this type greenhouse but cooling is seldom a problem since the ground keeps the plants cool as well as warm. Growing is usually done in pots placed on benches. If space is available oil barrels painted black and filled with water can be placed in the bottom of the excavated greenhouse to act as solar heat collectors. When the sun isn't shining, the barrels will radiate heat and help to maintain an even temperature inside the greenhouse.

FULL-SIZE CONVENTIONAL FRAME GREENHOUSE

The last project of this chapter is a modern greenhouse, twenty-four feet long and large enough for raising a considerable number of plants, either for private use or a small commercial venture. The design should pass most building codes with very little change. Moreover, since it might be considered a temporary structure by the tax assessor, it is possible that no increase in taxes would result from its construction.

The first step is to find out how far from the street or road the front wall must be located. Your friendly building inspector is the person to consult for this information. Generally, it will be the line of buildings already constructed. When this is known, the foundation site can be located and measured in.

Lay out the front line of the foundation by measuring equal distances back from the street or sidewalk in two locations twenty feet apart. Drive stakes at these points and stretch a chalk line between the stakes. Next, stand between the chalk line and the street, facing the chalk line, and determine where you want the left side of the building to be located. Mark this on the chalk line by folding a small piece of tape around the line. Use a plumb bob to find the point directly under the tape. Drive another stake there, attach a chalk line to it, and stretch it at right angles to the first line to locate the lefthand wall. Use a carpenter's square to make this corner as square as possible. Now continue to use the plumb bob, square, and additional chalk lines to lay out the entire foundation. Finally, square it up by measuring diagonally from one corner to the other and adjusting the rear wall line until the diagonal measurements are

the same. You will probably never get them perfect; no one ever does.

When the foundation is squared up, dig the trenches for the footings. The trench can be 1 foot wide and 4 feet deep. It will have to be widened at the bottom to about 16 inches to accommodate the footings.

MATERIALS LIST FOR FULL-SIZE GREENHOUSE

1. 26 cubic feet concrete for footings
2. 675 12 × 6 × 8 concrete blocks. Lightweight is recommended.
3. 70 running feet of 2 × 6 for sill
4. 38 43.5-inch 2 × 4's for studding. 48-foot studs.
5. 76 feet of 2 × 4 for wall plate
6. 24 running feet of 2 × 6 for ridgeboard
7. 26 8-foot 2 × 4's for rafters
8. 12 feet of 2 × 4 for end frames
9. 2 doors, frames and hardware.
10. 1600 square feet of .037 thickness flexible fiberglass made for greenhouses. For economy polyethylene can be used and replaced gradually by fiberglass to spread costs over a long period. Rigid fiberglass panels are also available.
11. Heaters, exhaust fans, shutters, electric wiring, and water pipe
12. 2 cubic yards crushed gravel for the floor. 48 running feet of 2 × 10 planking for walkways.

If the soil is firm no form will have to be built for the footings since the soil can be shaped properly to receive the concrete. A good concrete mix for footings of this type is 1 part portland cement, 2½ parts sand, and 3½ parts gravel. The footings should be 3 inches thick. The concrete for this footing can be mixed in a wheelbarrow or mortar box.

When the footings are curing, which will take three days, you can be installing the water and electric lines. Water lines will have to be buried at least 4 feet or protected by heating cable. Water lines could be ⅝ or ¾-inch diameter plastic or copper. The electric line should be #2, 3-wire cable insulated for burying. Connections at either end might have to be done by a licensed tradesman.

Both water and electric lines can be buried in the same trench if expedient. This digging also can be done by hand. Dig under the footings and don't forget to leave the ends of the lines long enough to make the connections inside the walls.

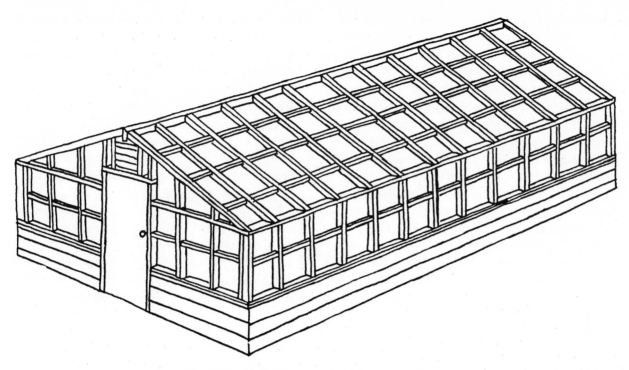

Fig. 2-13. Full-size conventional frame greenhouse.

After the footings have cured properly, the concrete block wall can be started. Lightweight blocks should be used if they are available, since they have greater insulating value. Bags of mortar mix are available for block laying, and generally it is easier and cheaper to use this mix than to mix your own. Besides the blocks and mortar you will need a trowel, carpenter's level, chalk line, and a pair of gloves.

Start by laying the corner blocks. Notice that the corner blocks have one flat face. This, of course, is laid to the outside. Set the first block on a full width of mortar about an inch thick. Level it up and square it with the footings very well since this first block determines the line for the rest. Do this at each corner. By the time you finish, the mortar should have stiffened enough to permit placing the chalk line between the first and second corner blocks. Use this as a guide to place three additional blocks in each direction. Notice that the blocks overlap to tie the corners together. In addition, it is well to fill the holes in the corner blocks with mortar and push a concrete reinforcing rod from top to bottom of the wall after the blocks are all in place to further reinforce them.

All blocks except the corner blocks should be filled with insulation.

Lay mortar bead 1 inch thick the width of the face shell of the block. In addition, the inside end of the block should be "buttered" with a similar bead of mortar. Push the blocks down and level them out so the joint is about $3/8$ of an inch thick. Be sure to level the block in both directions and keep the joint the same thickness. It is customary to build up each corner until only a corner block is left to be placed. Then the spaces between the corners are filled in. The door frame should be placed in position when the ground level is reached since it will be recessed three tiers of blocks. Half blocks are available for filling in sections where full blocks cannot be used. Also blocks can be cut to fit by scoring them with a chisel, or a masonry blade which will cut blocks can be purchased for your electric saw.

The cement block wall of our greenhouse extends two feet (three courses) above the ground level. Anchor bolts are placed in the top row of blocks for use in tying the wooden frame to the cement blocks. The wall then should be allowed to cure before further work is done on it. Curing will take about two weeks in summer weather.

When the block joints have hardened enough so some pressure can be put on them, they can be cleaned up and painted or stuccoed. Stuccoing is probably the cheapest, most satisfactory way to cover the blocks with a permanent good-looking finish. Instructions for doing this are readily available at lumber yards and hardware stores. Likewise, the cement block wall can be covered with wood siding by first installing wooden strips and then nailing the siding to it. Strips are attached to concrete block walls with special concrete nails or by drilling the blocks and installing plastic anchors.

After the foundation wall has hardened and is in place, the framing can be put up. The first step is to fasten the sills to the wall. The sills should be a double 2 × 6 of knot-free softwood such as redwood or treated fir. Bolt the sills to the wall by drilling holes to

correspond to the location of the anchor bolts placed in the wall. At the corners the plate should be cut to overlap so the opening in the joint doesn't extend from inside to outside. The sill should be treated with two coats of a good preservative and the joints between the sill and the wall should be caulked with a good grade non-hardening caulking compound.

Once the sills are in place, the studding and other framing can commence. Professional carpenters do the framing on the ground and raise an entire section into place at once. However, the amateur working alone with perhaps little space to work in will probably find that placing the framing boards one at a time in place will be the easiest. First procure 38 2 × 4's for studs and cut them all to length. They should be cut 43.5 inches long. When they are cut to length, measure off and place the corner studs in place. Plumb these corner studs with a level in both directions and brace them in place by

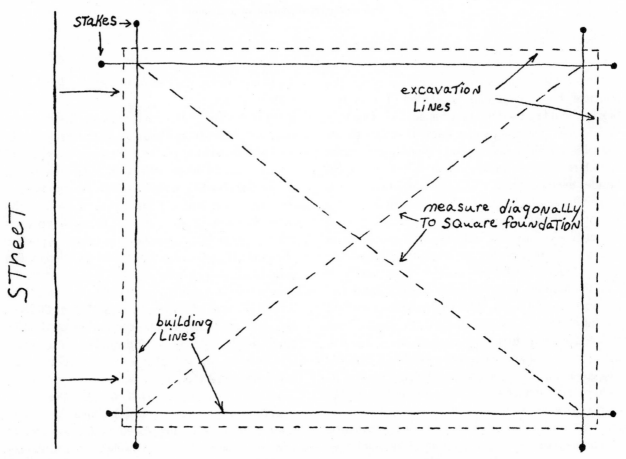

Fig. 2-14.   Squaring the foundation.

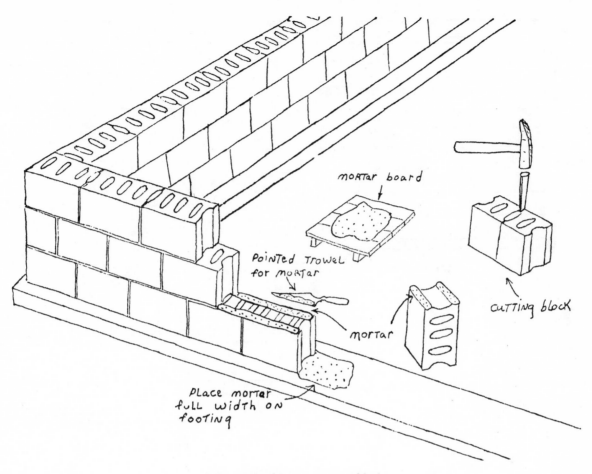

mortar board

Pointed trowel
for mortar

mortar

cutting block

Place mortar
full width on
footing

Fig. 2-15. Laying concrete blocks.

tacking a 1 × 4 from the stud to the sill. Next stretch a chalk line 3 feet off the sill from the outside of one corner stud to the other all around the building. Next find the center stud, mark on both sides of the building, and install a double stud by nailing two studs together. This is necessary because of the top plate being spliced at this location. Plumb these center studs also and brace them in place.

Now, the top plate can be a 12-foot 2 × 4. It will of course, take two to each side. Nail them in place with the center joint evenly spaced on the center stud. All that remains to finish framing the sidewalls is to nail the other studs in place 2 feet apart. The top plate and sill will indicate the correct location.

With the side wall studding in place the end wall studs can be considered next. Note that the two center studs which will be on each side of the door frame are 8 inches longer than the other studs. Toenail these in place and then install the top plate,

which is cut 66 inches long. Across the top of the doorway nail a 3-foot-long 2 × 4 to complete the frame. Both ends are the same.

The next step is to install the roof rafters. First nail the ridgeboard in place. This should be a 2 × 6, 24 feet long if available. If it isn't, use some combination of lengths that will avoid having the joint in the center such as would be caused by having two 12-foot lengths joined at the center.

Temporarily nail the ridgeboard in place, directly in the center of the building. Use a short length of scrap 2 × 4 to hold the ridgeboard 48 inches above the door frame on each end. The rafter detail is shown in Figures 2-13 and 2-18. It is important that the rafter heel cut fit the plate exactly so it won't extend past the side rafters, which could cause damage to the covering. Lay the rafters on 24-inch centers and toenail in place, using 16D nails on each side of each rafter.

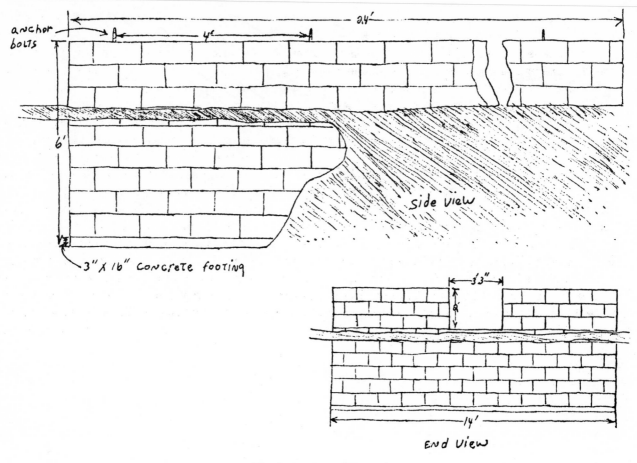

Fig. 2-16.   Foundation.

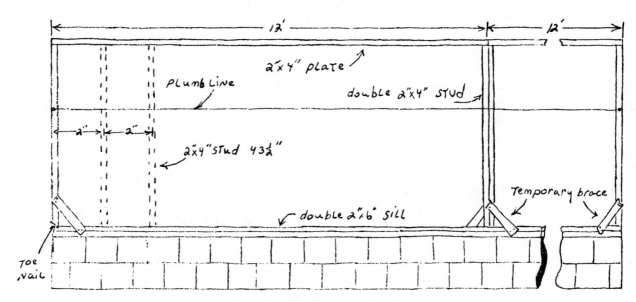

Fig. 2-17.   Installing the wall studs.

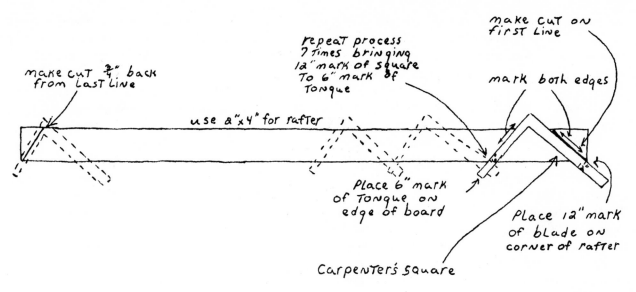

make cut ¾" back from Last Line

repeat process 7 Times bringing 12" mark of square To 6" mark of Tongue

make cut on first Line

mark both edges

use a"x4" for rafter

Place 6" mark of Tongue on edge of board

Place 12" mark of blade on corner of rafter

Carpenter's square

Fig. 2-18. Master rafter.

Forming the angles for the rafters can be trying for the novice carpenter. Generally it is best to make a master rafter and use it for marking the rest. This greenhouse rafter pitch is called a ¼ pitch since the rise in the center is ¼ of the width of the building. Further, by comparing the span by the length of the rise we find that the roof rises 6 inches for each foot of span. This is all the information we need to find the correct pitch for the rafters. First select an 8-foot 2 × 4 to use as a master rafter. Square one end by sawing if necessary and place it on two sawhorses where it will be comfortable to work with. Now take a carpenter's square and hold it so the blade (2-foot part) is in your right hand and the tongue in your left hand. Apply the square to the rafter so the 12-inch mark on the back surface of the blade coincides with the corner of the 2 × 4 nearest you. Further, pivot the square so the 6-inch mark on the tongue lines up with the edge of the rafter nearest you. Use a hard pencil to mark across the 2 × 4 along the back edges of both the tongue and blade. Now move the square to the left and place the 12-inch mark of the blade on the pencil mark where the tongue 6-inch mark was previously located (see Fig. 2-18). Also, as before, line the 6 inch mark of the tongue with the edge of the rafter. Notice that this places the square in exactly the same position as before except it will be moved over about 13⁷⁄₁₆ inches. Repeat this procedure seven times, marking each line each time. The first pencil mark you made will be the line for the wall plate and

the last will be the line for the ridgeboard. Now, very carefully measure and mark a line ¾ inch back from the previous ridgeboard mark. This will be the final ridgeboard mark. Finally saw the 2 × 4 on the final ridgeboard mark and on the opposite end at the wall plate mark.

This rafter can be used for marking all the rest, but be sure to put it in position before you mark any more to see if it is correct. After the roof rafters are in place install the 2 × 2 purlins and side rails. The purlins are made from 2 × 2 stock to minimize shading; however, they can be made from 2 × 4's too at the discretion of the builder. At each end over the doors a 21-inch-square opening for the exhaust fan and shutters is provided. Note details in Figure 2-19.

When the framing is complete the fiberglass covering can be applied. Notice that it is applied horizontally on the sides of the greenhouse and vertically on the roof. The waste from the roof can be utilized at the ends. Make sure the covering is pulled tight to eliminate wind rippling. Greenhouse fiberglass usually comes in 4-foot rolls; use 1 × 2 wooden strips or the equivalent to fasten the edges of the rolls to the rafters. Whatever waste is left from the fiberglass covering the greenhouse can often by utilized in building cold frames. The door can be solid or a door with windows. In the winter a considerable heat savings can be realized by building an entryway around the entrance doors.

The inside of the greenhouse must be covered

with polyfilm plastic to create a double wall in cold climates. This will effect up to a 40 percent heat savings. The polyfilm of course, is fastened to the inside of the 2 × 4 rafters. Use only the polyfilm made especially for greenhouses.

When this is done, the exhaust fan and shutter can be installed in the opening previously framed in. In addition, the heater or heaters should be installed. This size greenhouse will need a 60,000 Btu. heater to maintain the 60-degree air temperature in −20-degree weather. Actually, most operators opt for a heater much smaller than this and content themselves with providing supplemental heat just to keep the plants from freezing during the coldest days, since as soon as the weather moderates the greenhouse will warm and the plants start growing again. However, both the exhaust fan and heaters should be equipped with an automatic temperature regulating thermometer. In addition, every greenhouse should have

an automatic alarm system to warn the operator of too low or too high temperatures. Automatic misters and waterers can also be installed at the discretion of the operator after he gains experience. Level the floor and cover it with 2 inches of pea gravel. Walks can be formed with concrete blocks or wooden planks.

When the greenhouse construction is finished, the "furniture" can be installed. This model greenhouse can use a 3-foot growing bench on each side and a 4-foot bench in the center. The space under the benches can be used for growing plants with supplemental lighting or it can be used for storing potting soil, tools, and other necessities of greenhouse operating. Don't forget that hanging pots can be used also to raise plants if more space is needed.

No attempt will be made to give instructions for setting up the plants in the greenhouse, since this will vary considerably among operators. Notice that this

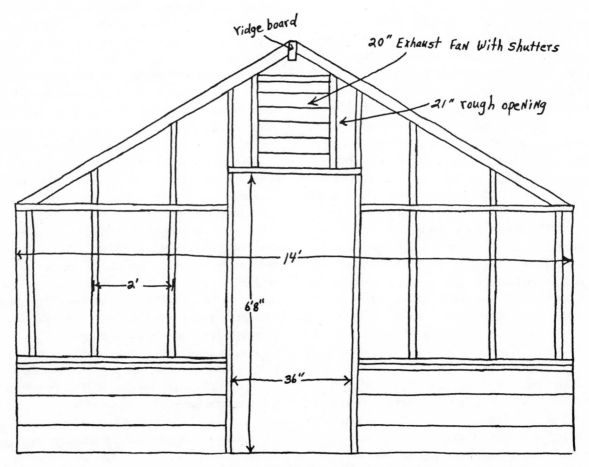

Fig. 2-19.   End view.

greenhouse can be made longer with no loss of symmetry if conditions warrant it at some later date. Also, it is highly adaptable to whatever personal innovations you may care to incorporate.

Control diseases and insects by keeping the doors shut tightly and sterilizing all tools periodically. Also, try not to introduce any new plants to the greenhouse without a two-week quarantine period and a careful inspection.

Some tools that are useful in the greenhouse are the dibble board and dibble. A dibble board is a board with evenly spaced holes drilled in it. The dibble is a pointed stick. They are used by laying the board on a seed flat and poking evenly spaced holes with the stick in the seed flat to plant seeds in. A masonry trowel for transferring soil and fertilizer is also useful as is a tamping block, rubber bulb for watering plants, hand sprayer, hand cultivator, scoop, sieve, and sharp knife. All of these tools can be handmade if you don't desire to purchase them.

If none of these greenhouse structures exactly fit your ideal, use the ideas mentioned to design your own. Also, almost every need of the prospective builder can be satisfied from commercial sources these days. Following is a list of greenhouse suppliers. No specific recommendation of the companies listed below is given or implied. The addresses are listed only as a convenience to the reader. See the classified ads in gardening magazines for other company names.

Environmental Dynamics
P.O. Box 996
Sunnymead, California 92388

Peter Reimuller
Post Office Box 2666
Santa Cruz, California 95063

Turner Greenhouses
Post Office Box 1260
Goldsboro, North Carolina 27530

McGregor Greenhouses
1195 Thompson Avenue
Santa Cruz, California 95063

Greenhouse Specialties Co.
9849 Kimker Lane
St. Louis, Missouri 63127

Redwood Domes
Aptos, California 95003

Sunshine Greenhouses
P.O. Box 3577
Torrance, California 90510

Greenhouse gardening is a fascinating but challenging occupation. No one ever learns enough about it to produce guaranteed results but it is always possible to learn more by reading the many excellent publications dealing with the construction and operation of greenhouses available today. The U.S. government, in particular, offers a wealth of valuable information. The following pamphlets should prove helpful:

Building Hobby Greenhouses
Agriculture Information Bulletin No. 357
U.S. Government Printing Office
Washington, D.C. 20402

Sash Greenhouses
Leaflet No. 124 U.S. Department Of Agriculture
Superintendent Of Documents
U.S. Government Printing Office
Washington 25, D.C. 20402

Also write to *United States Department Of Agriculture, Agricultural Research Service, Crops Research Division*, Beltsville, Maryland 20705 and ask for the publication *List of Sources of Information on Greenhouses*. This is twelve pages of sources of every type of greenhouse information.

The many challenges of greenhouse operation keep its practitioners on their toes. Maybe that's why there are so few ex-greenhouse operators.

Chapter 3

RED BARN GARAGE

Many semicountry dwellers, with an acre or less to live on, keep animals, raise a garden, and house the automobile could find this building an answer to their prayers. It can be made as large as desired but one measuring 20 x 30 feet will cover most requirements.

All sorts of adaptations are inherent in this design. If there are no horses, both stalls can be used for goats and vice versa. When the room isn't being used to smoke meat or dry produce, it can be utilized as a workshop. The entire loft can be used for storing hay or other feed if desired. Approximately six tons of hay can be stored in this space if the hay is loose. The hay is fed to the animals through doors cut through the loft floor directly over the animal stalls. This loft can be used for a studio or an apartment also if modified to some extent.

It would ideally be set up with the animal stalls facing south in order to permit the doors to let in sunlight in the winter, which is important in animal hus-

bandry. If horses are kept in the stalls, window bars of wrought iron should be placed across the frame to prevent the animals from breaking the glass with their heads or from kicking the windows out. It wouldn't be too unusual for a 1200-pound horse to try to leap out the window either, even if it is barely large enough for him to get his head through. Horses seem to suffer from poor space-estimating ability.

Now, if after glancing at the plans and directions for this project, a homeowner decides it is too big a task for his untried abilities, let me reassure him. There is nothing about this building that can't be done by anyone who can hold a saw, hammer, or mason's trowel in his hands. Just proceed cautiously, doing each step in its proper place, and your building will take shape as well as if you were a carpenter with decades of experience. The hardest part is performing the initial steps. Perhaps if you do this in your spare time it will take a minimum of six months to complete. But, do you know any other way you can increase your estate $6000 to $7000 during leisure hours right in your backyard, in this amount of time and have fun doing it?

Don't forget also that this building can be used to house people. Many times a building of this type in conjunction with a conventional house will allow two dwellings to be built on the same lot and the farmstead will still exude the quaint charm of a rural setting.

It is also very adaptable to raising small animals such as hamsters, chinchillas, or beneficial insects such as praying mantis, and of course, can be used as a "factory" building for propagating "mousies," "waxworms," red worms, or any of the other insect larvae that are so much in demand for fishbait. Naturally, it can house that cottage industry that you want to start but don't have a place for.

LAYING OUT THE FOUNDATION

The first step in building this barn is to lay out the foundation. Generally, since it will be built on a small tract of land, the property lines can be used for guidelines. First establish a straight line at the property line or use the street or another building to orient the nearest side of the prospective foundation. An unorthodox, but effective way to locate a building if no other building, street, or marked property lines are close enough for reference is to use a magnetic compass for orientation. Do this by first deciding exactly where you want the southwest corner of the building to be located. Then sharpen a 4-foot length of 2 × 4 and drive it securely in the ground at this point, with the width oriented as much north and south as possible. Make sure it is straight up and down. Then lay a magnetic compass on the top of this stake at the center (see Fig. 10-1). Note where the north and south poles of the compass needle are and drive six-penny finishing nails into the stake at the indicated north and south poles of the compass. Remove the compass and put it away.

MATERIALS LIST FOR RED BARN/GARAGE

1. Approximately 100 8 × 8 × 16-inch concrete blocks
2. 20 2 × 4's for shoes and plates
3. 150 8-foot 2 × 4's for studding
4. 40 running feet of 2 × 4 material for window braces
5. 8 8-foot 2 × 6's for stall liners
6. 26 4 × 8 sheets of ⅝-inch exterior plywood for wall sheathing
7. 735 square feet of #15 builder's felt
8. 16 20-foot 2 × 8's for floor joists
9. 60 running feet of 2 × 8 for floor joist bridging
10. 19 4 × 8-foot sheets of ⅝- or ¾-inch plywood for the upstairs floor
11. 32 8-foot 2 × 6's for rafters
12. 32 10-foot 2 × 6's for rafters
13. 16 10-foot 1 × 8's for rafter bracing
14. 32 panel clips for rafter joints
15. 32 4 × 8-foot sheets of ⅝-inch plywood for roof sheathing
16. 725 square feet of roofing material
17. 108 running feet of 2 × 4 for gambrel studding
18. 160 running feet of batten boards
19. 132 running feet of fascia
20. 2 4 × 8-foot dutch doors
21. 2 conventional entry doors
22. Loft door
23. 8-foot garage door
24. 4 windows (size to be determined by builder)
25. Anchor bolts and nails

Now the six-penny nails can be used as a north-and-south sighting plane. Proceed to lay out the foundation by measuring north 30 feet from the original stake. Use a thin pole or a 2 × 4 edgewise for a surveyor's pole and adjust it until it is directly north of the original stake as indicated by sighting across the nails. A level should be used with the surveyor's pole to make sure the top and bottom are perfectly vertical. When this second position is located, drive a stake at this point. Now the north and south line of the foundation is located and you can proceed to lay out the rest of the foundation from this north-south line according to the suggestions on laying a greenhouse foundation in chapter 2.

SQUARING THE FOUNDATION

A method often used by carpenters for squaring a foundation is called the *6-8-10* method. After the preliminary corners are found and strings stretched all around the foundation, select a light, easy-to-handle pole and adjust its length to exactly 10 feet. Then put a marker on the front wall string exactly 6 feet from either corner. This marker can be a short length of tape or simply a chalk mark. Further, put a marker on the side wall string exactly 8 feet from the same

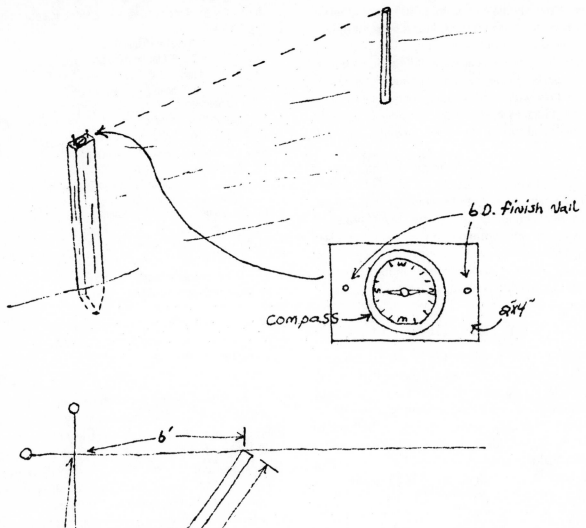

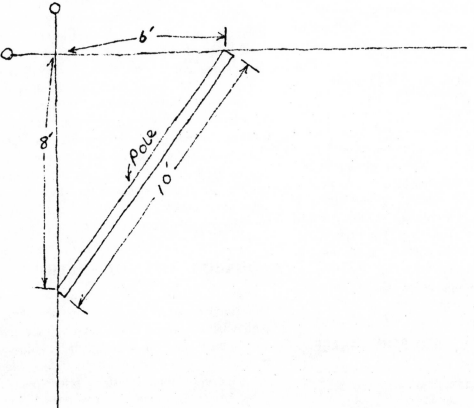

Fig. 10-1. *Top:* Locating a building line. *Bottom:* The 6-8-10 method of squaring a corner.

corner. Now the 10-foot pole should reach exactly from the 8-foot mark on the side wall string to the 6-foot mark on the front wall string if it is held level between the two marks (see Fig. 10-1). If it does not, then adjust the *side wall* string until it does. With this corner squared, repeat the procedure at either back wall corner and the entire foundation will be "squared" and "true."

FINDING THE GRADE LEVEL

The next step is to find the grade level. First, drive a stake in the ground at what looks like the highest level. Further, drive a nail in the stake and tie a string to the nail. Place a line level on the string and check all points which will be inside the foundation. If the slope of land is more than 4 inches some earth has to be removed or the foundation wall has to be built two blocks instead of one block above the natural soil line.

LAYING OUT THE EXCAVATION LINES

Now the excavation lines can be laid out. Generally, this is done with batten boards. Three feet outside each foundation corner erect a fence of scrap 1 × 4 boards with the horizontal rail 18 inches high. The "fence" should extend past each corner 3 feet. Do this at all four corners. Now extend the original foundation strings to the batten boards so they cross directly over the original corner stakes. Saw slits in the batten boards to level the lines and weigh each line with a brick so the line will be tight but portable (see Fig.10-2). Further, measure 30 inches outside the original lines and make another slit in each batten board. This second slit indicates the excavation line which the equipment operator will use to dig the trench for the cement block foundation.

Now either the building line or the excavation line can be quickly found by transferring the brick-

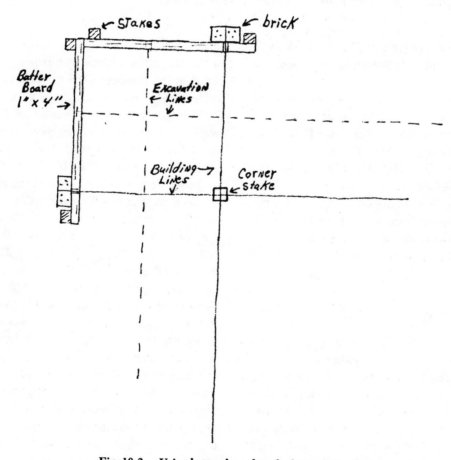

Fig. 10-2. Using batten boards to find excavation lines.

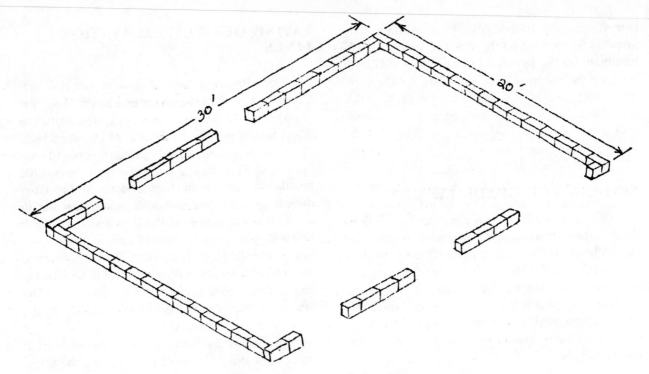

Fig. 10-3.   Top row of foundation blocks.

weighted string from one slit to the other. Of course, if you dig it yourself, this will also determine where you wield the pick and shovel.

Now, with the excavation lines laid out, the depth of the excavation will be the next consideration. Generally this should be below the frost line—4 feet below grade in the North, at least 3 feet in the South—but in all instances it should be dug down to firm mineral soil. Place footings under the wall. They should be at least 3 inches thick and 16 inches wide. Consequently, the excavation will have to be widened at the bottom to accommodate them. After the footings have set about three days, the block laying can commence.

BLOCK LAYING

The methods of block laying will be the same as for the full-size conventional greenhouse in chapter 2. We suggest the building be built at least one course of blocks or 8 inches above ground level to prevent water seepage problems. The blocks will have to be left out of the door openings to permit entry at the ground level (see Fig. 10-3). Don't forget to place the anchor bolts or anchor clips in this top row of blocks. If anchor bolts are used, plug the opening in the cement block with paper or a similar material at the bottom of the top course. Then fill the opening with concrete to the top of the course. Set the bolt in position with a washer at the head. The washer, of course, provides greater anchorage than the head of the bolt used alone. The bolt should extend 4 inches above the block. Locate the bolts by snapping a chalk line 3½ inches from the inside edge of the 8-inch blocks. Imbed the bolts, spaced 2 feet from each corner, 4 feet apart on straight walls. Also the door frames can be anchored to the blocks with bolts or clips, with clips being more expedient. Place the clip at the joint under the top course of blocks.

After the perimeter walls are in place, the interior partition walls can be laid. Six-inch instead of 8-inch blocks can be used for the interior walls if desired. Generally, the interior walls should be buried at least 8 inches, extended 4 inches aboveground. Make sure the bottom course of blocks rests on mineral soil, however. Poured partition footings can be used also. They should be at least 4 inches wide and 4 inches aboveground, and buried at least 8 inches or to a depth where they can rest on undisturbed mineral soil. Imbed anchor bolts in the interior footings also.

Use a concrete mix compounded of one part cement, three parts sand, and five parts ¾-inch gravel for poured walls.

FLOOR

At this time the type of floor that will be used can be considered. If the building codes specify concrete, it will be easier to install it now than when the building is put up. Actually, the floor in the animal stalls should be left as undisturbed dirt if possible. The floor in the automobile section can be traffic-compacted crushed gravel and the floor in the other two sections can be made from crushed gravel or treated lumber.

In no case should horses or other animals be required to stand for long hours on bare concrete. The floor should be covered with planks or with a thick layer of straw if a concrete floor must be used.

In suburban localities, local building codes often specify that the stable floor be drained into a dry well. Probably the local building inspector will notify you of this when you go to get the building permit. He may have plans for a dry well also. He might want to know what you plan on doing with the manure. In these days of organic gardening it usually can be sold to eager vegetable and flower raisers, and some of the cost of the feed can be returned. Also, any nearby farm will be glad to get it, especially if you deliver it to the fields. Naturally, if you build on sufficient acreage, none of these problems will be encountered.

THE ART OF DEALING WITH BUILDING INSPECTORS

Dealing with building inspectors is more of an art than a science. They vary from very conscientious, experienced men to outright con artists. Some even try to stop private citizens from doing their own building, or at least derive as much income from them as possible if they do. Here are two ways a homeowner can force fair treatment from a hostile, opportunist-type building inspector: (1) Very earnestly call him up two to three times a day and ask questions about the building. After this goes on for about three weeks, the inspector is likely to shout, "Don't call me again. I'm not your contractor." (2) Make a great show of writing down or recording every word the inspector says. He

will probably become very close-mouthed when faced with this situation.

The most self-serving way to deal with the building inspector is to use his knowledge to improve your structure, but don't allow him to bully you out of building or into hiring any of his contractor friends.

WALL FRAMING

Anyway, after the flooring and partition footings are in place, the framing can commence. Essentially, wall framing consists of the bottom horizontal members called shoes, top horizontal members called plates, and the vertical members between the top and bottom called the studding. Generally, all of these members are made of 2 × 4 lumber. It is recommended in this building that both the shoes and plates be doubled.

Make arrangements to buy, rent, or borrow an electric hand held or table saw. Even if you buy one, it will pay for itself before this project is half-done.

You can start by framing in the west end wall. Select two 10-foot 2 × 4's as knotfree as possible. Saw each end of each piece if necessary to square the ends, butt them together, and make sure the overall length of the two is near 20 feet. Next square the ends of a third 10-foot 2 × 4 and nail it so the center, or 5-foot mark, falls directly on the joint of the previous two 2 × 4's. Use ten-penny nails to nail the 2 × 4's together.

Complete the assembly by nailing two 5-foot lengths of 2 × 4's at each end. This completes the shoe, spliced together for maximum strength. Next, carefully measure and saw the shoe to a length of 19 feet 5 inches. This is necessary because the side walls are cut a full 30 feet long and the thickness of each side wall must be included in the width since building measurements are taken across the outside. Before the studs are nailed to the shoe, lay the shoe alongside the anchor bolts in the foundation wall and mark the location of each bolt hole on the plate. Drill the holes ¾ inch in diameter for ease of assembly.

The next step is to fabricate the plate. This is done identically to the shoe except that the top board of the double 2 × 4's is left a full 20 feet long to tie the end wall into the side wall (see Fig. 10-4). In all cases the splices should be made so they fall directly over the end of a stud, and the plate and shoe splices

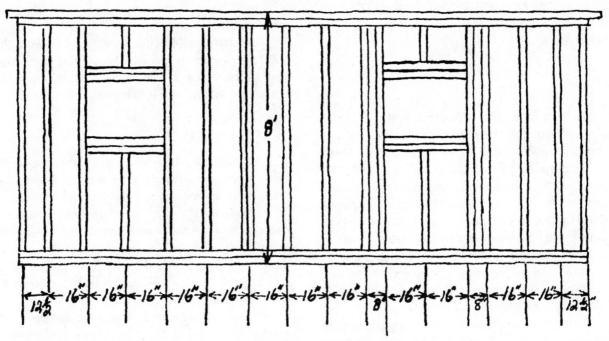

Fig. 10-4. West wall frame.

should not fall on opposite ends of the same stud. If good straight 20-foot 2 × 4's are available, they should be used to avoid the splices.

After the shoe and plates are made up, lay the plate on the shoe with the 19-foot, 5-inch section of the plate flush with the ends of the shoe. Use a pencil to mark the location of each stud on both the plate and shoe. This will eliminate measuring each one after they are installed. The studs are cut 7 feet 6 inches long except for the short lengths over and

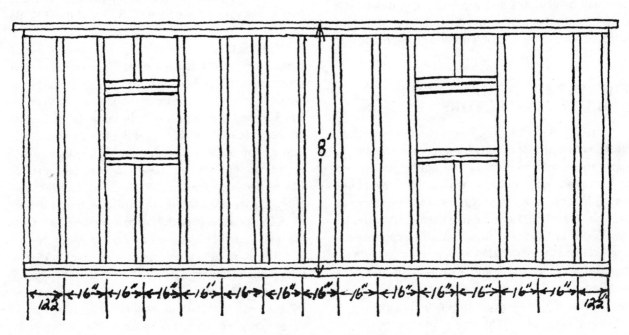

Fig. 10-5. East wall frame.

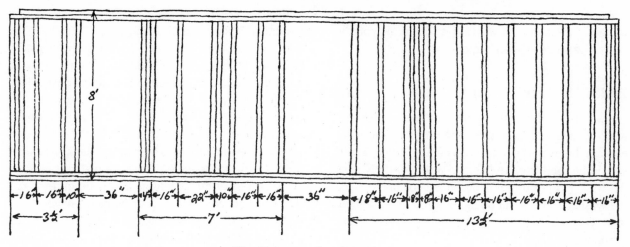

Fig. 10-6. North wall frame.

under the window frames. One hundred fifty 8-foot studs will be required in all. Study Fig. 10-9.

Notice at the top and bottom of each window frame a double 2 × 4 is required to prevent warping. Before the west wall is made up, the rough openings for the windows should be checked with the suppliers in your locality to see if they have windows that will fit. Then make the openings according to the available windows. Fail to do that and you may have to do what the author did and settle for a window much smaller than he really wanted during one building

project, simply because no window was available that would fit the rough opening called for in the plans.

The studs should be fastened to the plate and shoe by driving sixteen-penny nails through the plate and shoe and into the end of the stud or by toenailing two eight-penny nails on either side of the stud into the plate and shoe.

After the wall is completely framed, use a 50-foot tape to measure diagonally from both top corners to both bottom corners to see if it is square. If it isn't,

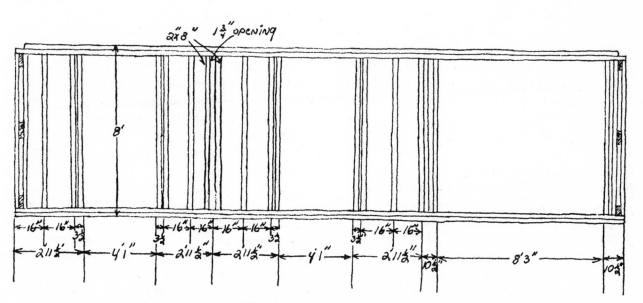

Fig. 10-7. South wall frame.

strike it at one corner to square it up. When it is square, nail a temporary 1 × 4 brace diagonally across the frame to keep it square.

RAISING THE WALLS

With this done, the frame can be hoisted into place. Many workmen injuries have resulted from not enough help at this stage. Generally, three adults should be used to raise this size wall. Carefully raise the wall and position it over the anchor bolts. Place the washer and the nut on the bolts but don't tighten them yet. They will be tightened when all the frames are nailed in place.

When the frame is in place, make sure it doesn't come crashing down again by bracing it in at least two places by extending 2 × 4's from the frame to the ground. At least the first and second frames being raised into position should be made plumb. Do this by driving an eight-penny nail into the end of the plate and hanging a plumb bob from it. Check the frames for alignment by stretching a chalk line from one end of a frame to the other at the side of the plate. If it is found to be either out of plumb or crooked, straighten the offending member by pounding on a piece of scrap wood placed against it.

Continue to fabricate and raise each wall into position. If, as frequently happens, a wall must be shimmed between the shoe and the concrete to level the frame and space is left under the shoe as a result, a mixture of one part portland cement and three parts sand must be flushed under the shoe to close up this space. This mixture should be allowed to dry three days before the bolts are tightened down. Nail the frames together at the corners with sixteen-penny nails, at least two in each location.

PARTITIONS

After the exterior framing is up and in place, the interior partitions can be put in place. The interior partition framing in this building is made identical to the outside walls. This simplifies construction for the amateur builder. The inside of the animal stalls should be lined with 2 × 8 planks if horses are to be kept in them, or a divider of 2 × 8 planks can be used to separate the stalls. If the stalls won't be used for horses, a solid partition of 2 × 4 studding covered

with plywood or a grillwork to promote ventilation can be utilized. Some builders may desire to have the partition between the stalls made so it is easily removed to make a larger enclosure for use as an animal nursery or a breeding stall. In that case, place 2 × 8 studdings 1¾ inches apart in the outside south wall (see Fig. 10-7) and the partition wall (partition A in Figs. 10-8 and 10-9) and bolt 8-foot 2 × 8 planks on edge between them. The bottom plank should be treated with a good waterproof preservative.

The rest of the partitions are made up of 2 × 4 studdings covered with ½- or ¾-inch plywood. All partitions have a double-thickness shoe bolted to the concrete divider walls, but a double-thickness plate is optional in the interior walls. When the partitions are complete, the floor joists can be installed.

FLOOR JOISTS

Most codes call for 2 × 10's to be used with the 10-foot span between the walls in this building. Generally, 20-foot 2 × 10's are available but if they are not use 12-foot 2 × 10's and splice them over the plates. Use only knotfree, straight boards, but if a crowned or crooked board must be used, position the crown up since it will straighten in time. Nail the joists together at the splices with eight-penny nails and into the plate with sixteen-penny nails. Also notice that the first floor joist is nailed 3½ inches from the gable end. Each succeeding joist is nailed on 2-foot centers (see Fig. 10-10).

After all the floor joists are in place, cut and nail in the joist bridging. Generally, solid bridging is the most advantageous to install. Simply cut 2 × 10 stock into 21-inch pieces. Nail the bridging between the floor joists at the maximum distance from the cross members. Also, the bridging should be staggered for optimum utility and to permit nailing through the joists into the ends of the bridging pieces (see Fig. 10-10).

Also nail in extra bridging over the horse stalls so an opening can be provided for dropping hay down to the horses from the mow.

By this stage in the building, you have probably noticed that you are not tall enough to work effectively from the ground. A ladder, of course, provides the easiest-to-obtain platform. If two sturdy ladders are available, they can be used in conjunction with

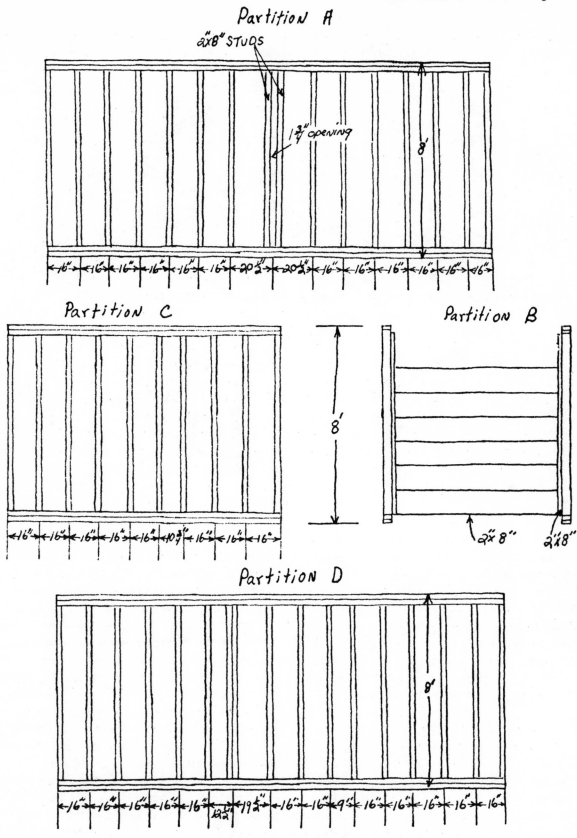

Fig. 10-8. Interior partitions.

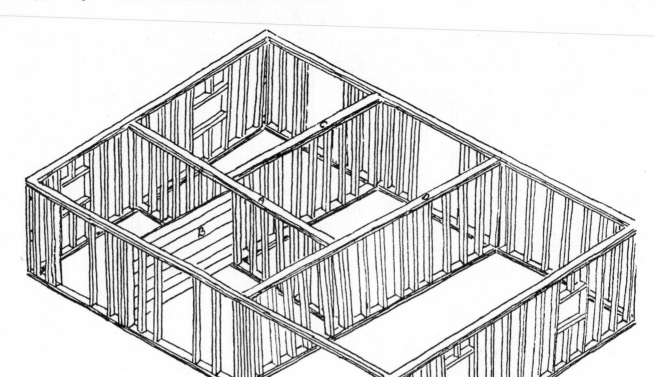

Fig. 10-9.   Complete frame.

ladder jacks to provide a working platform. The old standby of carpenters is the wooden scaffolding, erected on the spot. This makes a fine, safe platform but it does cost extra money and time to build. Fortunately, in most populated areas pipe scaffolding can be rented from building material suppliers or hardware or paint stores. You can also use 2 × 10 planks placed across sawhorses. After a few floor joists are in place, a temporary platform in the form of a few plywood sheets can be laid on the joists to work from.

WALL SHEATHING

The next logical step in construction is to apply the wall sheathing. Building codes often call for building felt to be used under exterior sheathing. Number 15 or, as it is commonly called, 15-pound felt is used. Apply it horizontally and overlap the edges 2 inches. Further, it should overlap the foundation 2 inches. It will take three runs of 36-inch-wide felt for the side walls of this building. A staple gun is the ideal tool to use to fasten the felt to the studding. Place a ½-inch staple every 4 inches on all edges.

After the felt is applied, the sheathing can commence. Ideally, ⅝-inch exterior grade plywood will be used for this, although ½-inch or even ⅜-inch may pass the code in some areas. Every plywood panel should butt together on a stud. This building is designed to accept pieces of plywood. Be sure the panel is positioned so it is ½ inch lower than the upper edge of the upper plate. Use eight-penny nails positioned every 6 inches apart on each stud and each edge. Each end panel sheathing should extend past the corner ⅝ inch to cover the ends of the side panels (see Fig. 10-11). On the 30-foot walls there will be 1 foot of waste on each panel which can be utilized in building the horse mangers. Cut out the

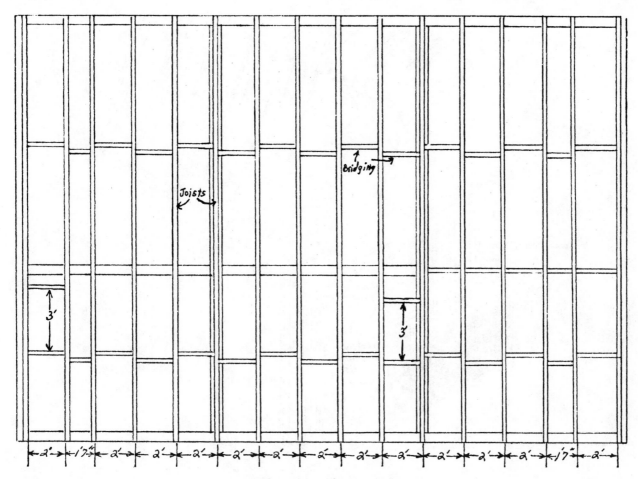

Fig. 10-10. Floor joists.

window openings after the panels have been installed.

HAYLOFT FLOORING

After the side wall panels are installed, the ceiling or hayloft flooring can be installed. Use ¾-inch exterior plywood if available. Start at the center by snapping a chalk line from one end wall to the other on the 10-foot line directly in the center. Align the first row of plywood panels carefully on this line and the remaining rows will be straight. Nail to the floor joists every 8 inches with eight-penny nails. Do not place the outer panels at this time since they need to be out of the way for installing the rafters. Always butt panels together over a floor joist. If you "miss" a joist, it will be necessary to install an additional bridging to brace the butt ends of the paneling.

MAKING AND INSTALLING THE RAFTERS

When this is all done, it will provide a platform for fabricating and installing the rafters. If you don't wish to make rafters, your local lumberyard will no doubt do it for you. However, you can do it yourself handily enough by following the simple procedures outlined here. First, select 32 16-foot 2 × 6's. Make sure they are straight and knotfree. Fir or pine will have sufficient structural strength. Cut a 9-foot length and a 6-foot, 6-inch length from one 16-foot 2 × 6. These two boards will form two angles of one side of the gambrel rafters.

Now take the boards, an 8-foot straight edge, a 20-foot steel tape, and a carpenter's square and climb up to the loft floor. Make a line (A in Fig. 10-12) 7 feet, 9 inches long on the loft floor, lengthwise of the building about 3 feet from the edge. Use the carpenter's square to find the corner and project a

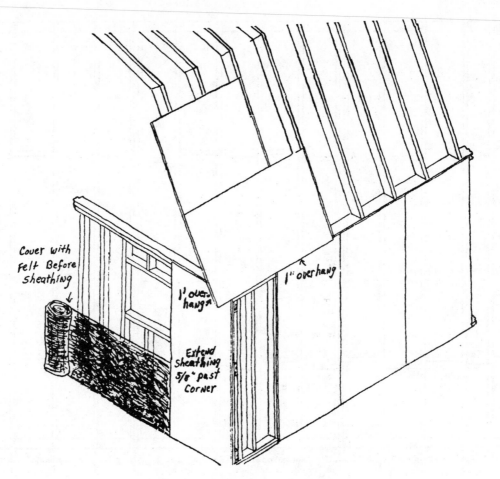

Cover with
Felt Before
Sheathing

1' over-
hang

1" overhang

Extend
Sheathing
5/8" past
Corner

Fig. 10-11. Sheathing the stable/garage.

second line (*B*) 4 feet, 3 inches long at right angles to
the first line towards the center of the building. Now
try the 9-foot length of 2 × 6 for connecting the ends
of line *A* and *B* as shown (see Fig. 10-12). If your
measurements are correct, this should just fit. If it
does, project line *C* 3 feet in the same direction as
line *A*. At the 3-foot mark of line *C*, project the right-
angle line *D* 5 feet, 9 inches long. Now try the 6-foot,
6-inch 2 × 6 between the ends of lines *C* and *D*. It
should just fit. If it doesn't, go back and check the
measurements. If it does, proceed to find the angle
cuts for each of the two boards. To find these angle
cuts project lines *D* and lines *A* until they intersect.
Then draw a line (*E*) from the intersection of lines *A*
and *D* approximately 6 inches past the junctions of
lines *C* and *B* (see Fig. 10-12). Then lay the previously
cut 2 × 6's, one at a time, in their proper position and
mark both edges where line *E* falls. Connect the
marks with a square and saw them off. The angles for

the ridgeboard and the plate can be found with the
square by simply extending a line at right angles to
lines *A* and *D* in both cases. Study Figure 10-12.

Notice that a 1 × 8, 5 feet long, is used for a
brace across the joint on both sides of the rafter, on all
except the end rafters (see Fig. 10-12). Also a panel
clip should be used at the joint, or a 1 × 8 × 12-inch
wooden gusset plate can be made up and nailed
across the joint. Nail 1 × 6 collar beams across the
rafters after they are in position.

It will be necessary to tack one rafter together
temporarily and check it with a temporary ridgeboard
to see if it fits. If it doesn't, make any adjustments
necessary and then disassemble the rafters and use
each board as a pattern for making up the rest of the
rafter assemblies. Notice that they are spaced on 2-
foot centers and thirty-two will be required in all (see
Fig. 10-13). Always use the pattern pieces for making
all of the others to decrease the chance for errors.

When the time comes for installing the rafters, temporarily bolt the lower end of the first rafter to the floor joist using one 1/2 × 3-inch bolt. Then tack it to the ridgeboard with an eight-penny nail. If both ends line up well, drill the second hole in the rafter and floor joist and install the second bolt. Then toenail the top end of the rafter to the ridgeboard with two ten-penny nails on each side of the rafter. The two end rafters have to have a spacer block nailed to them to bring the rafters flush with the inside joist.

The ridgeboard has to be held in position with a fixture until several of the rafters are in place. Make up this fixture by tacking a 1 × 6 to a stand made by nailing a 4-foot 2 × 4 to the loft floor (see Fig. 10-13). Use duplex nails or leave the heads of the nails slightly raised for easy removal.

After all the rafters are nailed in position, plumb them up and nail a scrap 1 × 6 brace across them to keep them true while the roof sheathing is applied.

Notice that the brace is underneath, not on top of the rafters. The ends of the floor joists extend beyond the angle of the rafters and they will have to be sawed off to the rafter angle.

LOFT SHEATHING

The next step after the rafters are in position is to nail the rest of the loft sheathing into place. It has to be slotted to fit past the rafters. Mark for these slots by holding the panel against the rafter and projecting the dimensions on the panel with a square and pencil. Use a saber saw to saw out the slots. With this done, the end gable studs can be installed.

FITTING THE GABLE STUDS

Fitting the gable studs looks more complicated than it is. Simply stand a 2 × 4 in the proper position

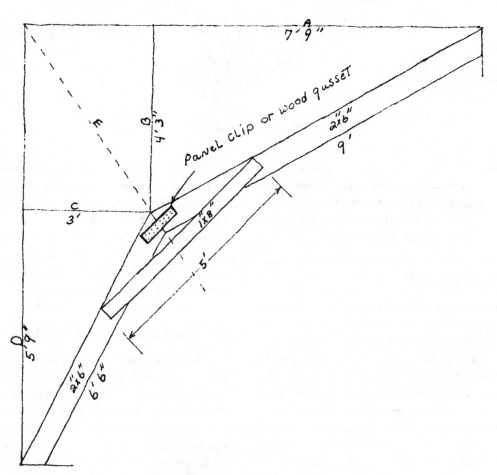

Fig. 10-12.   Gambrel barn rafter.

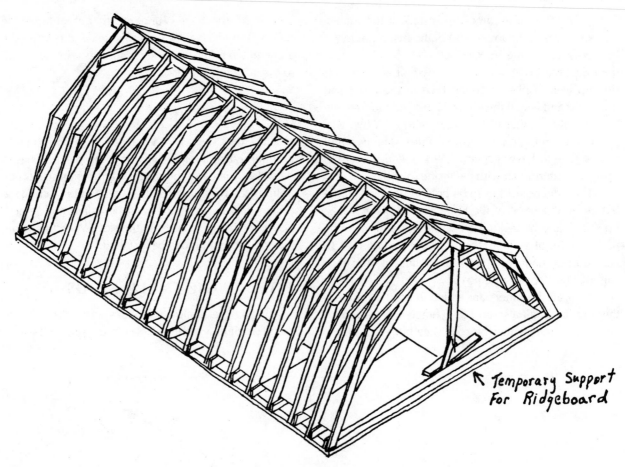

Fig. 10-13.   Location of gambrel rafters.

on the plate, use a level to make sure it is straight up, and draw a pencil line where the gable rafter intersects the stud. Notice that the west end has a loft door opening (see Fig. 10-14). This takes an opening liner of 2 × 4 plus a double 2 × 6 header.

ROOF SHEATHING

Now, with this done, the roof sheathing can commence. As with most roofing work, the first course must be started straight with the building. Generally this is done by snapping a chalk line to show the proper position for the upper edge of the plywood. Since a 1-inch overhang is desirable, snap the chalk line 47 inches up from the end of the rafters. A good method of doing this is to start six-penny nails on either end of the rafters and stretch and snap the chalk line between them. Do not place the joints of the panels parallel with each other since it could

weaken the roof. One way to install them is shown in Figure 10-11. When the peak is reached, the ridgeboard has to be shaved to prevent a space at the top of the roof. Use a skill saw set at an angle or a drawknife to slant the ridgeboard to the angle of the sheathing. Notice that the panels project 12 inches beyond the end rafters. The panels should be nailed every 8 inches with eight-penny nails.

INSTALLING THE FASCIA

When the roof sheathing is complete, the fascia can be installed (see Fig. 10-15). Notice that the 1 × 6 end fascia is made like a gambrel rafter. This is nailed to the ridgeboard at the top and through the roof sheathing along the slant of the roof. The side fascia consists of 1 × 6 boards also and it is nailed under the side eaves, butted against the roof sheathing. When this is done, the roofing can be applied.

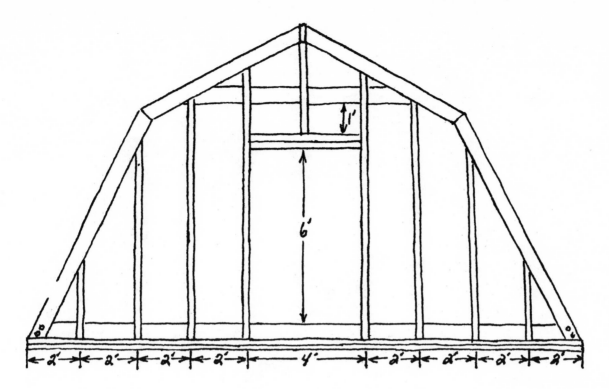

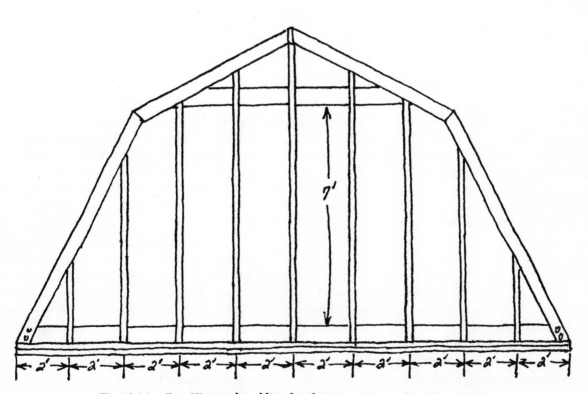

Fig. 10-14. *Top:* West end studding detail. *Bottom:* East end studding detail.

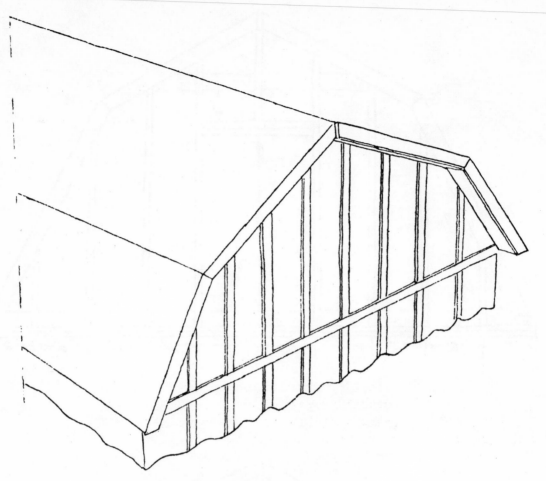

Fig. 10-15. Roof fascia and batten boards.

SHINGLING

All sorts of commercial roofing is available and most would be satisfactory for this application. We used asphalt 3-in-1 shingles that weigh 300 pounds to the square for our roof. This was a good choice since they are simple to handle, require very little expertise to install, and can be put on while working from ladders. If you use this type shingle, be sure yours have a seal on each tab. The heat of the sun will eventually seal the tabs of the shingles to prevent the wind from lifting them.

Before applying the asphalt shingles a metal starter strip should be nailed along the eave. Be sure the starter strip extends beyond the wall sheathing 1¼ inches so it extends past the siding at least ½ inch. This prevents the water from running down the wood. Starter strips are available at lumberyards and hardware stores.

The first row of asphalt shingles at the roof is called the shingle starter strip. It is a standard shingle nailed on upside down so the notches between the shingle tabs are extended towards the peak and the flat edge of the shingle is along the eave. Use six large-headed roofing nails per strip.

Apply the succeeding rows of shingles in the normal position, overlapping each about 5 inches. The notch between the shingles is used as a guide in regulating the amount of overlap. Place the nails 1 inch back and 1½ inches on each side of the notches.

When the peak is reached, use a row of shingles applied parallel with the ends of the roof. Overlap this row about 5 inches also. A metal ridge roll also is convenient to use for this application and gives the roof a finished appearance.

When working from a ladder, some method of securing the ladder so it doesn't slip is recommended.

Many roofers use a ½-inch nylon rope tied from the top of the ladder over the roof ridge and secured on the other side to a door, window, or wall anchor.

DOOR AND WINDOW FRAMES

After the roofing is put on, the door and window frames can be made up and installed. As mentioned before, be sure to check what is locally available in window sizes before the openings are left in the studs. Window frames are made according to a definite standard procedure. First, cut two 1 × 4's to the size required to line the vertical sides of the rough opening. Then carefully measure the horizontal length of the rough opening, deduct the thickness of the two vertical 1 × 4's and saw out a 1 × 6 to fit between them. These will form the top and sides of the frame. The windowsill is made from a 2 × 6. It is sawed to be placed flush with the back edge of the vertical sides of the frame and notched to extend past the sides of the vertical frame for 3½ inches on each side. This is to cover 4-inch window casings. This window frame should be installed flush with the inside edge of

the studs. If it is desired to use 2 × 8 stall liners in the animal stalls, be sure to use 1 × 6's for the vertical and horizontal members. Further, use a 2 × 8 for the windowsill.

Once the window frame is made up, place it in the rough opening and use shingles to square it up. When it is square, nail it to the studding with sixteen-penny nails. Make sure it is flush with the outside sheathing before nailing. When the window is in position, nail 1 × 4 casing all around the perimeter. A drip cap made from a 1 × 2 pine strip can be installed as an optional installation.

Many times windows are made up by the manufacturer complete, so the window frame and sash can just be installed in the rough opening. All that has to be done then is to nail the window trim in place.

The door frames of 1 × 6 boards on the north wall are nailed inside the studding which forms the 36-inch rough openings for the doors (see Fig. 10-16). The door frame is squared up inside the rough opening with shingle wedges and then nailed securely in place with ten-penny nails. A drip cap and 1 × 4 casing is also used with these doors. The two dutch doors

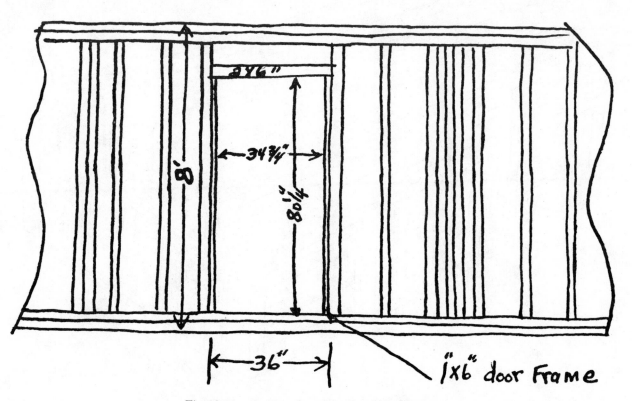

Fig. 10-16.   Section of north wall with door frame.

on the south wall are also framed in this way, but 2 × 8 headers must be used for this length of opening.

The garage door is framed by lining the inside of the 8-foot opening with 2 × 8 planks. Generally adequate instructions come with garage doors so they can be hung securely. Try looking at a neighbor's garage door installation if you feel insecure about installing one. For this type of installation an overhead track-type door should be satisfactory, although tilting, folding, and sliding doors are also good choices. Generally, whatever is available within the budget is a good choice since any of these types of doors are satisfactory if installed correctly and maintained well.

The dutch doors used on the south wall probably must be handmade since purchasing custom-made doors like this is nigh impossible. Perhaps the easiest and fastest way to make a dutch door is to cut out a

piece of ¾-inch exterior grade plywood to the desired shape. Line one side with tongue-and-groove 2 × 6's (see Fig. 10-18) by placing number 10 flatheaded wood screws through the plywood into the liners. When it is assembled, saw the door apart and then place a cleat across the top section so that it overlaps the bottom. This can be a 1 × 4 fastened to the top section with wood screws or nails. For a "professional" look countersink all nail holes and fill the holes with putty. Personally, I don't find the head of a nail offensive; in fact, I find it reassuring to see the correctly placed nail or screw heads giving evidence of the fasteners buried in the wood doing their darndest to keep my building together. Naturally, the nails should be evenly spaced, however, if they aren't covered.

When the door is done, proper hardware should be secured for it. Many carpenters weigh a door on a

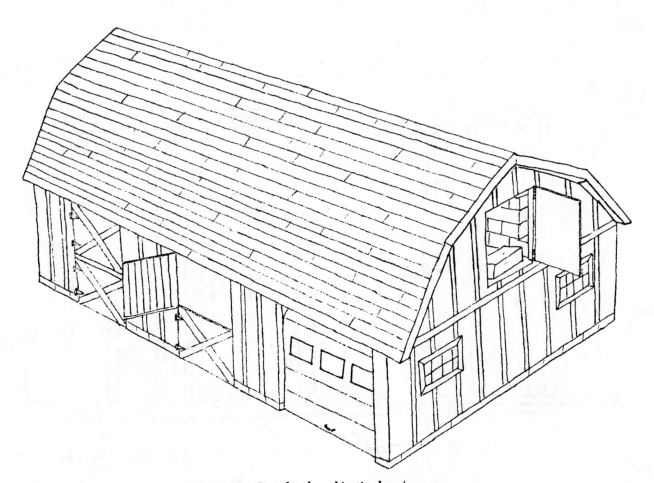

Fig. 10-17.   Completed combination barn/garage.

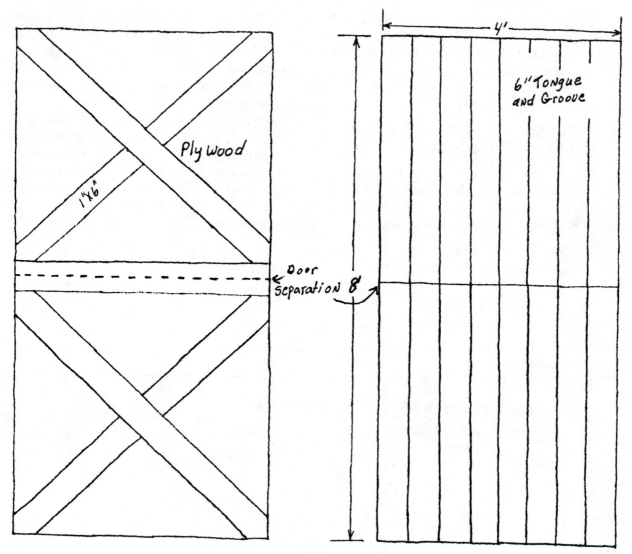

Fig. 10-18.   Dutch door.

feed scale or even a bathroom scale to determine what size hinges to use. Use a T hinge. Your hardware should be able to tell you what size is needed. Of course, this has to be very strong to form a kick-proof door. No use having a heavy door if the horse can kick the hinge off. The door should be secured with a bolt lock and at night the bolt should be padlocked to prevent anyone from bothering the horses.

Goats also are becoming a valuable animal and they should be made secure if they will be bothered. Each one of these stalls can accommodate two goats

with all the paraphernalia needed to milk and care for them.

RUSTICATING THE EXTERIOR

No additional siding needs to be used for the exterior of the building, but 1 × 2 batten boards should be placed vertically on 16-inch centers to project a rustic appearance. The barn can then be painted red and trimmed with white. The very best way to finish the outside of this project, though, is to tear down an old barn and use the weathered boards as board and batten siding on your barn. Weathered boards should not be painted but they should be coated with three coats of a good waterproof preservative.

ARRANGEMENTS FOR DRYING PRODUCE AND SMOKING MEAT

The northwest corner of the building can be used for drying garden produce or for smoking meat (see Fig. 10-19). Make sure the room is well ventilated for at least two weeks after smoking meat before an at-

tempt is made to dry vegetables, unless some smoke flavoring of the vegetables is not objectionable.

Meat can be smoked very well in this room by placing a plate of wood chips on the element of a hot plate. Drying heat can be generated by a small thermostatically controlled electric heater such as a "milk house heater." Provide a ventilator by extending a 4-inch diameter galvanized smoke pipe through the loft floor. By providing this pipe with a damper the amount of ventilation can be controlled. If meat or fish is soaked in salt water before being hung to smoke, a container should be placed to catch the salt water drippings if the room has a cement floor.

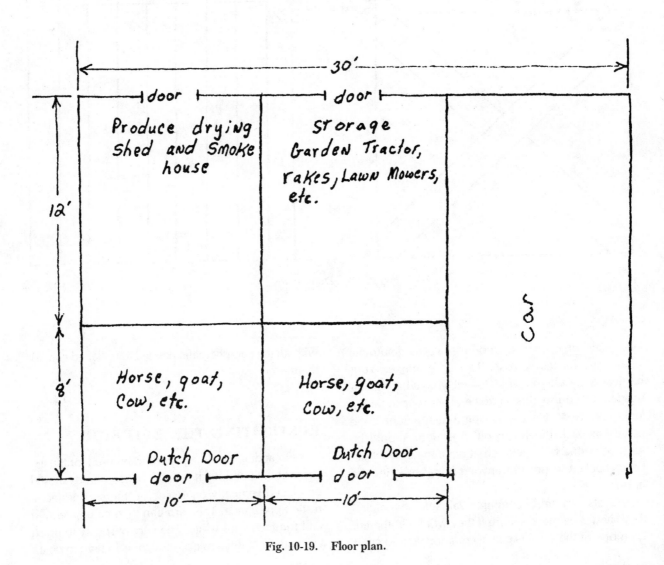

Fig. 10-19. Floor plan.

Build drying racks in the room by covering frames made of 1 × 2 furring strips with ¼-inch mesh wire. The frames can be as wide as desired, and a different tier can be used for each foot of height. The same racks that will be used for drying produce can be used for smoking meat and fish also, but be sure that no salt water comes in contact with galvanized wire.

No special equipment is needed in the tool storage room except for a few sections of perforated boards nailed to the walls to hang tools from and perhaps a sheet of ¾-inch plywood lying on the floor to use as a platform for repairing and servicing garden tools. The garage stall can have an overhead snow tire platform as well as a lifting hoist for making repairs on the car.

The horse stalls or goat stalls should be built with a hay platform while the goat stalls should be made with a milking platform and other necessities of goat husbandry. Get a copy of *The Homesteader's Handbook* for complete information on the proper way to set up the stall and care for these animals.

Chapter 4

PLAY BUILDINGS FOR KIDS

Build any one of the projects contained in this chapter and the kids will no longer have to leave home to find a place to play. In fact, you may even "gain" a child or two. By all means let the kids help build these projects since they will learn important skills, develop a protective attitude towards the finished project, and derive more satisfaction from playing with it. An attempt has been made to provide information for building something for a child whether he has a bias towards rivers, the frontier, or outer space.

KENTUCK KAMP FORT

The Kentuck Kamp fort is built along the lines of an Adirondack shelter. From a practical standpoint it fits in with many lawn schemes wherever rough-sawn boards or large natural stones, logs, or ties are used in any building or decoration. If you have a wooded set-

ting available as a location for this building, by all means build it there. It will fit in so well that your boys might not ever come home again—except for meals, of course.

The Kentuck Kamp was originally used by the fast-traveling woodsman Daniel Boone a long time before anyone ever heard of the resort area commonly called the Adirondack Mountains today. Nor was this camp an original design of Boone. He reportedly was taught to build it by the North Carolina supply wagon drivers that the English General Braddock employed during the French and Indian wars.

Daniel soon grew adept at building one, however, and he "throwed" one up whenever he was going to stop for a few days. This delighted the settlers who followed Boone since they watched for and gratefully utilized the shelters that he left as he moved on. It is also rumored that he once said bitterly that if he had had time to build a Kentuck Kamp, the hostile Indians would never have been able to seize his son James, whom they tortured to death.

Several years later when Boone went to settle the Kentucky Territory, he lived first in a Kentuck Kamp and only reluctantly moved to a large house when he became prosperous. In a few years Boone was back in the Kentuck Kamp at Point Pleasant, West Virginia, however, since conniving lawyers arranged to have him stripped of his huge land holdings in the Kentucky Territory. It is one of the great tragedies of history that this brave man who settled and opened so much hostile land to settlers should have lived in poverty most of his life.

The original design of the Kentuck Kamp had the front wall left out. This made it possible to heat and light the interior of the structure with an open fire built in front of it. It was not exactly foolproof that way, however, since wayward winds occasionally swirled smoke and sparks onto the bedrolls of sleeping campers. Also, invariably some hardy camper would have to rise up during the night and replenish the fire. We included the front wall in our design for obvious reasons.

MATERIALS LIST FOR KENTUCK KAMP FORT

1. 24 8 × 8 × 16-inch concrete blocks or approximately 10 cubic feet of cement
2. 12 ¼ × 8-inch carriage bolts
3. 4 8-foot 2 × 6's for floor stringers
4. 100 running feet of 2 × 4 for floor joists
5. 3 4 × 8 sheets ⅝-inch plywood or the equivalent for flooring
6. 14 8-foot and 2 6-foot 2 × 4's for studding. 4 12-foot 2 × 4's for plates and sills
7. 7 10-foot 2 × 4's for rafters
8. 3 6-foot 2 × 4's for overhang
9. 250 square feet of half-log siding
10. 150 square feet of roof sheathing and asphalt shingles or roll roofing
11. Approximately 3 pounds ten-penny common nails. Door
12. Inside furnishing, etc

Site Selection

Some special considerations are apparent when selecting a site for the Kentuck Kamp playhouse. The most important is to avoid building beside a driveway, highway, or railroad track. Deep water, dangerous animals, and people should also be taken into consideration when selecting a site. Some other common but often overlooked situations to avoid are areas where water stands after a rain or where the yard will be muddy as a result of underground moisture. Also, do not build too near large dead trees or electric lines. Green trees, however, are desirable since they provide shade and a natural setting. As in all building, if your township is zoned, it is wise to consult your building inspector even before you start.

Foundation

The cheapest way to make a foundation for such a structure is to build a piling at each corner, although Boone probably just set his on stones. When you want to build a piling for a minimal-weight building such as this, it is not necessary to sink the piling in the ground more than 1 foot or to mineral soil. If the soil is too light or moist, the piling can be made so that it is flared on the bottom for maximum flotation. Anyway, start the form for the piling by digging an 8-inch diameter hole. Further, form a cylinder of heavy roofing paper that will just fit in the hole and project 6 inches above it. This is the form for the concrete. A tin can with both ends cut out will also work for a form.

Use the 1-2-3 mixture for pilings of this type. This mixture is one part portland cement, two and one-fourth parts sand, and three parts small gravel. Small amounts of concrete such as this can be mixed in a pail or even on a wide board. Mix the ingredients dry until they are well blended; then just add water until the mixture is pliable. Be sure to tamp it in the form so the air bubbles are removed from it. After the mixture starts to harden, set one ¼ × 8-inch carriage bolt in the center of each outside piling. The bolt head should be sunk about 3 inches in the concrete.

Be sure to level each piling again after the bolts are inserted, and do not attempt to build until the concrete has cured for three days. The concrete should be kept covered for at least twenty-four hours to allow slow curing. Concrete blocks can also be used. Place one 8-inch block underground and top it with another. Fill the center core with concrete and set the bolt in it.

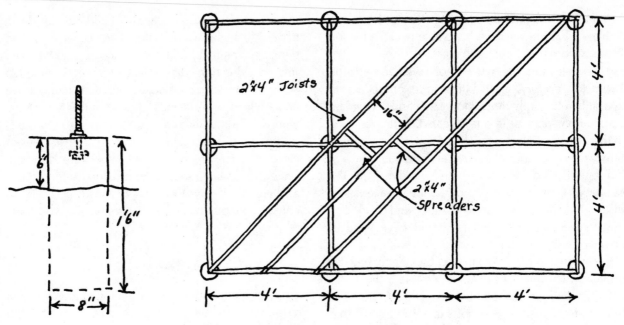

Fig. 8-1. *Left:* Piling. *Right:* Girders and floor joists.

Floor

After the pilings are set, build the floor frame. The first wooden members are 2 × 6 stringers placed on edge from one piling to the other. They have to be drilled for the ¼-inch carriage bolts. Use a flat washer under the nut on the bolts and tighten the nut until it just starts to compress the wood. The floor joists are sturdy knotfree 2 × 4's nailed on 16-inch centers diagonally between the stringers. The two center joists in each set have spreaders placed between the longest joists.

The flooring is ⅝-inch plywood or composition board. Of course, 1-inch boards can also be used. Be sure to use well-seasoned boards for the floor and treat them with a good preservative prior to installing them.

The shoe and plate are single 2 × 4 stock and all studding is 2 × 4 also. The frame for the overhang is likewise 2 × 4 stock. The waste from the rear wall studding can be utilized in the overhang.

Rifle Ports

All windows are made like rifle ports. They are 12-inch diameter holes sawed in the side wall sheathing. A cover is made for each porthole so that it can be pivoted down to cover the opening when the building is "under siege." The cover pivots on a ¼-inch carriage bolt. This bolt has the head outside and the threads inside the building, where it is equipped with a wing nut so the covers can be dropped from the inside. Each wall has four portholes. These portholes can be covered with screen if the danger of "attack" isn't too imminent.

Wall Frames and Rafters

Build the front wall frame by sawing out a plate and shoe 12 feet long. Nail 6-foot 9-inch studding on 24-inch centers between the shoe and plate. No allowance is made for the door since it is hung between the two center studs. See Figure 8-2. The rear wall of the Kentuck Kamp is made the same way except that the studs are 3 feet 9 inches long. See Figure 8-3.

The simplest way to assemble the frame is to make the front and rear wall frames first, then prop them up and lay each outside rafter in place. Note that the rafters have to be notched for the front and rear wall plates (see Fig. 8-4). When the rafters are nailed in place, spike the front and rear frame shoes to the floor and then finish installing all of the rafters. The rafters are 9 feet 6 inches long and have 12

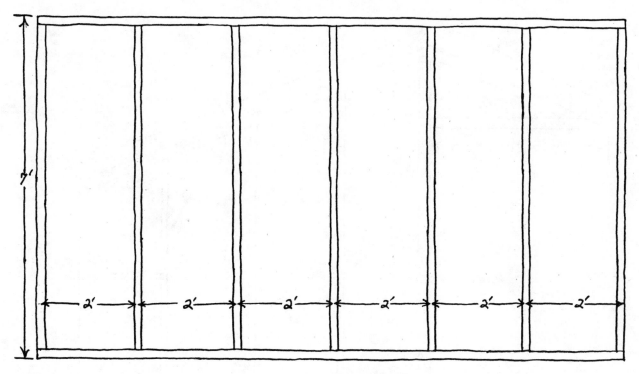

Fig. 8-2. Front wall frame.

inches of overhang at the rear. Once they are all placed, the side wall studs can be set in place, plumbed, marked, and sawed. The side wall studs are also placed on 2-foot centers. No stud is needed at the front and rear and no shoe or plate is needed on the side walls since the studs are toenailed directly to the floor and rafter.

Siding

No sheathing need be used with the Kentuck Kamp, instead, the siding is nailed directly on the studding. Half-log siding is available from most lumberyards. Sawmill slabs can be peeled and used also, and of course, rough-sawn boards directly from the sawmills can be used.

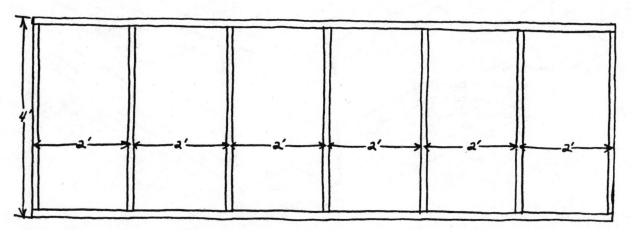

Fig. 8-3. Rear wall frame.

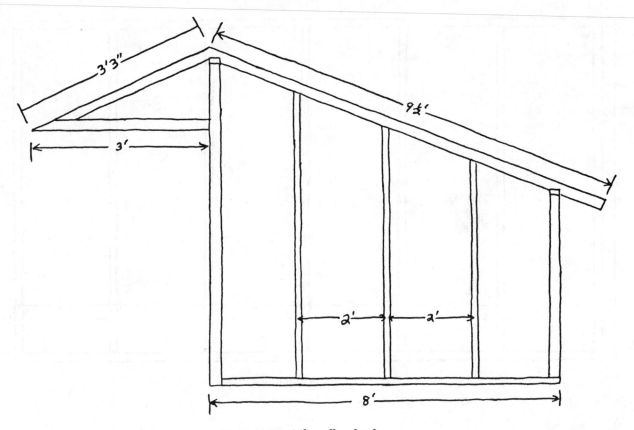

Fig. 8-4.   Side wall and rafter.

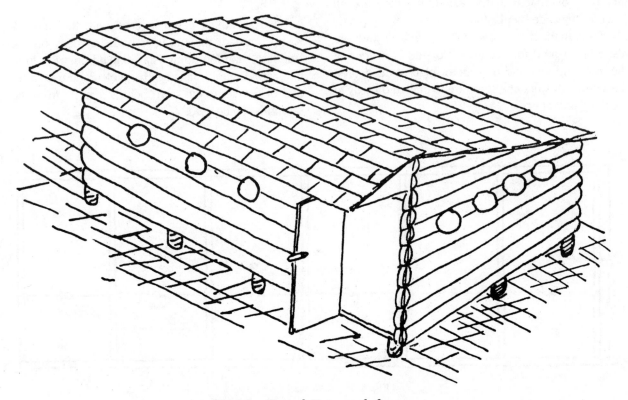

Fig. 8-5.   Kentuck Kamp ready for use.

Roof Sheathing

The roof sheathing can be ½-inch plywood. If a large snow load accumulates, it should be scraped off since the roof will not stand an extremely heavy load. The roofing can be any conventional shingle or roll roofing.

Paint

The exterior of the building can be painted a rustic brown or gray, and the inside a light green or white to make it as cheerful as possible.

Furniture

Furniture for the Kamp includes bunks and a table and benches. The bunks are made to fold up against the wall. One simple way to do this is to suspend the bunks from the walls. They are hinged in three places and a rope is knotted through a hole at each end of each bunk. The ropes are secured to the walls with large threaded screw eyes. Each bunk is a ⅝-inch plywood panel 30 inches wide and 5 feet 5 inches long. When not in use, the bunks are folded against the wall and kept in position with a screen door hook and screw eye. See Figure 8-6. The bunk should be placed within a foot of the floor to prevent little children from injuring themselves if they fall out of bed.

The table and chairs can be made as a picnic table is made. It is expected the table will be built inside the building since it will be extremely difficult to bring it in after the door and other framing is in place. The tabletop can also be used for a bunk.

Build the table by first sawing out a 3 × 5-foot panel of ⅝-inch particle board. Next, fabricate a frame of 2 × 4's with the outside dimensions the same as the hardboard panel. These 2 × 4's are placed vertically. Next, make the legs by sawing out two 2 × 4's for each end. These legs are 32 inches long. Nail them to the top and then cut out the two 2 × 6's that brace the table and project from the sides to form the seat. A 2 × 6 is also used for the seat. Study Figure 8-6. When the table is all done, it should be sanded and painted.

Beside the table a camping sink with a hose drain to the outside is convenient. Also, battery-

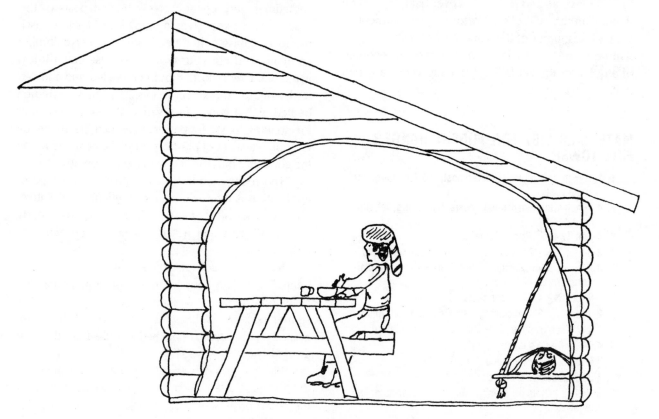

Fig. 8-6. Kentuck Kamp furnishings.

operated camping lights can be utilized to provide safe lighting so the cabin can be used day or night.

FOREST RANGER FIRE TOWER

The next project for the kids leaps ahead over a hundred years. It is called the Forest Ranger Fire Tower. In such a tower keen-eyed men have watched for dangerous forest fires for the last hundred years. They have been attacked by bears, shot at by poachers, and have often climbed down from their towers to singlehandedly put out fires that would have wiped out thousands of acres of timber if allowed to spread. Generally, the activities of these men have gone unheralded and maybe it is time we all pause for a few moments to pay them tribute.

Before building such a tower each parent should ask himself if he is willing for his child to take some risk. Also, it is to be expected that the neighborhood children will climb on it and it is possible that sooner or later one of them may fall. Injured feelings and possible litigation could be the result.

On the other hand many people have had such towers for years and no one has ever been injured on them. Further, a spokesman for the Department of Natural Resources of the state of Wisconsin asserted that no record of any injury had ever been recorded of any Forest Ranger falling from a tower or any part of it.

MATERIALS LIST FOR FOREST RANGER FIRE TOWER

1. 1 8-inch minimum diameter post, 14 feet long, for main post
2. 4 4-inch minimum diameter posts, 6 feet long, for support posts
3. 4-foot ³⁄₈-inch diameter steel cable
4. 2 6-foot 2 × 12's with 3¹⁄₂ × 12-inch carriage bolts
5. 4 2 × 6's approximately 6 feet 6 inches long for platform braces
6. 5 6-foot 2 × 4's for floor joists
7. 2 6-foot 2 × 6's for closing the ends of the floor joists
8. 1 6 × 6-foot section of ⁵⁄₈-inch-thick particle board
9. 4 6-foot 4 × 4's for studding
10. 4 6-foot 2 × 4's for wall plates
11. 4 33¹⁄₂-foot 2 × 4's for studding
12. 3 4 × 8 sheets of ¹⁄₄-inch tempered masonite or the equivalent
13. 1 12-foot and 3 8-foot 2 × 4's for the plate under the windows and the stud for the center of the window openings
14. 6 1 × 8-inch boards
15. 64 square foot of roof covering, either sawn 1-inch lumber, ¹⁄₄-inch plywood, or sheet metal. Wood must be covered with roll roofing
16. 1 × 6 lumber for ladder, 6 feet of rope, nails, etc

Risks can be minimized by insisting that a definite set of rules be followed by users of the tower and violators be banished from climbing. Further, a cushion of wood shavings at least a foot thick can be provided at the base of the tower to break a fall if an accident does occur. All wagons, toys, and other objects should be kept out of the "drop zone."

Support

A fine support can be made for the Forest Ranger Tower from a single large center pole ringed by four shorter poles. The center pole should be 8 inches in diameter on the smallest end and should be at least 14 feet long. Each short post should be 6 feet long. Used posts are often available from utility companies, sometimes very cheaply. New treated posts of this type are very expensive. In many localities it is possible to purchase a live tree from a farmer or timber company and cut your own posts. Use cedar if it is available. Green posts should be peeled and allowed to dry out for at least six weeks. Then they should be treated with a good preservative. A usable container for soaking posts in preservative can be made by wrapping a sheet of plastic around the post and filling the container thus formed with the preservative.

The recommended preservative for this type of application is the toxic, water-repellent preservative. This type of preservative will make a post nearly impervious to water if it is soaked for the optimum time.

Softwood such as pine can be successfully treated in twenty-four hours of soaking. Cedar and redwood should be soaked for six days. All of the shorter posts as well as the center posts should be treated to the depth that they will be buried in the ground.

Raising the posts should be done according to a definite procedure. First the hole should be dug for the center post. After this post is set in place, each one of the shorter posts should be dug in one at a time. The center post is buried 4 feet; each short post 2 feet. Before the center post is set up, a flat surface 11½ inches wide should be sawn on its opposing sides. If it is possible to secure the services of the local telephone or electric light company to help set up this center post, fine. If not, and you have to go it alone, proceed as follows: First dig the hole and position the pole so the butt is within a foot of the hole. Next, start at the small end of the pole and raise it with a tractor bucket or with people power until it starts to slide into the hole. Then raise it a little at a time and prop it up. Exercise care so that it doesn't push too much dirt down into the hole. Once the pole slides down into the hole, plumb it up with a level and backfill around it. Then place each of the short posts, and backfill and tamp them in very well.

After all of the posts are in position, they should be joined together with a cable. Use a ³⁄₈-inch diameter steel cable, and wrap it around the shorter posts 1 foot from the top. Use cable clamps to fit each end of the cable to the eyes of a turnbuckle, and tighten the turnbuckle to draw the cable tight. Do this on a warm day if possible.

Platform

When the cable is tightened and the posts are securely backfilled, work on the platform can be started. Use a ladder to level up the platform.

The first two boards to put in the platform are the cross girders under the floor. They are 6-foot 2 × 12's and they are placed on a flat surface sawn on the top of the post. The 2 × 12's are secured at the center with three ½-inch bolts placed through the 2 × 12's and through the post. Additional bracing for these girders is provided by 2 × 6 members nailed to the cross girders and to the tops of the short poles (see Fig. 8-7).

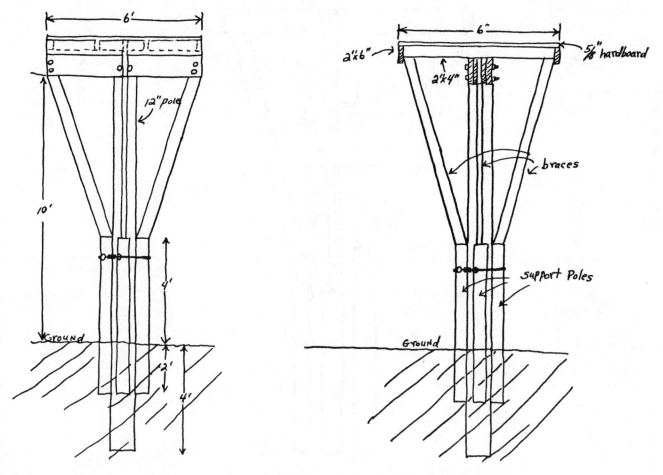

Fig. 8-7.   **Ranger tower platform.** *Left:* **Front view.** *Right:* **Side view.**

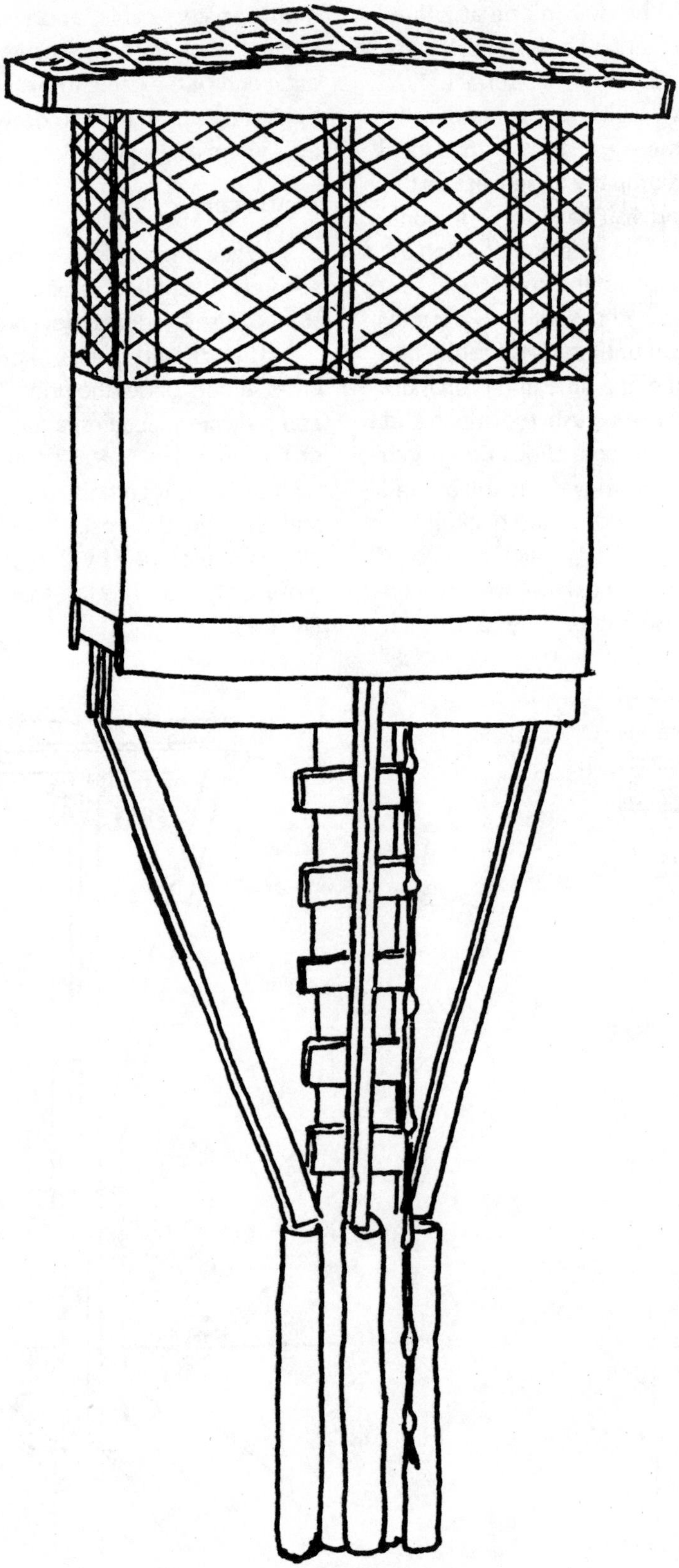

Fig. 8-8.   Ranger Tower with access ladder.

The next structural members for the platform are the floor joists, which are 6-foot 2 × 4's nailed across the 2 × 12's. The joists are placed on 24-inch centers. A 6-foot 2 × 6 is nailed across the ends of the joists. A 2 × 6 brace is placed from the floor joists to the tops of the column poles on the side opposite to the brace for the girders. Use sixteen-penny nails for fastening ‡he milled lumber and twenty-penny nails for fastening the 2 × 6's to the posts.

Use ⅝-inch particle board for the floor. The floor is applied before the walls are framed in so it can be used as a platform for the rest of the Ranger Tower. After the floor is applied, the entrance hole is cut in it and the ladder is installed. One way to give the children access to the tower is to use a knotted rope and shallow steps cut into one of the short posts to get to the top of the short posts. From there on up a ladder is formed by nailing boards to the center post (see Fig. 8-8). The purpose of the rope at the bottom is to discourage toddlers from making the climb.

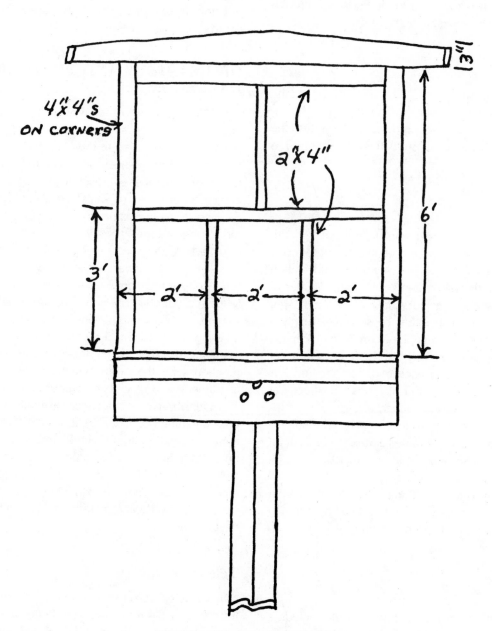

Fig. 8-9.   Side view of Ranger Tower.

Walls and Windows

The walls are built so viewing is possible from all four sides. This is done by installing windows in the upper half of each wall. The lower half is solid. Start building the walls by nailing a 6 foot 4 × 4 upright at each corner. Next, toenail a 68½-inch 2 × 4 between each 4 × 4 at 36 inches height from the floor for the plate. Then the studs can be put in place. Study Figure 8-9.

The studding is 34½-inch 2 × 4's installed on 2-inch centers. It is toenailed to the floor and through the plate into the end grain of the studs.

Sheathing

When the studding is all nailed in place, the sheathing should be installed. Sheathing can be ¼-inch hardboard or the equivalent. Installing the sheathing at this time will strengthen the structure so the roof work can proceed.

Roof

After the sheathing is complete, nail a 2 × 4 with the width vertical around the perimeter of the tower outside of the top of the 4 × 4's. One stud is then placed under the perimeter 2 × 4 at the center of each window opening. For safety and comfort, the window openings can either be screened or fitted with windows. The rafters placed on 24-inch centers are formed by sawing 1 × 8 boards so they are 8 feet long, 3 inches wide at each end, and the full 7½ inches wide in the center. This forms a roof peak at the center of the tower. Further, a false rafter is installed alongside each outside rafter. The false rafter is held in place by a 1 × 4 nailed across the ends of all rafters. The roof sheathing can be either ¼-inch plywood or sheet metal (see Fig. 8-10).

This completes the Ranger Tower. It can be painted a bright color if desired or it can be made to blend into the landscape by painting it green with brown trim.

Furniture

The furniture inside the tower should include a center pedestal for the "instruments" and at least one wall should boast a topographical map, fitted with thumb tacks and strings for cross sightings on fires. Of course a snack table and chairs should be included also, because even Forest Rangers have to eat.

While many children will find the Ranger Tower an answer to their fondest dreams, perhaps your family has a child who likes to dig into things a trifle more complicated. This child may be fascinated by space, heavenly bodies, and other things celestial. If that same child happens to like photography, the next project will be very worthwhile because it is a combination astronomy observatory and photography darkroom.

OBSERVATORY AND PHOTOGRAPHY DARKROOM

The idea of an observatory where astronomers can study the stars, sun, planets, and other celestial phenomena has a rich history. In fact, the first observatory was built in A.D. 647 near Kyungju, Korea. Other observatories were built to prepare accurate astronomical tables so ships at sea could determine their positions and courses with accuracy. Some famous observatories are the French Observation de Paris, where the speed of light was first measured, and Mount Palomar Observatory in Pasadena, California, which boasts a 200-inch reflecting-type telescope. Modern observatories are usually dome-shaped. The dome houses the telescope and revolves to bring the telescope into the right viewing plane. There are also special buildings or rooms used in conjunction with the dome which are used to house instruments and special photography equipment.

Our observatory, of course, is much more simple than anything used by a real scientist. In fact, it is merely a small building with a hinged roof. The purpose of the hinged roof is to provide an unblemished view of the sky. The walls of the backyard observatory, of course, keep all extraneous light from signs, street lights, and car lights from falling on the lens of the telescope.

Telescope

The telescopes used for astronomy are either the reflecting or the refracting type. Reflecting-type telescopes can cost millions of dollars and are not to be

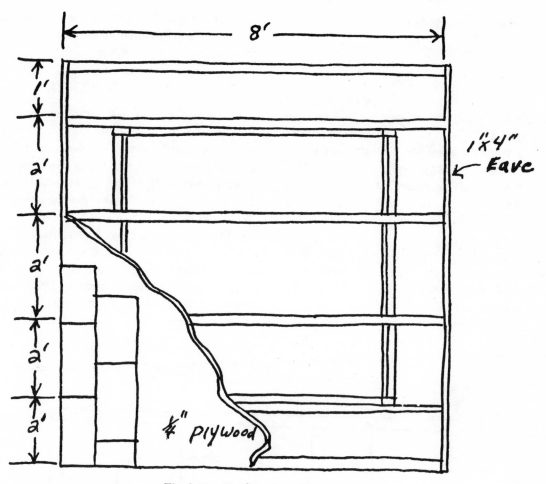

Fig. 8-10.   Rooftop view of Ranger Tower.

considered for the amateur astronomer. A suitable refracting-type telescope for backyard astronomy can be purchased for about $200.

There is adequate room with careful planning for the telescope in addition to the lights, trays, and other equipment used in the photography darkroom.

No floor is used in the observatory because a wood floor would be too unstable to use with the telescope. A thick concrete floor would, of course, be stable enough but it would raise the cost considerably.

Wall Frames

Start building the observatory by making the frame for the front wall. Cut two 2 × 4's to 7-foot, 6-inch lengths for the shoe and plate. Next, cut six 2 ×

4's to 6-foot, 3-inch lengths for the studdings. Position the studs on 16-inch centers except for the two center studs, which are placed 26 inches apart to make room for the door frame (see Fig. 8-11). Nail the front frame together and put it aside until the rest of the frames are done. Each plate and sill has a tie splice. This is used for fastening the side walls and end walls together. The rear wall is made exactly the same as the front wall frame except that no door opening is provided.

The side wall frames are made with a plate and sill and studs spaced 16 inches apart. When all the wall frames are fabricated, set them up and spike them together.

A gable is nailed to the upper plate of both the front and rear wall frames. This gable is made from a 7½-foot 1 × 4 board tapered from zero width at the outer ends to the full 4-inch width at the center.

Wall Sheathing and Roofing

The wall sheathing can be ⅜-inch exterior ply-wood or the equivalent. This can be installed before the roof is put on. The roof is made from two sheets of ⅝-inch hardboard. The center is sealed by a rubber strip. Asphalt shingles are used for the roofing. The roof is hinged at the walls so it can be pivoted out of the way for using the telescope. One side of the roof has a cleat fastened to it so it overlaps the other. This cleat creates a seal by means of a rubber strip fastened to it. Reinforcing strips of 1 × 4 boards are fastened to the inside of the roof panels to minimize warping.

No windows are built into this observatory since they would be unnecessary. Water and electricity is supplied to the observatory from the house. A garden hose and a waterproof electric cord will supply the utilities with little expense.

A simple pedestal should be built for the tele-scope and a sink, bench for the trays, and a table for the enlarger should be provided.

MISSISSIPPI RIVER BARGE

The next project in this chapter comes straight from one of the most colorful eras in American his-tory: the day of the Mississippi riverman. This is not to say that there is no cargo being hauled on the "Big Muddy" today; it is still an important waterway. However, the day of the swashbuckling rivermen and the danger from river pirates is all but over.

One of the most colorful of the rivermen in those days was the river pilot. The services of good pilots were so eagerly sought after that they were afforded every measure of respect, and they often received as much for a month of their services as a skilled carpenter received for a year's work. Such an occupa-

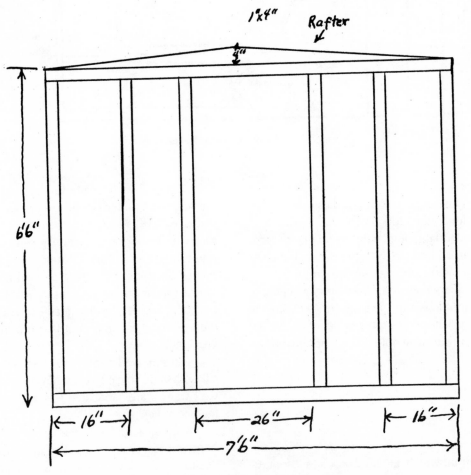

Fig. 8-11.   Front wall frame of observatory.

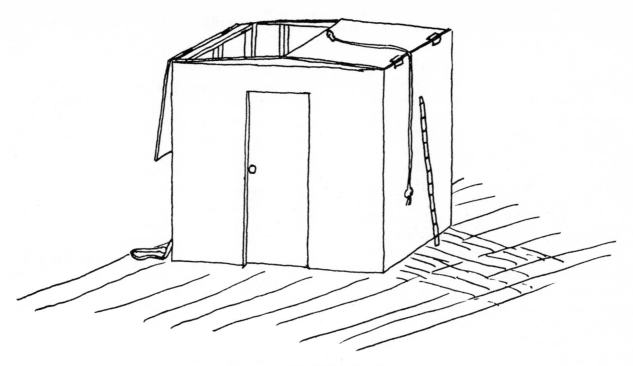

Fig. 8-12. Backyard observatory.

tion was bound to attract some unusual people and it did. One of the most outstanding was a young lad named Samuel Clemens who in later life received worldwide fame as a writer under the pen name of Mark Twain.

This brings up a story that has been handed down in my family since the days of my great-grandfather, who was a Mississippi riverman, decorated Civil War veteran, and rugged independent backwoodsman all of his life.

Grandfather Jim was a deckhand and general roustabout on the cargo barges. He said a deckhand was as far removed from a pilot as a private from a general, and, in fact, he very seldom saw the pilot. Therefore, when Grandfather Jim saw a young fellow lounging about on the aft section of the barge he sought to draw him into conversation. After an exchange of pleasantries Jim asked the fellow where he was from. When the stranger replied "Boston," Jim immediately assumed he was a paying passenger and a "Yankee traveler," green to the river and probably heading further west. Always ready for a joke, Jim took the fellow for a tour of the boat, deliberately attaching the most ridiculous names to parts of the

barge. After he had completed the tour he kept the stranger buttonholed for the better part of a hour spinning completely untruthful tales of life aboard the ship: attacks by ruthless pirates, shipwrecks, and the horrible food and working conditions that the deckhands were forced to put up with. For good measure he fabricated a few stories about the beautiful women waiting in the little towns along the way. The stranger listened very intently to every word, showed him the greatest respect, and thanked him very intently and gratefully when Jim exhausted his supply of stories and took his leave.

Grandfather was so tickled by the fact that the stranger swallowed every word he said that even before the stranger walked away he felt such a knot of laughter rising in his chest that fighting it back actually strained a muscle in his side. He could hardly get out of his bunk the next day and, in fact, it was two days before he could get around well. When he did, he went looking for the stranger after his watch one afternoon.

As he walked by the wheelhouse he happened to glance at the pilot, mostly to see whom they had picked, since they had changed pilots at St. Louis two days before. He could scarcely believe his eyes when he saw the "Yankee traveler" standing all alone at the wheel, guiding the huge craft through the snag and whirlpools of the river. The outrageous lies he had told actually fell on the ears of the pilot himself. Probably no one except the immortal Mark Twain himself would have let the deckhand play out his hand that way.

When Grandfather Jim finally realized what had happened, he slunk away and never ventured near the wheelhouse again. When he got to Prairie du Chien, he collected his wages, went back to the farm for an extended period, and never, never worked a barge that had a pilot named Clemens again. Years later when Twain wrote his famous book *Life on the Mississippi* he mentioned the incident but, remarkably enough, Clemens apparently never mentioned it to a single soul otherwise and no one on the river ever knew exactly whom he was talking about.

Laying Out the Barge

Start building the River Barge by laying it out with stakes and strings. This gives you a chance to visualize it in a given location. The Mississippi River Barge is 8 feet wide and 16 feet long. It should be set on posts placed at 2-foot intervals across the width and at 4-foot intervals along the length. It is expected each post will project 18 inches above the ground at the lowest point. The posts should be at least 3 inches in diameter and they should be treated to prevent decay. Fence post sections will do nicely. See Figure 8-13.

MATERIALS LIST FOR MISSISSIPPI RIVER BARGE

1. 13 4-inch diameter minimum poles for foundation
2. 6 8-foot 4 × 4's for girders
3. 7 8-foot 2 × 4's for floor joists under pilot house

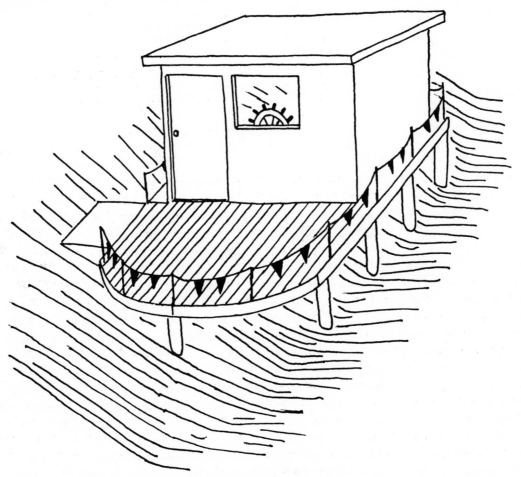

Fig. 8-13. Mississippi River Barge.

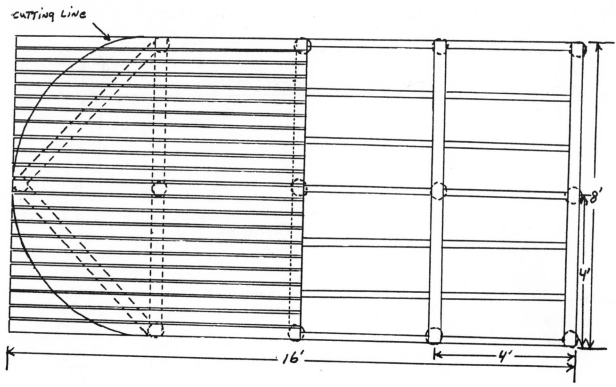

cutting line

Fig. 8-14.   River Barge deck.

4. 21 8-foot 2 × 4's for decking
5. 2 4 × 8-foot sheets of ⅝-inch particle board
6. 10 8-foot 2 × 4's for pilot house studding
7. 4 10-foot 2 × 4's for roof rafters
8. 7 4 × 8-foot sheets ⅜-inch exterior plywood
9. 65 square feet roofing
10. Pilot house window, wheel and inside furnishings. 1-inch dowel, rope, etc.

Start laying out the barge at the lefthand rear corner. Drive a tall stake there and project all the rest of the measurements from it. The first line to project will be the lefthand side of the barge. This line will be 12 feet long. Find it by tying a chalk line to the starting stake, pulling it tight, and tying it to another stake about 13 feet from the starting point. At 4-foot intervals along this line drive stakes to mark the locations of the posts in the lefthand side of the barge. The four outline posts will form a line 12 feet long. The center row of posts will be 16 feet long. See Figure 8-14. When the lefthand row is outlined, go back to the lefthand rear corner and use a carpenter's framing square, the chalk line, and a measuring tape to find a

point at right angles to the lefthand rear post which will mark the 8-foot width of the barge. Drive a stake there. Then go to the front stake of the lefthand line and project the front stake of the righthand line using the same methods. All that remains then is to measure off for the posthole locations.

The posts should be set into firm soil and tamped very well. This barge is well adapted to being built on a slope or hillside. In fact, that is where it should be built. Having a steep dropoff on one side enhances the excitement of using the barge since the "riverman" can pretend this is deep water.

If a slope is used, of course, some posts will be much longer than the minimum 18 inches. Sawing off round posts so the tops are all level is handily done by making a temporary jig for guiding the sawblade. The jig is simply two pieces of 1-inch board nailed at right angles to the post. The boards are nailed right on the cut-off mark. Care is taken to nail them on level so they will guide the saw in making a level cut. See illustration 8-15. Use a coarse-toothed hand saw or a wood saw.

End View   side View

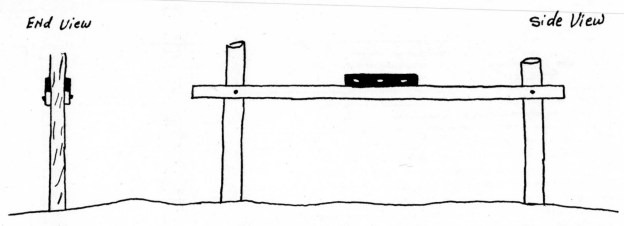

Fig. 8-15.   Squaring the tops of posts.

Installing the Decking

When the post tops are all leveled, the decking can be installed. The rear end (stern) of the barge will support the pilot house; thus the stern of the barge will include floor joists covered with flooring.

However, the first construction stage is the same for the entire length. Spike 8-foot 4 × 4's on the tops of the posts across the width of the barge. These will be the girders. The bow section has a 4 × 4 extending from each side to the single post in the center row (see Fig. 8-14).

When the girders are all in place, nail 2 × 4 joists on 16-inch centers on the 6 × 8-foot section that will be the floor of the pilot house. Cover the joists with ⅝-inch particle board or the equivalent. All of the rest of the deck will be covered with 2 × 4 boards. They will be separated by ½-inch cracks to allow rain to fall through. The decking in the bow section is allowed to extend past the girders and is finally cut on a radius to form the bow (see Fig. 8-14). This radius can be marked by stretching a string from the center of the barge, 4 feet from the extreme end of the bow.

Pilot House

After the deck is complete, the pilot house can be made up and put in place. It measures 6 × 8 feet and is equipped with a "steering wheel," two bunks, and even a tiny galley. This allows the barge to be useful even on rainy days. The door opens onto the deck so quick action can be taken to dispel "pirates" or other undesirable boarders. A few barrels or boxes can be placed on the deck to simulate cargo.

Start building the pilot house by first fabricating the framing for the front wall. The shoe is 6 feet long, and the plate 7 feet in length (see Fig. 8-16). The studdings are spaced on 24-inch centers. The door frame is 24 inches wide. The overhang of the plate is used to tie the front and side walls together. The door, located on the righthand side of the front wall, is fabricated from a ¾-inch-thick plywood panel 23 inches wide and 72 inches high. A window is located in front of the wheel (see Fig. 8-13).

The rear wall plate is 7 feet long and the shoe is 6 feet long (see Fig. 8-16). The studding is also placed on 24-inch centers. The roof rafters are 9½-foot-long, 2 × 4 boards spaced on 16-inch centers. The side studdings are placed under the roof rafters (see Fig. 8-17), marked accordingly, sawed, and nailed in place. The sheathing for the side walls and the roof is ⅜-inch exterior plywood or ¼-inch tempered masonite for the sides and ⅜-inch plywood for the roof. The roofing can be asphalt shingles.

When the outside is done, the railing around the deck can be made up and installed. The railing is simply a ⅜-inch diameter nylon rope strung through 1-inch diameter wooden dowels set into the periphery of the deck (see Fig. 8-13). Each dowel is drilled for the rope before it is set in place. Brightly covered streamers hung from the rope impart a festive appearance.

Inside the pilot house a wheel and wheel stand is

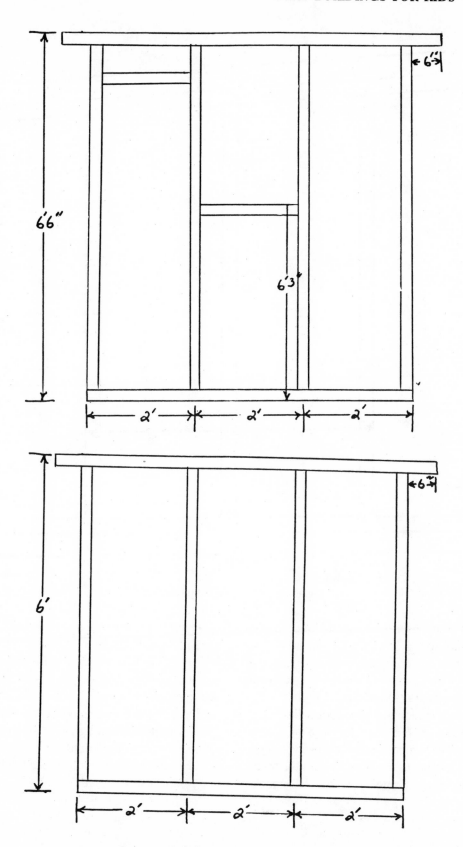

Fig. 8-16.   *Top:* Front frame of pilot house. *Bottom:* Rear frame of pilot house.

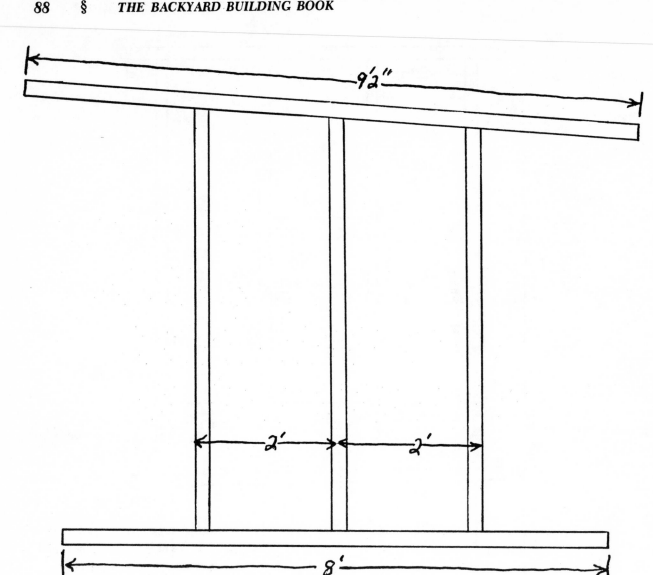

Fig. 8-17.   Side frame of pilot house.

built. Build the wheel by setting 1-inch wood dowels into a hub made from a 3½-inch section of 4 × 4. Pivot the wheel on a ¼-inch bolt anchored to a 4 × 4 stand. An automobile steering wheel also can be utilized if you do not desire to build your own.

Use your imagination to create your galley. One way is to use a camping stove for cooking and a plastic camping sink which contains its own water for washing dishes and hands. By all means use the traditional sailor sleeping arrangement, the hammock.

Suspend the hammock from eye bolts into the studding of the width of the pilot house.

Although the Mississippi River Barge is a lot of work to build, it will be very useful. Besides a place for the children to play in good weather or poor, it will provide extra sleeping quarters when there are house guests, turn an ugly unused slope into a place of beauty, provide an outdoor eating deck for adults and children, and generally make the homesite more interesting and attractive.

Chapter 5

SAUNAS AND A FURNISHED SCREENHOUSE

SAUNAS

When we moved from southern Wisconsin to extreme northern Wisconsin we encountered a very different lifestyle from the one we were accustomed to. We found many things interesting and delightful, but one of the most intriguing was the sauna baths and the way the natives in the Upper Peninsula of Michigan and in the northeastern corner of Wisconsin made and used their saunas.

The sauna bath is a Finnish custom, and it no doubt came to America with the thousands of Finlanders who immigrated to this country around the turn of the century. Local historians say that the immigrant Finlanders built their sauna house first and lived in that until they could get a permanent house built. This gives some indication of the reverence that the Finlander holds for his sauna bath.

A sauna bath is largely a method to induce wholesale perspiration. Unlike a Turkish, or steam bath, the conventional Finnish sauna subjects the

body to very high temperatures and a very low humidity. This causes the pores of the body to open and literally gush forth perspiration. As any doctor knows, induced sweating is the best method known for cleaning the skin.

A sauna bath does much more then clean the skin, however. It eliminates colds and relieves rheumatism, muscle spasms, and pain from overtaxed muscles. It "boils" away blackheads and pimples and imparts a healthy glow to the skin. It has an important psychological effect also as it relieves nervous tensions, pressure, and preoccupation. It is said no one can come out of a sauna bath in ill humor. Personally, it makes me feel like a new man and I can easily recharge myself with a sauna bath so that I feel as good after a day's work as before I started, not to mention that it is the fastest, easiest way I know to lose from one to three pounds.

However, no one should go into a sauna right after an extremely heavy meal. Generally speaking, a person troubled with heart disease, high blood pressure, or respiratory ailments should avoid the high heat of the sauna bath. It also should be avoided immediately after heavy exertion. Many people report very negative effects from the sauna after consuming alcoholic beverages. However, they also report that a sauna has a very beneficial effect on the "morning after" blahs.

Since the sauna is a Finnish custom and the Finns have been refining it for about 2000 years, their customary way of enjoying it should be followed. First, build a fire in the sauna stove and heat the room to at least 140°. While the room is heating, find or cut a bundle of birch twigs about 2 feet long and tie them together. This bundle of twigs is called a "whisk," and it is used for beating or whisking the body. More about this later. Then arrange for a container of hot water, cold water, and soap to be available in the sauna house.

Enter the sauna naked or with a loose towel draped around the waist. Sit on the lowest bench at first. When you become accustomed to that, move to the highest level bench in the sauna and when that becomes enjoyable, increase the heat by building up the fire until a temperature of at least 165° is reached. When the heat is as high as is comfortable, lie down in the prone position on the upper bench and elevate the feet. Maintain this position as long as is comfortable, which is about 15 minutes for many people. This first phase is called the perspiration phase. Follow this by a roll in the snow or dip in the lake if possible to cool down. A cold shower will also work, as will pouring cold water over your head. After the cooling off period rest a short time and then return to heat. Repeat this as often as you feel the need. Some hardened sauna users do this five times or more.

After the perspiration stage comes the steam phase. Steam is produced by simply sprinkling water on the stone, either by dipping the whisk in the cold water container and then sprinkling that on the stones or by using a long-handled dipper to pour some water on the stones. This should be done while lying down if possible and for that reason the sauna should be arranged so the water can be reached from the top bench. A minimum of water should be used so the steam does not become too stifling. After steaming for about five minutes, enter the whisking stage.

Whisking is beating the body lightly with a bundle of birch or cedar twigs. This loosens the old skin softened by perspiration and stimulates blood flow to the capillaries. Whisking starts at the upper body and progresses to the extremities. If you do not desire to use twigs, somewhat the same effect can be achieved by a brisk towel rubdown or scrubbing the body with a long-handled shower brush. Some people think a twig whisk is too much trouble as twigs do tend to dirty the floor of the sauna. Also, traditionally the birch twigs are cut in early summer when the leaves are on. They are then dried and kept for use as needed.

After the whisking comes the bathing. First, put hot water and a little soap in a container such as a wash basin. Stir this around until it makes a foamy lather. Then take handfuls of the lather and cover the body with it like a shaver lathering his face. Next, take the whisk and scrub the body with it very well. Then completely rinse off the soap with clear warm water. Take care to rinse off all the soap and also rinse the benches and stools and floor. After the washing period return to the perspiration stage for a short time to get the body very hot again. Then whisk for a short period again.

The next stage is to cool off very quickly. Finlanders do this by rolling in the snow or by jumping into a cold water lake or even by jumping into a hole in the ice. American sauna users take a cold shower.

The drying stage follows the cooling off period and if it can be done outside in the air, that is fine. Generally, the hair and face should be dried with a towel and the rest of the body air-dried. If it is necessary to dry inside, use a warm, dry room, not a warm, moist one since you might never get dry in a moist room. In the city some people use alternate hot and cold showers for cooling off, then dry with a towel.

Just as the sauna bather lies down when he is perspiring, he should lie down when he finishes the sauna. A rest of ten to fifteen minutes neither speaking nor thinking is recommended. After that the bather can dress and the sauna is complete. He will then be very thirsty and if he desires to gain back the weight he has lost he can drink copiously for a few minutes. Many of the native saunas were followed by a meal. This meal sometimes could be cooked right on the sauna stones while the bath was taking place. Avoid using odoriferous foods or foods which have to be boiled if you cook in the sauna, since they can affect the humidity and also spoil the clean air of the sauna.

All this is a long introduction to building a sauna, but without the tradition it just becomes another way of taking a bath and a fine legend will be cheapened.

A sauna should be built separately from the main house. This is because it is somewhat of a fire hazard, especially if wood heat is used, as many people think it should be. It also should be comfortably large but not too large to heat. Our sauna is 8 × 10 feet.

Drainage and Foundation

Start building the sauna by building the foundation. Care should be taken that the drainage is very good from the foundation of the sauna since water will run down into it each time the bath is used. If you are building in a suburban location, the drain will have to be connected to the septic system or the sewer system unless you have a water recycling unit. Very likely the local plumbing inspector will have some regulations concerning this if your property is zoned. In many states now the buildings must be built back a specific distance from the lake, river, or stream. Consult the local zoning administrator. In areas where field tile is used for drainage, the water from a sauna probably could be run directly into the tiles if soap remover is used in conjunction with the bath. A simpler way is to excavate the entire length and width of the foundation and fill the excavation with coarse gravel. This creates a leach bed which will easily take care of the small amounts of water used with a sauna.

MATERIALS LIST FOR SAUNA

Sauna foundation and floor
1. 15 6-inch diameter poles, 3 feet long
2. 8 1-inch diameter 12-inch length plastic pipes (optional)
3. 1½ yards of 2-inch gravel (optional)
4. 5 4 × 4's 8 feet long
5. 6 10-foot 2 × 6's
6. 5 4 × 8 sheets ⅝-inch particle board

Framing
7. 16 8-foot wall studs
8. 4 10-foot wall studs
9. 2 8-foot 2 × 4's for shoes

10. 2 10-foot 2 × 4's for shoes
11. 4 10-foot 2 × 4's for wall plates
12. 1 6-foot 2 × 4 for door and window frames
13. 14 8-foot 2 × 6's for rafters
14. 4 10-foot 2 × 6's for ridgeboard and cross beams
15. Sheathing to cover approximately 400 square feet
16. Siding to cover approximately 240 square feet
17. 160 square feet of roofing
18. Window and door
19. 18-foot 1 × 4 lumber for screen door

The actual bed for the building can be cedar posts placed into the ground or a foundation of cement blocks. Posts are preferable in some areas because of uneven ground or hard digging conditions. When posts are used, they should be placed on 30-inch centers on the perimeter. Three rows of posts should be used to provide 4-foot spacing for the 4 × 4 floor girders. See illustration 9-1. The floor joists can be placed on 16 inch centers, and they should be 2 × 6 boards or the structural equivalent.

Flooring

Ideally, two layers of flooring will be used with a layer of bituminous felt sandwiched between them. Each layer should be ⅝-inch particle board or the equivalent. Tongue-and-groove 2 × 6's also can be used, but in this case insulation such as sheets of foam or fiberglass should be fastened underneath the floor. Drain holes should be drilled through the floor to allow the water to run into the leach bed below. If desired, each hole can be fitted with a section of plastic pipe that extends to the gravel underneath the floor (see Fig. 9-2). In this way cold air can be prevented from seeping into the building around the bathers' feet. It is usually prudent to place racks on the floor so the bathers' feet are kept off its cold surfaces. Naturally, a concrete floor can be used. In this case one drain hole connected to a drainage system would be utilized. The entire floor would then slant to the hole.

Nailing the Studding

The authentic Finnish sauna should be built of logs. However, you can achieve a log effect by the use of split log siding. The next step after building the floor is to nail the studding in place. Since it is desir-

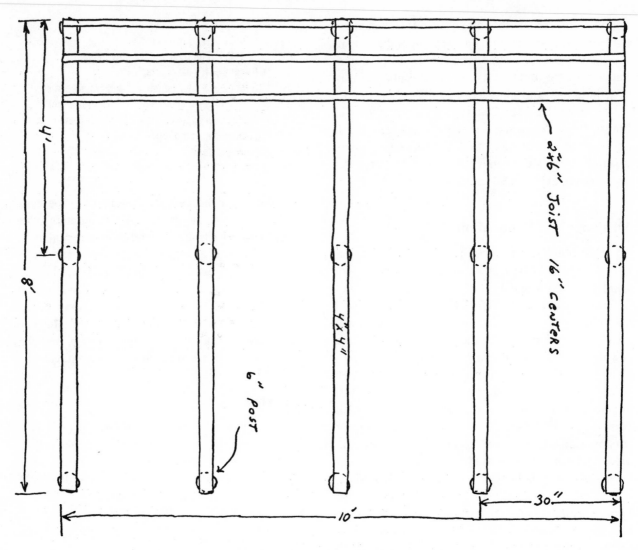

Fig. 9-1.   Floor joists and girders.

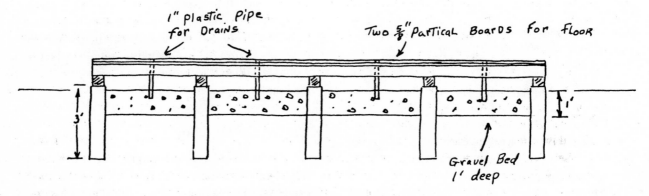

Fig. 9-2.   Side view of gravel bed and flooring.

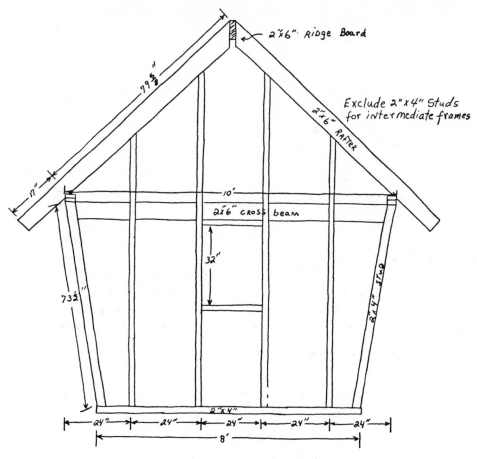

Fig. 9-3.   Sauna end frame.

able to have a flared wall, the studding will not be completely vertical. Instead, it will sit on the sills at an angle so that the top is actually 24 inches wider than the bottom (see Fig. 9-3). This angle not only imparts a dramatic unconventional look to the building, but also provides room for the top benches so they can be made wide enough for prone position bathing. All of the studs are made the same length and each has the same angle at the plate and sill. A double plate is used.

Start with an 8-foot 2 × 6. Square one end. Place the framing square at one corner of the stud so it will form a line that when it is sawed off will remove a right triangle piece with a ³/₄-inch base. This angle will of course be in opposite directions but exactly the same on each end of the stud. Mark this angle and cut it out. Check the stud to see if it is properly cut and then use it for a pattern for the rest of the side rafters. One slight deviation from normal construction

is that the angled studs have to extend clear to the outside of the back and front walls.

Door and Window

The door is framed into the front end and the window in the other (see Figs. 9-3 and 9-4). The door frame should be made of 2 × 6 material if it is available. This allows an inside and outside door to be utilized so heat can be conserved in the sauna. Any kind of commercial outside doors can be utilized if you desire to purchase them. Also two "garage entry" type doors with windows can be used to eliminate the window in the back of the sauna. Of course, if the sauna is being built in a populated area, the window glass should be stained or treated or else one door should be fitted with a shade to discourage window peekers.

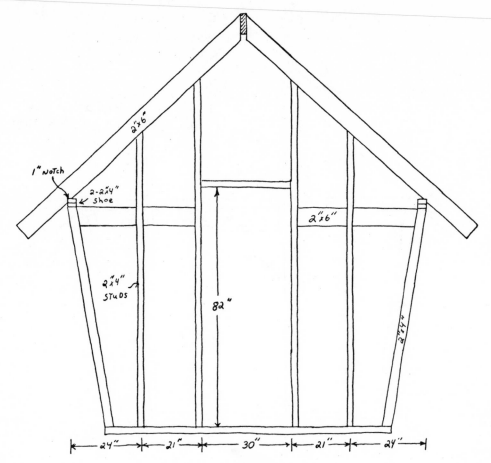

Fig. 9-4.   End frame with door.

Crossbeams

Crossbeams are placed on 4-foot centers. Ideally, the will be made of 2 × 8 stock, but 2 × 6 or the equivalent in poles is also adequate. After the building is done the crossbeams can be used for bed pieces for the bathing racks. This sauna has the capacity for six bathers all at the same time while it also can be utilized by only one bather without serious waste of fuel. For wall sheathing use ship lap or ½-inch plywood and half-long siding.

Rafters

The rafters should be made from 2 × 6 stock and placed on 16-inch centers, especially in territory where the snow load is substantial. Make the pattern rafter by laying an 8-foot 2 × 6 out on sawhorses. Use 5 inches for a measuring line. Scribe this line from one end of the rafter to the other. Lay the 12-inch mark on the blade of the square and the 5-inch mark on the tongue of the square at the measuring line. Move the square five times, since the run of the rafter is half the span of ten feet, to find the length of the rafter. Another way is to multiply five times the distance between the 12-inch mark of the outside edge of the blade of the square and the 10-inch mark on the tongue of the square. This distance is 15⅞ inches. Multiply this by the span of 5 feet and we have 5 × 15⅞, or 79⅜ inches, which is the total length of the rafter. After finding the correct ridgeboard angle of the rafter, a measurement from both points of this angle will reproduce the wall plate angle at the desired position on the rafter. This, of course, simplifies making the rafter and minimizes the chance for error.

In this rafter the heel or tail is left full width and the rafter is notched for the wall plate. A ridgeboard is used. Thus, after the rafter is made, saw half the ridge-board width from the length of the rafter at the ridge-board cut. This is ³/₄ inch. Now as long as you make each succeeding rafter just exactly the same as the first one by laying the first one on the succeeding rafter boards, no problems will appear even if some slight error has been committed in laying out the pattern rafter.

The ridgeboard will have to be placed on a temporary stand until a few rafters are nailed to it. This stand should project above the wall plate approximately 53³/₈ inches, although slight adjustments may be necessary to fit the angle of the rafters exactly.

After the rafters are in place, set the gable studs in place on 16-inch centers and mark and cut them. Then apply the roof sheathing.

Roofing

The roof material can be roll roofing or composition or shake shingles (see Fig. 9-5), but at least two layers of felt should be applied under the roofing. This minimizes the need for insulation under the roof. However, if insulation is desired, use 6-inch insulation in the ceiling and 4-inch in the sides. Then finish the inside with solid boards or paneling which will withstand heat and humidity. One-quarter-inch outdoor plywood treated with a water preservative should also be satisfactory.

Cold and Hot Water Barrels

After the shell is done, the inside furnishings can be built by hand or they can be purchased from commercial sources.

In a sauna that can't be equipped with running water some water storage facilities must be provided. Generally this consists of two large 20 to 30 gallon containers. The economical containers of this size are generally used barrels. It works very well to cut the tops out of the barrels and equip them with a wooden cover. The barrel which will be the hot water barrel is positioned next to the stove and equipped with pipes that project from the bottom and the top of the barrel through the stove (see Fig. 9-6). Several refinements can be incorporated into this water heating arrangement but good results can be obtained by simply running a copper pipe through the stove. The ends are connected too through the stove and slightly separated by one being higher than the other in the barrels. This creates a circulation caused by the heating of the water in the pipe. In fact, this water turns to

Fig. 9-5.   Finished sauna.

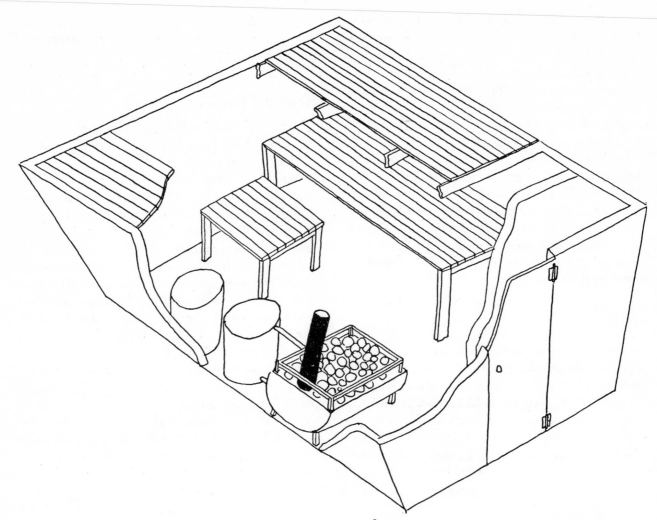

Fig. 9-6.   Interior of sauna.

steam and bubbles out the top. Cold water then comes in to take its place and is in turn heated. The size of the pipe in the stove largely determines how fast the water will heat.

Barrel Stove

Since we designed and used a barrel stove especially for our sauna, a brief description of how we did it may help a prospective builder.

First, take a 55-gallon steel drum. Cut it in half lengthwise with a cold chisel. Use the section with the large hole. Then go to the blacksmith and obtain a sheet of ¼-inch boiler plate measuring 25 × 36 inches from one end. Have the blacksmith cut a hole and weld a 6-inch pipe onto the boiler plate to use for a stovepipe collar. Further obtain 10 feet of 1-inch

angle iron and bolt it to the underside of the boiler plate so it will fit inside the barrel half. This is to secure the plate to the barrel. This forms the top.

Now have the blacksmith braze a large U-shaped (4-inch) water pipe to the barrel shell so that it lies just under the top of the stove. Make sure the ends are reduced so that it can be fitted with ¾-inch well pipe.

Next, make the door for the stove. Take another 8½ × 11½ piece of boiler plate and cut out an opening in it 6½ × 9½. Next, take a piece of ⅜-inch plate steel and weld a piece of ½-inch metal tubing to it to use as a hinge. Then weld two pieces of matching tubing to the boiler plate frame so that a metal rod can be placed through them to complete the hinge. The frames of boiler plate are bolted to the barrel and the plate steel door is hung from the hinge. The latch is a piece of 1-inch strap iron that pivots with a bolt. A small piece of angle iron is then welded to the barrel and notched so the strap iron latch will fit in it. Cut the opening for the door at the end of the barrel with the large bung. The stand for the barrel stove is also made from angle iron. Further, 3/4-inch pipe fittings must be brazed to the water barrel so the circulation pipes from the stove can be fitted to it. Connecting pipes are then made up which will join the water barrel and the stove. Copper tubing, although expensive, works well for this application but galvanized water pipes can also be used. A large dipper is used to remove the water from the barrel or the water barrels can be fitted with faucets by simply brazing the fittings to the barrels. The cold water barrel is placed beside the hot water barrel. After the stove is made up, a large container such as a section of barrel can be placed on the top of the sauna stove and filled with rocks. When they are well heated, water is sprinkled on them to create steam for the steam phase of the sauna bath.

Besides the stove and water pots, the racks are generally handmade. They are generally made from aspenwood if it is available since it is a poor conductor.

If it is not desirable to make up an automatic water heating unit, just sit a water container on the top of the stove. Generally only a gallon or so of hot water will be needed for the bath. Too much water and steam in the sauna could raise the temperature too high.

Three separate platforms at different altitudes can be used. The bottom will be used for bathing, the center for the whisking platform. Study Figure 9-6 for the proper method. Also a partition should be included to form a dressing room.

How to Convert a Room to a Sauna

Of course, not everyone lives in the country where they can build a separate sauna. This is fine also. Most large homes have a room that can be converted to reproduce the sauna conditions. A closet for instance will work fine. Just insulate all the walls with at least 3 inches of insulation. Install a bench and an electric heater with a controllable thermostat. Enter the room, build the heat as high as you can stand it and perspire away your problems. It

helps, of course, if you can reach the shower from the closet without parading through the living room or some other room where there is apt to be people. It is a good idea to plan your new house with a sauna room included. In that case it can be adjoining the bathroom. A single person or even a couple could use their bathroom for a sauna, but this of course wouldn't be too convenient if there was one bathroom and several people.

People who have a swimming pool and a pool room have almost the ideal artificial setup for sauna bathing. Just build a small insulated room off the pool and "sauna" away. Commercial units are also available for this type of installation if you don't desire to build your own. Be sure to have a room large enough to lie down in while sauna bathing, though, since this is part and parcel of the sauna.

SCREENHOUSE

One of the most delightful buildings to have in proximity to a sauna is a screenhouse that a bather can relax in after the rigors of the sauna. It is still better if the screenhouse can be made safe from prying eyes so the bather does not have to don clothes before entering the screenhouse. A screenhouse is, of course, a fine place to relax in after work or play or a place to eat outside, sleep outside, or do a dozen other outdoor things. This screenhouse is unconventional in design and very useful to a dozen different lifestyles.

The screenhouse described here is 6 × 9 feet, which is large enough for a double bunk, a card table and chairs, or a custom-made trestle table and benches. It is most suitable for a family of about four persons. If more room is desired, of course, the screenhouse can be made larger. The roof is made overlarge so it will catch rainwater, which is the best for sauna bathing. A catching basin and pipes could be used to direct the water from this roof to the cold water container inside the sauna. A simple filter could be provided on the outlet from the catching basin to strain the dust and other impurities from the water. The large roof also serves as a shaded area when the screenhouse will be used for other than sauna use. It is expected that the inside of the screenhouse will have a wood floor. Generally it is advisable to set the screenhouse permanently in one place.

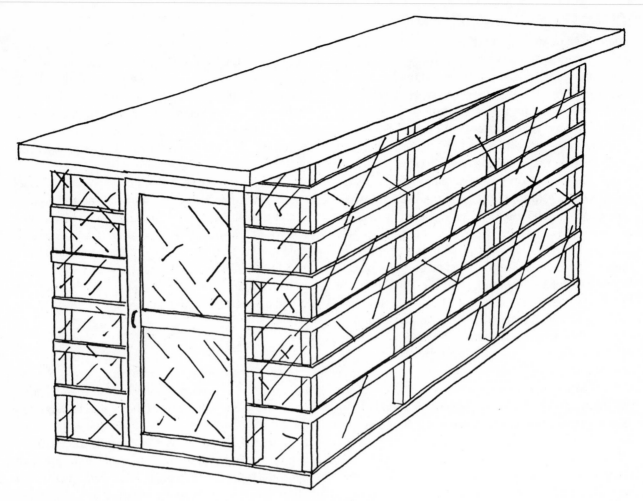

Fig. 9-7. Screenhouse.

MATERIALS LIST FOR SCREENHOUSE

1. 10 8-foot 2 × 4's for side and end frames
2. 8 6-foot 2 × 4's
3. 1 9-foot 2 × 4 for floor. 3 12-foot 2 × 4's for rafters.
4. 8 6-foot 2 × 4's for floor and roof
5. 54 square feet ⅝-inch plywood
6. 54 square feet ⅜-inch plywood
7. 60 square feet roofing. Nails, etc.
8. Approximately 200 square feet screen
9. 4 pounds ten-penny nails, 2 pounds ½-inch roofing nails

Floor

Start by building the floor. Cut two 2 × 4's 108 inches long and four 2 × 4's 72 inches long. Use ten-penny nails to nail the 72-inch 2 × 4's between the 108-inch framing members to form the floor frame (see Fig. 9-10).

When the floor is framed in, nail tongue-and-groove 2 × 4's or ⅝-inch plywood to the framing. This flooring should extend to the outside of the frame. After that, the studding is toenailed on the top of the floor. The studding is positioned on 36-inch centers (see Fig. 9-11). The front studs are 7 feet long; the rear studs are 78 inches. Note that the door frame is 3 feet wide (see Fig. 9-12).

Roof

The roof framing is 2 × 4's nailed across the studs on the outside. They are 12 feet long with an overhang of 18 inches both front and back (see Fig. 9-11). A center 2 × 4 rafter also is used (see Fig. 9-13).

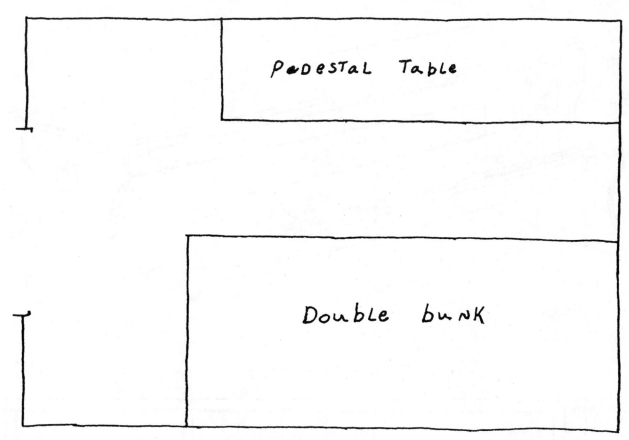

Fig. 9-8. Floor plan for screenhouse.

Additionally a 2 × 4 plate is used across the tops of the width studs (see Fig. 9-12). The roof should be covered with ³/₈-inch plywood or the equivalent. A smooth roofing such as noncorrosive metal should be used for the roof if it is desired to keep the water clean. If this screenhouse is not to be used for this purpose, a more economical roofing such as roll or composition roofing can be used.

Screen

The space between the studs is slatted with 1 × 3 furring strips of lumber. The furring strips are placed 1 foot apart. They are toenailed to the studding with six-penny finishing nails. When the slats are nailed in place, they provide shade as well as a base for nailing on the screen. Either plastic or metal screen should be used for this application. If this screenhouse will be used without the sauna, regular metal screen will be most satisfactory.

Screen Door

A standard commercially built screen door can be used. However, it is not difficult to build your own with a 1 × 4 lumber frame. Since nailing this type of corner is troublesome, a joint called a mortise and tenon joint must be utilized. This involves sawing a slot in the end of a board and creating a tenon joint on the end of another board to fit into the slot (see Fig. 9-14). A simple cross joint must also be used for the center brace.

Both joints can be formed with a hand drill and a hand saw. To make the mortise section of the joint, drill a hole ¼ inch in diameter through the side framing members. This slot should be the same distance from the end of the piece as the side panels are wide, generally 3¹/₂ inches. Next make saw cuts to form a slot ¼ inch wide. Also saw the connecting board to form a male tenon ¼ inch wide to fit in this slot. This joint will be used at all four corners. The crosspiece is joined to the sides by cutting a square notch ³/₈ inch

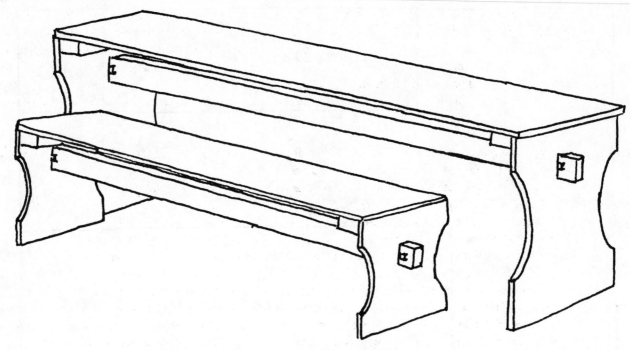

Fig. 9-9. Trestle table and bench.

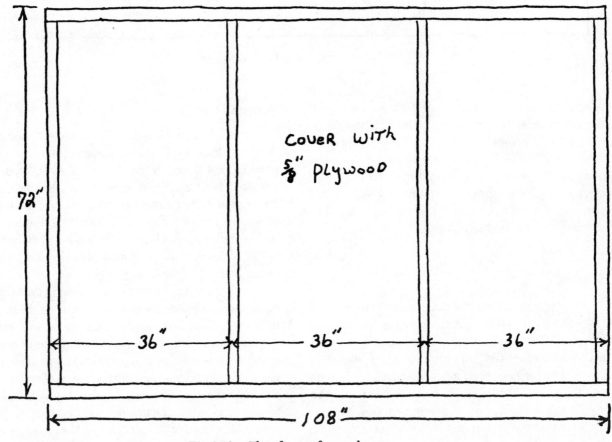

Fig. 9-10. Floor frame of screenhouse.

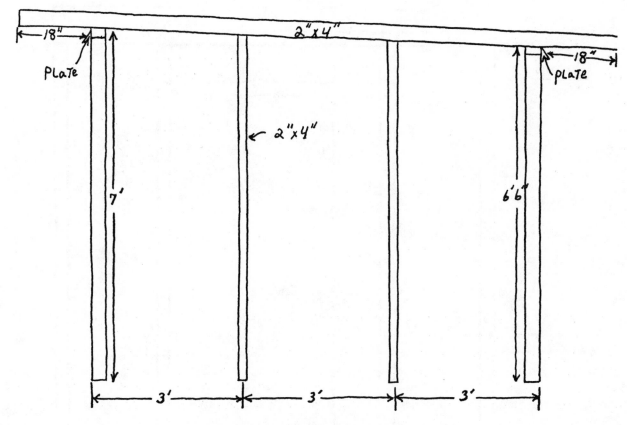

Fig. 9-11. Side frame of screenhouse.

deep as wide as the board. It is then fitted into the slot. Brass screws are used to join the joints together. The door is covered with screen that is held in place with screen bead.

Trestle Table and Benches

All the furniture to be used in the screenhouse can be handmade. It includes two benches and a table plus a double-decker bunk.

The table and benches, which are a matched set, are made in the trestle table design. Trestle tables, which are used for kitchen furniture, are made from very heavy stock. A card table doesn't need to be made this heavy. We can use ⅝-inch exterior plywood, sanded on one side for this tabletop. To prevent warping, 2 × 4 cleats are used. Start by sawing out a piece of exterior ¾-inch plywood 18 inches wide and 72 inches long. Sandpaper the corners. Next, cut three 18-inch pieces of 2 × 4 stock. Bevel each end of each piece. Fasten the 2 × 4's to the un-

derside of the plywood tabletop with 2-inch wood screws (see Fig. 9-15). The screws should be placed through the 2 × 4 into the tabletop. The legs are then fastened to the outside crosspieces.

The legs are also sawed from a piece of ¾-inch exterior plywood. Since they are visible from both sides, plywood that is good on both sides should be used. The initial sections are 15 inches wide and 27¼ inches high. They are made according to Figure 9-15. Shoes made of a double thickness of 2 × 4 are used at the floor to stabilize the table. The ends of the shoes are also beveled.

The 2 × 4's on either side of the pedestal legs are 25 inches long. They are tapered at the ends. The center joint or crossmember is a 2 × 6 long enough to reach from one end to the other of the pedestal legs plus a surplus of 4 inches on each end.

All joints are glued as well as fastened with screws. Two-inch wood screws are used in this application. When the table is done, it should be painted or stained with three or four coats of paint.

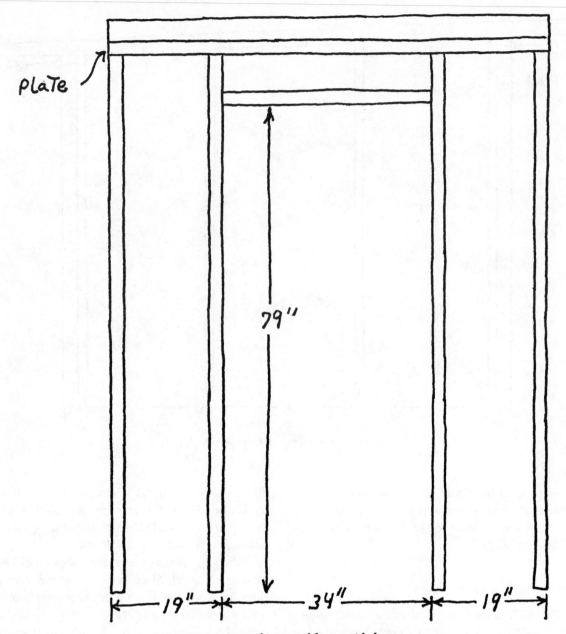

Fig. 9-12.   Screenhouse end frame with door.

The benches are made almost like the table. The benches are 60 inches long, 18 inches high, and 12 inches wide. They too are made from ¾-inch plywood or the equivalent. Study Figure 9-16.

The crosspin between the pedestal legs is 2 × 4 instead of 2 × 6 as in the table. The benches should be finished like the table. The beauty of these pieces will be a result of how well you sand and finish them.

Double-Decker Bunk

Besides the table and benches a double-decker bunk with sleeping room for two to four people can be included in this screenhouse.

The bunk is made with a simple 2 × 4 frame. It is 52 inches high, 30 inches wide, and 6 feet, 6 inches long. The mattresses also are handmade from expanded foam covered with plastic material. The table is made small so it can be used at one end of the screenhouse or it can be used alongside the double bunk. If slightly crowded conditions are not objectionable, the table can be used at the end of the bunk.

Start building the bunk by cutting four knotfree 2 × 4's, 6 feet 6 inches long. Next, cut four 2 × 4's, 4 feet 4 inches long. Notch the 6-foot, 6-inch 2 × 4's so they can be fitted into the crosspieces. Each notch is 1⁵⁄₈ inches deep so a comparable notch in the crosspiece can be fitted into it and still maintain a level surface on the top (see Fig. 9-17). All pieces are attached to the legs with wood screws, through the legs and into the pieces. Further, three 2 × 4 crosspieces on which the mattresses rest are installed between the sides of the bunk. It is expected a sheet of plywood will be used under the mattresses if foam is used. If springs are used, then the springs should set above the plywood. An edge is formed by nailing a 1

× 4 to the sides of the bunk beds. For strictly sauna bathing and resting when the bather may have water on his body the plywood can be utilized without a mattress. A board bunk also is a fine place for resting on a hot day since it will usually feel cool.

FIREPLACE

Most outdoor type people need a collection of outdoor furniture which can be used when desired and of which no care whatsoever has to be taken. If it rains on it, it won't hurt it. If you forget and leave it out over the winter, very little damage will result. Just as important is that it be strong enough so the children can roughhouse on it and little harm will result. It also must have good looks and exude a rustic charm so the yard and buildings will be complemented by it.

One of the most useful of such items is a back-

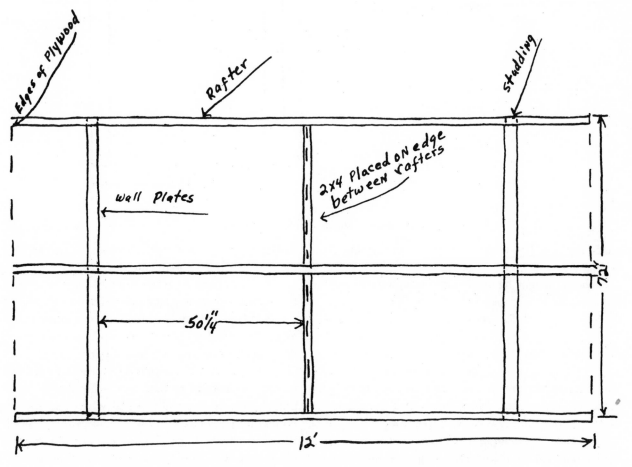

Fig. 9-13. **Top view of screenhouse roof frame before covering it with plywood.**

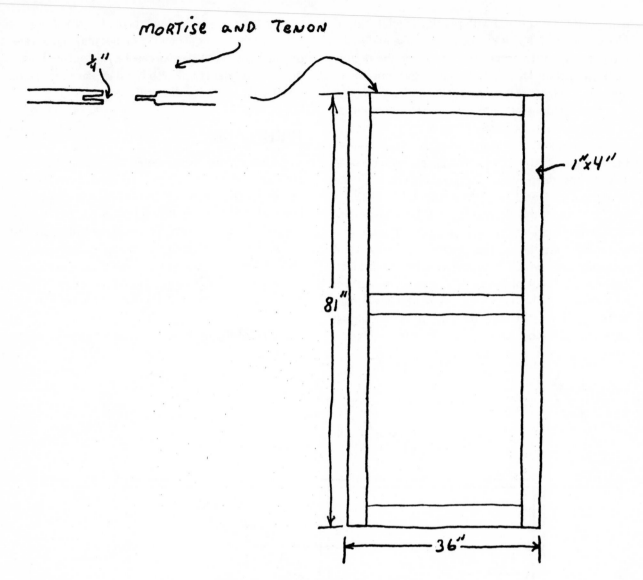

Fig. 9-14.   Screen door for screenhouse.

yard fireplace. The very best fireplace to my way of thinking is simply a circle of stones around a fire pit. This should ideally be made large enough so burgers and a roast can be cooked at one time. Such a pit also works very well for cooking a pot of beans or mulligan. The pit can also be used for cooking an entire meal at one time. Likewise, it can be used for smoking meat and drying food to preserve it. Also if you occasionally like to have some way of heating metal to the red-hot stage, for making your own knives or other tools, this pit will do the job.

Start by excavating an area 4 feet in diameter at least 1 foot deep at the top of a knoll if possible (see Fig. 9-18). First place cement tile in the bottom pro-

jecting to the top of the ground from the center. This tile serves to let air into the fire.

Further cover the bottom with flat stones at least 6 inches in diameter. At the side of the pit use colored round stones to form a wall so the fire doesn't drift away. The drain tile should be kept free of debris. A good plug for the draft tile is a round stone that will just about fit into it. By removing or installing these stones the amount of draft to the fire can be controlled. This is especially useful when the fire has burned down to coals and very high heat is desired. We even make a forge of ours by setting the vacuum cleaner to "blow" position and feeding the air into one end of the drain tile.

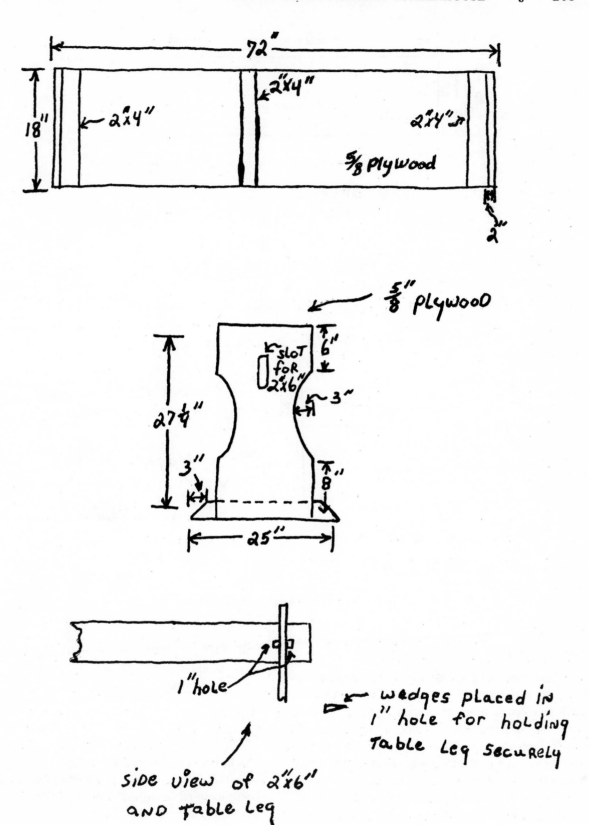

Fig. 9-15. Dimensions for trestle table.

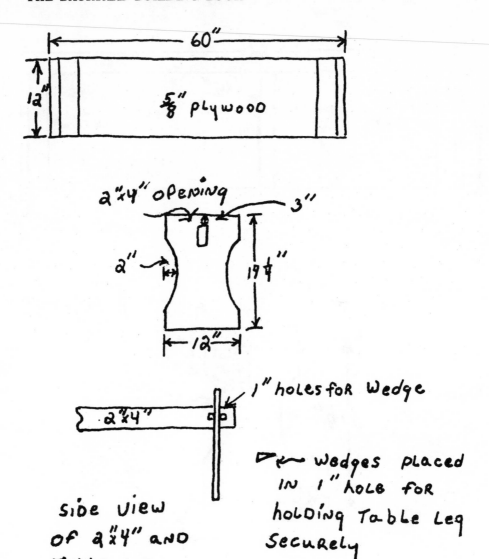

Fig. 9-16.   Dimensions for trestle table bench.

Spit and Grill

The most useful accessories such a fireplace can have are a spit and grill. The entire spit is made from well pipe and a piece of 1/4-inch iron rod. The rod, which is the actual spit, is sharpened at one end and driven through the meat being cooked. If it is not desirable to actually spit the meat, it can be tied to the rod with fireproof string.

The spit rotates in 1/4-inch holes drilled through the pipe. The handle of the spit should be made from wood. A treelimb or similar contrivance could be used. It is held on with a cotter pin placed through the

end of the steel rod (see Fig. 9-18). The grill can be made of expanded metal which is available at most hardware stores.

PICNIC TABLE

In conjunction with the fire pit a rugged picnic table will deliver many hours of enjoyment. The very best picnic tables to my way of thinking are made from logs. The top of the table is made from rough sawn lumber. Redwood is fine but fir, spruce, or pine will also do the job.

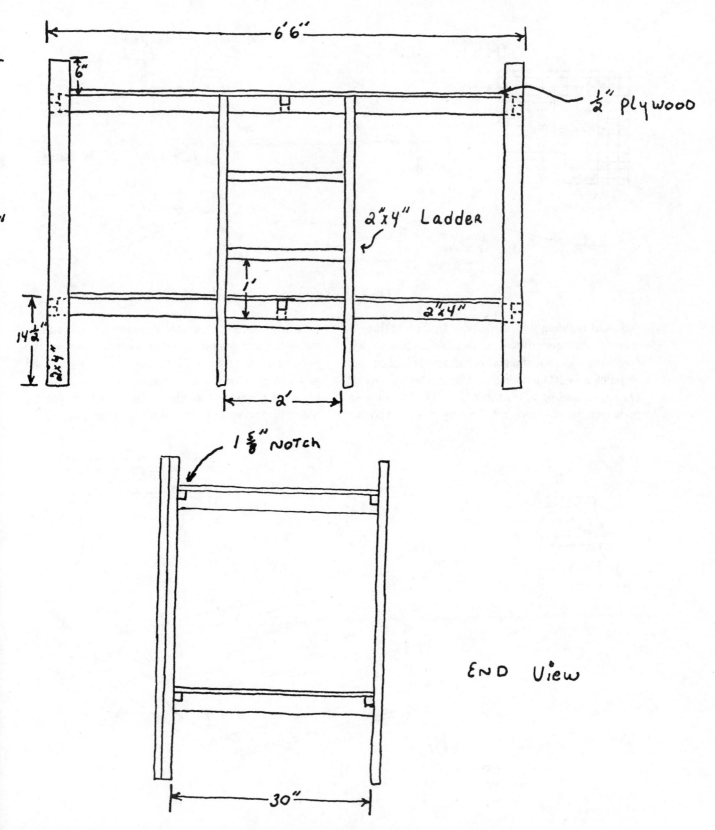

Fig. 9-17. How to build double bunk.

Fire Pit

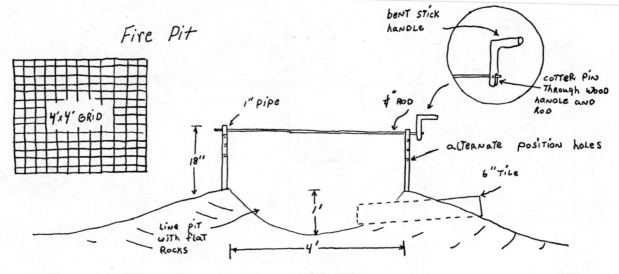

Fig. 9-18. Fireplace.

Start building this picnic table by cutting three 2 × 10's into 72-inch lengths for tabletop pieces (see Fig. 9-19). Next, cut three 5-inch diameter fence posts or poles into 30-inch lengths. Use the bench saw or chain saw and jig to rip two right-angle flat surfaces on two of the poles. Then lay out the three top pieces on a level surface, separate the boards ½ inch, square the ends, and position the two sawn poles across the ends of the top pieces. Clamp or temporarily nail the poles in position on the boards. Then drill ¼-inch holes all the way through the poles and top pieces. Make two holes in each top piece. Then place 6 ½-

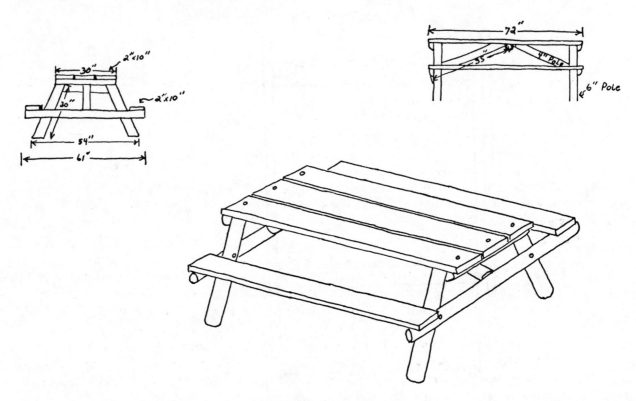

Fig. 9-19. Picnic table.

inch carriage bolts with the head at the top surface of the table through each hole. Place a nut and flat washer on each bolt and tighten them enough so the head is countersunk into the tabletop. Do this at all hole locations.

Now saw one flat surface on the remaining pole and place it at the centerline of the table. Use ¼-inch carriage head bolts to secure it across the top pieces also. This completes the top; the legs can be made up and attached next.

The legs are made from 30-inch-long, 8-inch diameter peeled poles or fence posts. Lay the poles out on a level surface parallel to each other and separated by about 54 inches. Next, cut a 4-inch pole, 55 inches long. Lay it across the legs 14 inches from the ends. Now drive a spike through the pole into each leg. Don't drive the spike down so the head is tight, since it must be removed. Next, pivot the other ends of the legs so they are separated by about 34 inches. This forms the correct angle for the notch which must be cut into the legs for the 4-inch crosspieces. Use a saw or scribe to make the marks for the notches. Pull the spikes out, remove the crosspiece, saw out the notches and replace the

crosspieces in the notches, drill the holes, and bolt them in place with 2¼ × 6-inch carriage head bolts at each joint.

Now attach the legs to the tabletop. Find the correct angle for this by laying a straight edge across the tops of the legs. Saw out this indicated line. Further notch out for the crosspiece at the tabletop. Drill two holes at each crosspiece and bolt them together with ¼-inch bolts. Next install a 35-inch-long diagonal brace of 4-inch diameter pole from the center of the crosspiece on the legs to the center of the crosspiece on the tabletop (see Fig. 9-19). Make up the legs for the other end the same way. Attach them and install a 2 × 10 plank between the crosspieces to form the bench. Finish the tabletop with at least four coats of a good clear preservative. If the heads of the bolts on the top of the table are objectionable, they can be countersunk and the hole filled with a section of wooden dowel. A 1-inch diameter countersunk hole and a 1-inch diameter dowel works very well for this.

Hardly anything can hurt this table and about the only care it will require is to be set on end in the winter so ice doesn't freeze to the top and spoil your winter outdoor picnics.

Chapter 6

A WINDMILL, A WIND GENERATOR, AND A WIND MOTOR

WINDMILL

A smoothly rotating replica of a Dutch windmill on the lawn adds grace and charm to the most decorative residence. Moreover, it will transform a drab corner of the yard or garden into an eye pleaser that will delight the homeowner. Almost anyone who has a few tools can build one.

MATERIALS LIST FOR WINDMILL

1. 4 6 × 21-inch pieces of ⅛-inch masonite for propeller blades
2. 4 15-inch lengths of 1-inch diameter dowel
3. 6-inch diameter, 3-inch-thick wooden hub
4. 2 running feet ½-inch diameter plastic water pipe
5. 4-inch length of 4 × 4-inch lumber
6. 28-inch 2 × 4-inch board
7. 9 running feet of 2 × 2-inch boards
8. 2 × 2-foot section of sheet metal for canopy
9. sheet ⅜-inch exterior plywood
10. ½ × 10-inch machine bolt / 3 nuts / 4 washers

Start by building the four-blade propeller. The first step is to make the vanes. Procure a sheet of ⅛-inch masonite. Saw off four pieces measuring 6 × 21 inches. Further saw out four pieces of 1 × 2 lumber 15 inches long. Use a drawknife, spoke shave, plane or lathe to create a 1-inch round dowel 3 inches long on one end of each piece of lumber.

Center the masonite blades on the 1 × 2 pieces and fasten them together with wood screws so the inboard ends are flush with the dowels. See Figure 6-2.

Some people find that they like latticework propellers better. To make them requires four 2-foot 1 × 2's, nine 6-inch lattice strips, and four 24-inch lattice strips. As with the masonite propeller, dowel 3 inches of one end and then nail the lattice strips to the 1 × 2 strips as shown in Figure 6-2.

Next saw off a 3-inch hub from the end of a 6-inch diameter cedar or hardwood post. A section of 2 × 8 will work if no round stock is available. Carefully find the center of this hub and drill a ¾-inch hole

Fig. 6-1.　Windmill.

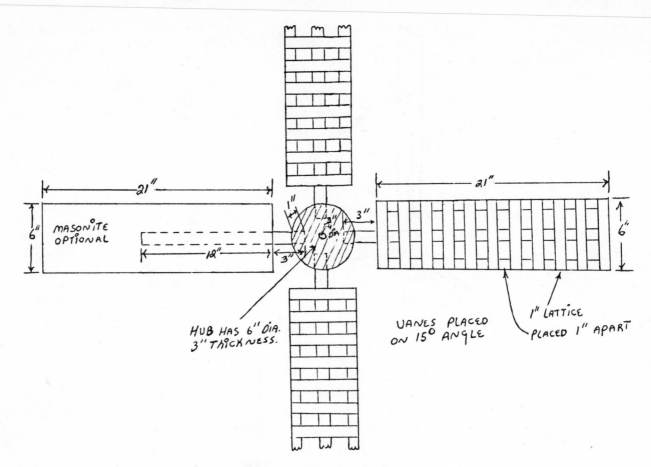

Fig. 6-2. Four-blade propeller.

completely through the piece. This is the pivot hole and will receive the axle. Next drill four 1-inch holes evenly spaced and centered at the circumference of the hub. These holes should be 1 inch deep. Now fit the dowels of the propeller blades into the hub and rotate them so they are 15 degrees from the perpendicular and parallel with each other. Study Figure 6-2. When you are certain they are positioned correctly, drive a #5 finishing nail through the hub to hold them in place. If any holes are oversized so the dowel is loose, it should be glued as well as nailed. With that done, the propeller is ready to fasten to the axle.

Obtain a 2-inch-long section of ½-inch diameter plastic water pipe. Press one end into the hole in the center of the propeller. If it doesn't fit securely, coat it with a good wood glue before it is pushed into position. Let it dry at least eight hours before mounting it. Next, procure a ½-inch machine bolt 8 inches long. Also get three nuts and three flat washers for this bolt. If the bolt has more than 2 inches of unthreaded

shank, have the threads cut to within 2 inches of the head. Refer to Figure 6-3.

Try the bolt inside the plastic pipe. If it fits very tightly, ream the pipe out with a ½-inch drill so the bolt will rotate smoothly. When it does turn easily, place a washer on the bolt and slide the threaded end through the propeller hub so the head of the bolt is on the outboard side of the propeller. At the inboard surface of the propeller place another flat washer. Then thread a nut on the bolt up to the end of the threads and back it up with another nut. Turn the nuts against each other to jam them. The bolt should turn easily in the hub of the propeller.

Next, cut a piece of 4 × 4, 4 inches long. Drill a half-inch hole at its center. Nail it on the width of one end of a section of 2 × 4, 28 inches long. Twelve inches from the opposite end of the 2 × 4 drill a ¾-inch hole through the center of the width of the 2 × 4. Then bolt the propeller through the ½-inch hole in the section of 4 × 4. Next, take a 6-inch-long section

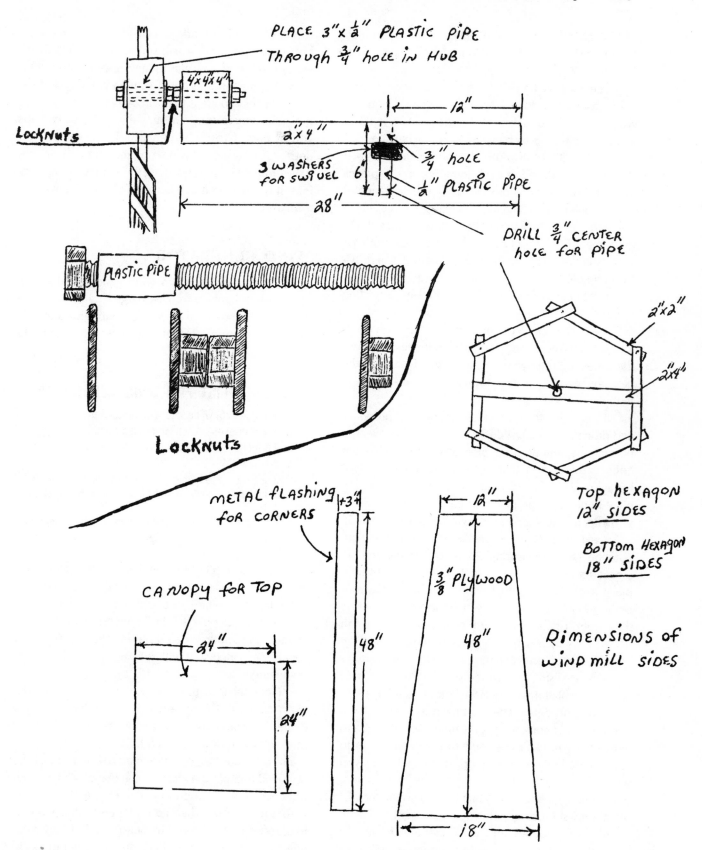

PLACE 3"x ½" PLASTIC PIPE
THROUGH ¾" HOLE IN HUB

4"x4"x4"

Locknuts

2"x4"

12"

3 WASHERS
FOR SWIVEL

6"

¾" HOLE

½" PLASTIC PIPE

28"

DRILL ¾" CENTER
HOLE FOR PIPE

PLASTIC PIPE

Locknuts

2"x2"

2"x4"

TOP HEXAGON
12" SIDES

BOTTOM HEXAGON
18" SIDES

METAL FLASHING
FOR CORNERS

+3"

12"

CANOPY FOR TOP

24"

24"

48"

⅜" PLYWOOD

48"

DIMENSIONS OF
WINDMILL SIDES

18"

Fig. 6-3.

of ¹/₂-inch plastic pipe and glue it into the ³/₄-inch hole in the 2 × 4 so the end is flush with the top surface of the 2 × 4.

The base is framed from two hexagon figures made from 2 × 2 stock. It is covered with ¹/₄-inch plywood. Cut six 18-inch 2 × 2's and six 12-inch 2 × 2's. Lay out the 18-inch pieces to form a hexagon approximately 3 feet in width. The ends can be lapped and one nail placed at each joint. Move the pieces until an even figure is produced; then place another nail at each joint to hold them in place. Further, nail a piece of 1 × 4 stock across the figure to brace it. Do the same for the 2-foot hexagon and brace it with a 2 × 4 nailed across it. At the center of this 2 × 4 drill a ³/₄-inch hole and ream it out so the ¹/₂-inch water pipe will rotate easily in its bore. Saw off any projecting corners.

Next, saw six pieces of ³/₈-inch exterior plywood into sections measuring 48 × 6 × 16 inches. They are the sides of the windmill. Use them to nail the hexagon figures together forming a stand 48 inches high.

Then take the previously fabricated propeller and propeller mount, slide 3 ³/₄-inch washers over the plastic pipe, and push the pipe down into the ³/₄-inch hole in the 2 × 4 that is the brace for the 2-foot hexagon. This should create a smoothly operating pivot joint for the propeller. Its purpose is to allow the propeller to orient itself to the wind. Study Figure 6-3.

Next, find a piece of metal roof flashing and cut out one piece measuring 24 × 24 inches and six pieces measuring 3 × 48 inches. Nail the 24-inch piece across the top to form a canopy for the propeller mount, and use the 3-inch pieces for covering the corners of the base. It will be necessary to toenail a 1 × 4, 24 inches long, on edge to the center of the propeller mount to fasten the canopy to.

For realism cut windows in the base and construct a platform around the bottom (see Fig. 6-1).

Now, no doubt, after you have had your Dutch windmill in operation for some time you will begin to wonder if you can't use some of the wind power to actually do some kind of work. Perhaps like us you would like to light a light from your very own homebuilt wind generator. Now that we can no longer take our energy sources for granted, government and well-financed institutions of all kinds are frantically developing alternate energy sources and wind power

is one of the most worked with sources. However, if history repeats itself, it will still remain for lonely inventors working with hardly any resources but their own imagination and initiative who will develop the mechanisms and ideas that will carry these projects to the point where they are actually feasible. Perhaps you or one of your children will be the genius who does. Also perhaps this next project, though simple, will stimulate your mind along these lines. At the very least it will deliver much personal satisfaction when it is finished.

WIND GENERATOR

The next project is a wind generator that will light 12-volt lights or trickle-charge small batteries. It also has the potential to provide enough current to take care of minimal lighting at remote cabins or workshops.

MATERIALS LIST FOR WIND GENERATOR

1. 6-foot 2 × 6, white spruce or the equivalent
2. 4 × 8 sheet of ¹/₄-inch tempered masonite
3. 2 8-foot 2 × 4's
4. 6-foot 4 × 4
5. 3 × 3-inch pipe nipple. ³/₄-inch pipe nipple. ³/₄ × ¹/₈-inch pipe nipple. ¹/₈-inch pipe nipple. 3 ³/₄-inch pipe tee's.
6. Bicycle tire, bicycle generator, bolts to hold tire to propeller

The first step in building this model is to obtain a 2 × 6-inch board, 6 feet long, that can be used for a propeller. Use white spruce if it can be found, but redwood, white pine, or similar wood that is straight-grained and knotfree can be used. The 2 × 6 should be well seasoned so it will not warp after it is put up. See Figure 6-4.

Place the 2 × 6 on the work bench and find the exact center of the piece. This is done by drawing a centerline both lengthwise and crosswise. Where the lines intersect, drill a ¹/₄-inch hole. The next step is to mark off and cut out the material that must be removed to taper the width of the blade. Measure out 4 inches on each side of the center hole. Draw lines across the 2 × 6. Then go to the ends. At each end mark off 4 inches of width, measuring from opposite edges. Connect the end marks to the center marks at

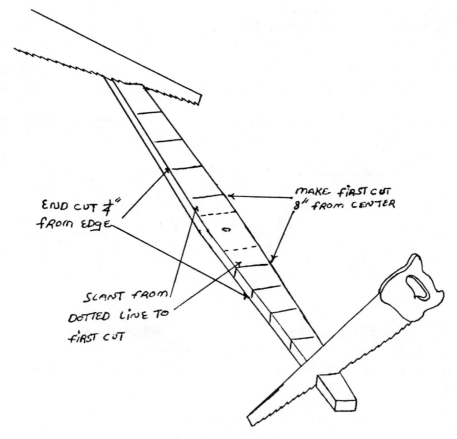

MAKE FIRST CUT 8" FROM CENTER

END CUT 7" FROM EDGE

SLANT FROM DOTTED LINE TO FIRST CUT

Fig. 6-4.

the junction of the center marks and the outside edge of the piece. Notice that this sections off a triangular piece 4 inches wide at the base with a height of 32 inches. Also check to be sure the triangles oppose each other. When you are sure you are removing material from opposite sides of the piece, saw out the marked triangles. With the width of the piece facing you, the edge of the propeller that hasn't been sawed off become the leading edge (see Fig. 6-5). Mark this edge for future reference.

With the width of the blade tapered, the next step is to form the thickness of the blade into an airfoil design tapering from ¾-inch thickness at the ends to the full 1½-inch thickness of the original board at the hub. Lay this out by drawing lines across the width 8 inches on either side of the center hole. Now take a hand saw and make diagonal cuts approximately ¾ inch apart from the 8-inch marks to each end of the piece. Caution: before making any saw cuts study

Figure 6-4. These saw cuts are to make it easier to remove the material which must be removed to form the flat side of the propeller; be sure to stop them about ¼ inch from the edges to prevent too much material from being removed. After the saw cuts are made, remove the material between the cuts with a wood chisel or drawknife. Use a drawknife to smooth the flat surface. Clamp the propeller in a vise or to a bench with C clamps to make it easier to work on. Also use the drawknife to taper the hub into the flat side of the blades. Now the blade is well on the way.

To finish the blade in the airfoil design, turn it over so the flat side is down and shave the corners with a drawknife (see Fig. 6-6). Some people make patterns to keep track of their progress as they shave the back of the blade, but it isn't really necessary. Just work slowly and carefully and remember that the propeller will turn clockwise and the thickest part of the airfoil design will be the leading edge. The trailing

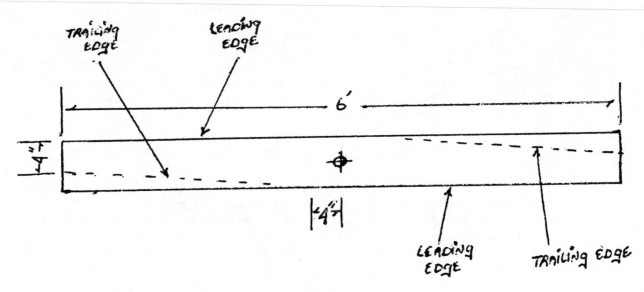

Fig. 6-5.

edge will be sharp to prevent turbulence behind the blade which will slow it down. Do the final shaping with a hand or power sander so no uneven dimensions are visible.

The propeller should be sealed with a good wood sealer and covered with at least two coats of varnish or outside house paint to protect it. When that is done, balance the propeller by mounting it on a

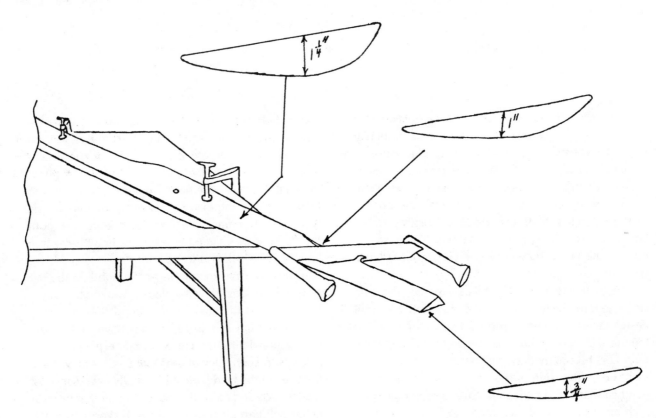

Fig. 6-6.

board nailed upright to the edge of the bench. Use a bolt through the center hole as a pivot. Make sure that the propeller turns free and then spin it several times. If it consistently stops in the same place, it is probably unbalanced. The easiest way to balance it is to drive four-penny finishing nails in the end of the propeller. Generally one will be enough. The propeller must be balanced again after it is mounted to the bicycle wheel.

After balancing the propeller, set it aside and procure a 26-inch front bicycle wheel with tire and axle. Also obtain a 12-volt bicycle generator and light. These small generators will put out about 2 amps, which makes them useful for 12-volt lights, and they can be used to trickle-charge 12-volt batteries. Very often these parts are available used. The generator and light kit cost about $12 new at this time while the wheel and tire may cost about $13 retail.

When the parts are procured, attach the wheel hub to the stand and the propeller to the wheel. The first step, if the wheel is used, is to remove the axle and check the bearings and bearing races. Do this by unthreading the locknut and hub from one side of the axle. Remove the components, wash them in gasoline or solvent, and check the bearings and bearing races for chipped or missing balls or chipped races. Replace all failed parts, coat the bearing with light bearing grease, and reinstall the components. It will be necessary to install the axle offset to one side to adapt it to the stand. Do this by threading one bearing race on the axle as far as possible. (At the center of the axle is an unthreaded section that will stop the race.) Then reinstall the components in the proper order. Tighten the opposite race until the wheel is "set up" and then back it off slowly until the wheel revolves freely. The axle can be held in the hands to check this. Install and tighten the locknuts.

Next obtain a steel, heavy-duty $\frac{1}{8} \times 2$-inch pipe

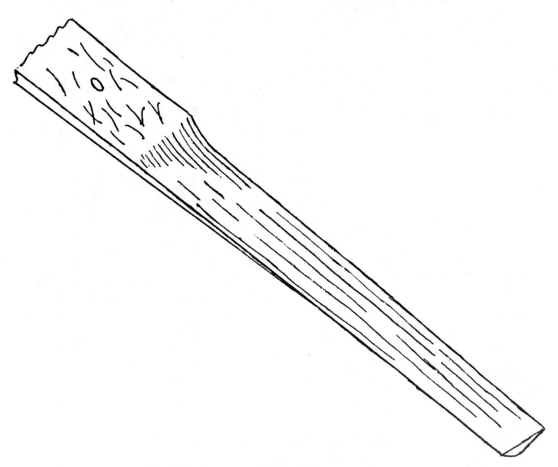

Fig. 6-7.   Correct air foil design for the propeller.

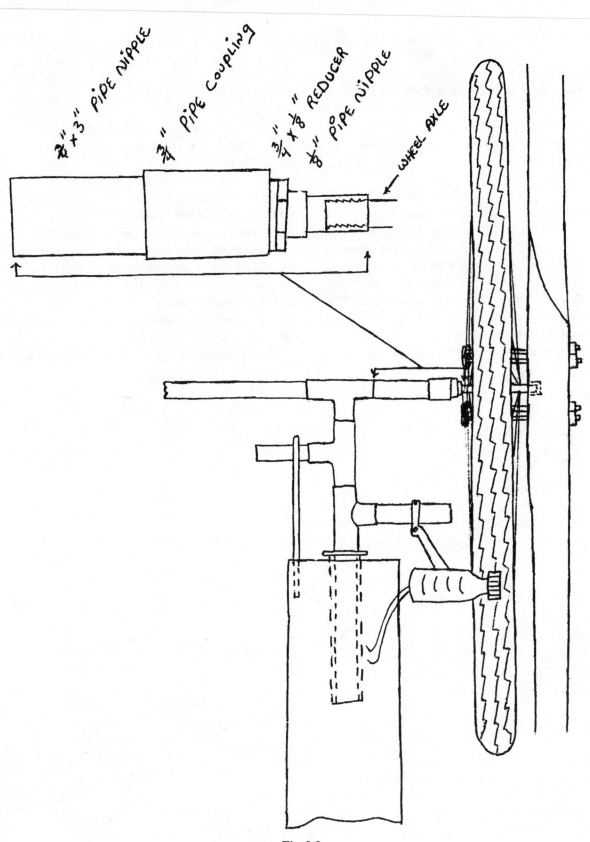

Fig. 6-8.

nipple, hacksaw the threads off one end, clamp it in a vise, and use a $\frac{5}{16} \times 24$ tap to cut threads 2 inches deep in the sawed end. Then install a $\frac{5}{16} \times 24$ hex nut on the axle and turn it against the bearing locknut. This will be used as a jam nut to prevent the axle unthreading from the pipe nipple. Finally thread the long end of the axle into the pipe nipple as far as it will go and tighten the jam nut against it. Now the cycle wheel is ready to install to the mount.

Next make up the mount for the propeller, vane, and generator. First thread a $\frac{3}{4} \times \frac{1}{8}$-inch reducer bushing into a $\frac{3}{4}$-inch pipe coupling (see Fig. 6-8). Then thread a $\frac{3}{4} \times 3$-inch pipe nipple to the opposite end of the coupling. Next thread a $\frac{3}{4}$-inch pipe tee to the $\frac{3}{4} \times 3$-inch bushing with the center outlet of the tee pointing down. Then at the center outlet of the tee thread a 3-inch pipe nipple and another tee. This tee will have the center outlet pointing to the rear. Next a close nipple and another tee with the center outlet

towards the front, and finally a 6-inch pipe section threaded on one end only. Tighten all threads very well after the correct alignment is determined. If a joint tends to unthread after it is placed in operation, drill a .125 hole through the walls of both pipe sections and install a cotter pin. This is useful also for joints that can't be tightened in the correct alignment. When the mount is made up, thread the $\frac{1}{8}$-inch pipe nipple into the $\frac{3}{4} \times \frac{1}{8}$-inch reducer bushing. This will fasten the wheel to the mount. The next step is to fasten the propeller to the wheel.

Drill four $\frac{1}{4}$-inch holes through the hub of the propeller evenly spaced in a $1\frac{1}{2}$-inch radius around the center hole. Next drill a $\frac{3}{4}$-inch diameter hole 1 inch deep enlarging the center hole at the back side of the propeller to provide space for the end of the wheel axle.

Then select a sturdy 6-foot 4×4 hardwood if available. Find the center of one end and drill a $1\frac{1}{8}$-

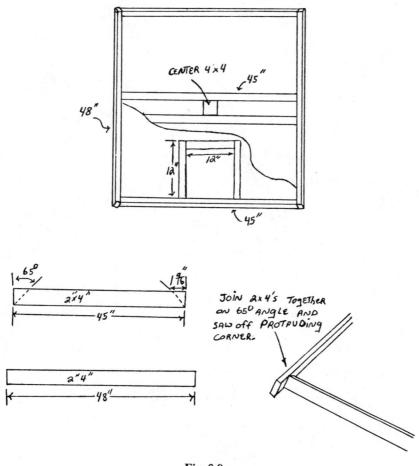

Fig. 6-9.

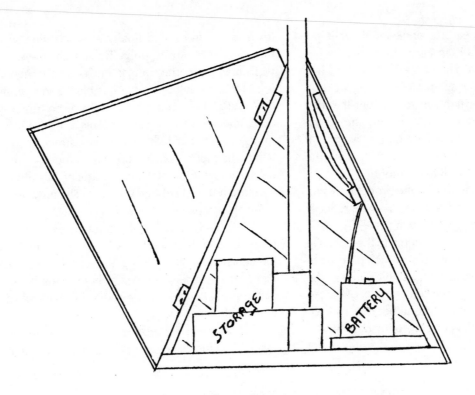

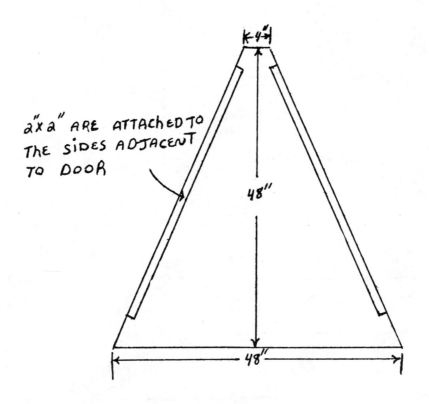

Fig. 6-10.

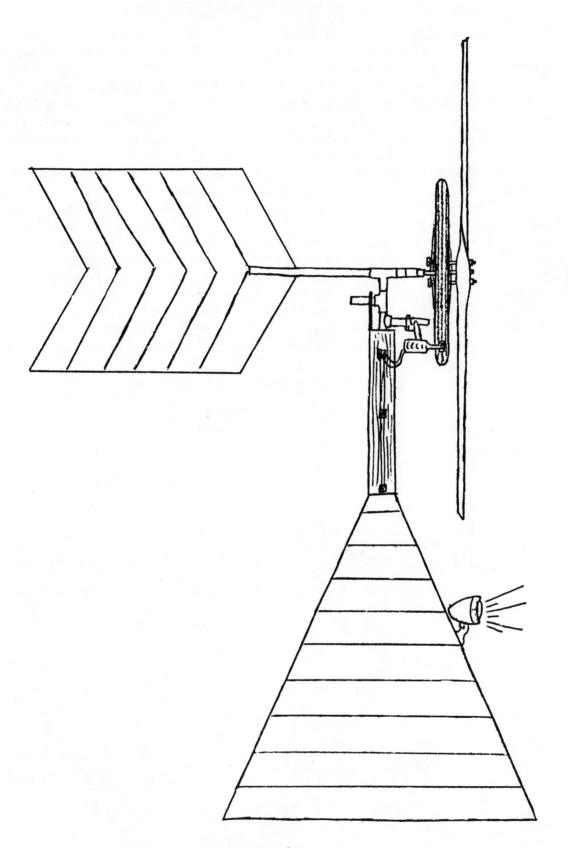

Fig. 6-11.   Wind generator.

inch hole 6 inches deep directly on the centerline. Next cut 6 framing lumber 2 × 4's into the following dimensions: four 2 × 4's 45 inches long and two 2 × 4's 48 inches long. At each end of each 45-inch 2 × 4 cut a 1⁹/₁₆-inch triangle to form the correct 65-degree angle for the side walls of the stand (see Fig. 6-9). Spike two 45-inch 2 × 4's to the 4 × 4 flush with the end opposite the 1¹/₈-inch hole. Next nail the 48-inch 2 × 4's to the ends of the previously nailed 45-inch 2 × 4's. Finally slide the remaining 45-inch 2 × 4's into place and nail securely to form the square base. Saw off the projecting ends of the 48-inch 2 × 4's. When the base is complete, stand it up and nail in the floor.

The floor can be ¼-inch plywood or the equivalent. If a sheet of tempered masonite has to be purchased to make up the wind vane, the waste can be used for the flooring. When the floor is nailed in place, form a battery box centered at the surface which will eventually be the front. Next cover three

sides of the base with scrap plywood. Considerable waste would result from using full sheets of plywood for this. The fourth side will be made from a sheet of 3 × 8 plywood, hinged and latched to form an access door. *Note:* if it is not desirable to charge batteries, with this unit no battery box need be installed. The space inside the base can be used for tools, toys, or gardening aids also. See Figure 6-10.

After the base is complete the propeller mount can be placed in the 1¹/₈-inch hole in the top of the 4 × 4. After considerable use this hole may become enlarged and allow the propeller to lean. If this happens drill out the 1¹/₈-inch hole to 1³/₈ inches and install a 6-inch length of 1¹/₈-inch steel tubing to use for a sleeve. After the sleeve is installed place the propeller and mount into place.

Since a propeller must face directly into the wind to be effective, a wind directional vane must be made up which will keep the unit facing into the wind (see

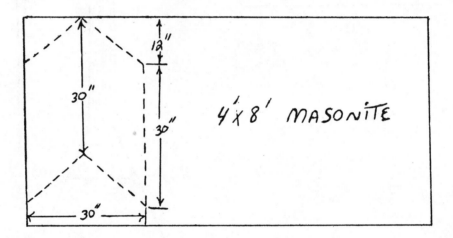

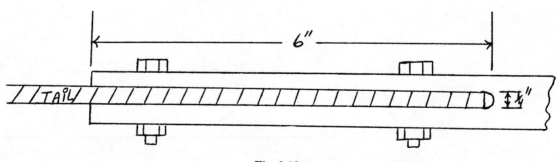

Fig. 6-12.

Fig. 6-11). Make the vane from ¼-inch tempered masonite. Streamline it as shown in Figure 6-12. Then procure a ¾ × 18-inch pipe section threaded on one end only. Measure off 6 inches from the unthreaded end and drill a ¼-inch hole directly through the center of the pipe. Next rotate the pipe 90 degrees and drill 2³⁄₁₆-inch holes directly through the center of the pipe. Finally, use a hacksaw to slot the pipe from the unthreaded end to the ¼-inch hole. When this is done the 18-inch pipe will have a ¼-inch slot 6 inches deep into the unthreaded end (see Fig. 6-12). Evenly spaced at right angles to this slot will be the ³⁄₁₆-inch holes. Next slide the masonite vane into the slot, drill through the ³⁄₁₆-inch holes, and install ³⁄₁₆-inch stove bolts to fasten the vane to the 18-inch pipe section. Then thread the pipe into the tee. Now the unit is ready to use except for installing and wiring in the generator.

Install a ¾ × 6-inch pipe nipple and attach the generator as shown in Figure 6-8. Remember that it is necessary to use two wires to connect the light to the generator for a complete circuit. Study the layout. If it is desirable to charge batteries with this unit, a "cutout" must be installed between the generator and battery to prevent the battery from discharging. Cutouts of this type are available from sources listed at the end of the chapter or build your own wind-activated device. No collector is needed for this wiring diagram since the unit is prevented from swiveling completely around, which would twist the wires, by stops drilled into the 4 × 4 base. Thus the wind charger should be set up facing the direction of the prevailing winds. Experience has shown that it will be inoperational only a tiny fraction of the time.

When the wind generator is done, move it to the windiest section of the garden or lawn and enjoy it. It is useful for illuminating a pool, lawn, or steps in the nighttime, as well as discouraging prowlers. During the daylight hours the smooth motion it produces will delight your eye each time the wind blows. Be sure to make up a simple hook to fasten the propeller during periods when windstorms are expected. If it is desirable to stop the propeller at any time, simply approach it from the rear and push it out of the wind. If high winds come up unexpectedly, it will simply blow over long before it becomes a hazard to life or limb. A simple fence can be constructed in front of the unit to keep small children from coming in contact with the whirling propeller.

WIND MOTOR

One of the greatest weaknesses of the propeller type wind motor is that it must be always facing the wind to be usable. Since the wind is constantly changing, this requires a mechanism to keep it oriented. Additionally, when high winds come up, the propeller should be stopped to prevent damage. The wind motor eliminates many of these weaknesses. It will run no matter where the wind is coming from and nothing short of a full-scale hurricane will do it any harm.

Moreover, it will work very well to turn a water pump or a propeller to keep a fish pond open in winter or produce a desirable current to cool it in summer. It is also useful for pumping water for a solar heating system or filling a container of a gravity-fed animal watering system. It also can be used as a source of free power for a workshop.

The following directions are for a wind motor using two halves of a barrel. For adding the two additional vanes when it is used for shop power just increase the length of the ½ × 3 center stock from 36 to 72 inches and add four additional strap iron braces.

MATERIALS LIST FOR WIND MOTOR

1. 55-gallon drum, either 1 or 2
2. 8 running feet of ½ × 1¼-inch strap iron and 24 ⁵⁄₁₆ × 1½-inch machine bolts, nuts, and washers.
3. 4 feet of 2½-inch pipe, 6 feet of 1-inch pipe
4. ¼ × 36-inch strap iron
5. Piece ¼ × 3 × 24-inch strap iron
6. Lengths of 1¼-inch diameter water pipes as needed to make the stand

The first step is to cut a 55-gallon steel drum in half. Use a cutting torch or a sharp cold chisel for this if you don't have a power saw. Make the cut from top to bottom. Then find enough strap iron to make four strips (eight strips for a shop wind motor) ½ × 1¼ × 24 (*B* in Fig. 6-13), and bend each strip at each end to form a 90-degree angle to fit the inside of the barrel. Drill through the strips and the barrel and bolt the strips to the barrel with ⁵⁄₁₆-inch machine bolts.

Next find a piece of metal stock ½ × 3 × 36 inches, 72 inches for a four-vane. Slot one end ¾ inch wide and 6 inches deep. Lay the other end on the strap iron strips (*B*) on one barrel and weld it in place. Then unbolt that strip from the barrel (to make

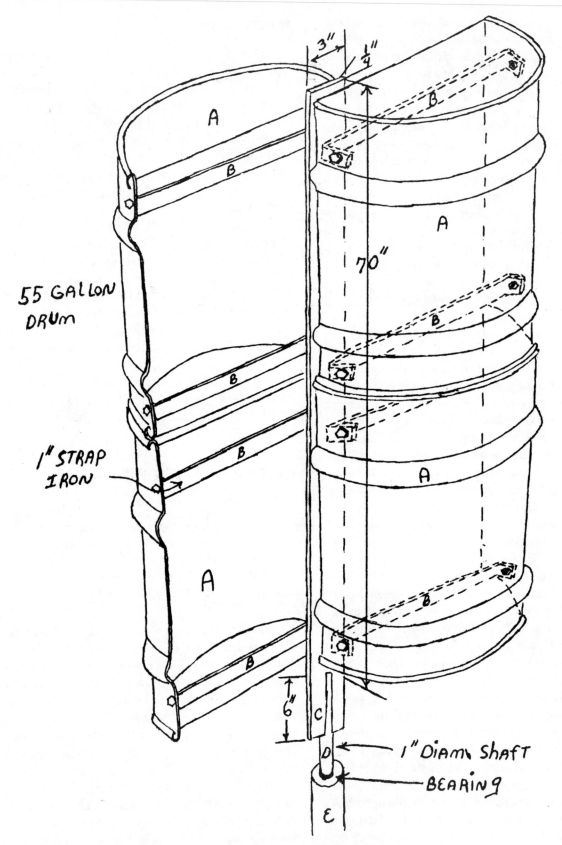

Fig. 6-13.   Vanes for high-torque wind motor.

it easier to work with) and weld the opposite side of the piece (C in Fig. 6-13) to the other barrel. When this is finished, reinstall the removed barrel half and you have formed the vanes of the windmill. The piece (C) should extend past the lower edge of the vanes 6 inches to form a mount for the propeller shaft (D in Fig. 6-13).

The propeller shaft, which can be 6 feet long and ³/₄ inch in diameter, is placed in the slot in piece C, aligned very carefully with the vanes, and welded in place.

The next step is to secure a 4-foot length of 2¹/₂-inch pipe (E in Fig. 6-13). This will form the housing for the ³/₄-inch diameter shaft and will be used as a bearing retainer. Moreover, it will make the shaft freezeproof. After the pipe is secured, go to the bearing supply house or your favorite salvage dealer and find two bearings which will have a ³/₄-inch inside diameter and a 2⁹/₁₆-inch outside diameter. These dimensions will give a tight fit on both the shaft housing and shaft, which is essential for proper operation. If you find the inside of the pipe (E) is irregular, it can be smoothed or enlarged slightly with a small grinding wheel turned by a ¹/₄-inch drill. If it isn't possible to insert the bearing into the pipe, warm the end of the pipe with a fire made of a few newspapers. Well pipe expands considerably when warmed. Then, without getting the fingers burned, place the bearing in the pipe and let it cool and shrink to fit. If the bearing is slightly loose, it still can be used by drilling a hole completely through the pipe slightly below where the top bearing will be placed, but offset enough to miss the ³/₄-inch diameter shaft. Then put a bolt in the drilled hole, put a nut on the bolt, and slide the bearing in place until it contacts the bolt. This bolt will serve two purposes. It will stop the bearing from sliding down into the housing and when a nut is placed on the bolt and, tightened, it will compress the housing enough to grip the bearing to keep it from spinning.

The bearings have to be placed in this order. First put the top bearing on the shaft (D). Then slide the bearing and shaft into the top of the housing (E). Next, tap the lower bearing onto the shaft and up into the housing (E). If the bearings aren't tight, place a bolt through the housing and turn it up to compress the housing around the bearing.

If you are building the two-vane wind motor for use in keeping a fish pond open, coat both the top and bottom of the shaft housing with roofing cement to prevent any water from leaking into the housing. Water in the housing will cause it to freeze up in cold weather.

Make the propeller which will turn under the water when the vanes turn above the water by drilling a 1-inch hole in the center of a piece of metal stock ¹/₄ × 2 × 18 inches.

Since this wind motor is adaptable for turning a generator and other devices inside a shop, it can be mounted on the roof of a building and made very useful. Generally, it will be desirable to increase the torque of this wind motor by adding two additional vanes when it is used for shop work.

All other directions are the same. Mount it on the roof by cutting a suitable hole in the roof and slide the shaft down until it is about 1 foot above the roof. Hold it in place with a bracket made by sawing two 4 × 4's into 1-foot lengths. At the center of each, cut out a 2¹/₂-inch radius so that when the pieces are placed together they will form a 2¹/₂-inch bore. Drill 2¹/₂-inch holes at right angles to the shaft so that bolts can be placed through the 4 × 4 to tighten them around the shaft. Nail one section of the mount to the roof so that the radius adjoins the hole in the roof. Place the shaft in position and then bolt in the other half of the bracket to secure it. Paint the mount or cover it with roofing cement. Further, place liberal amounts of roofing cement around the areas of the roof which could leak from this installation.

Inside the building use a 2 × 4 frame to make a steady rest for the shaft. Nail the 2 × 4's to the rafters so they project down from the rafters about 4 feet apart. Connect the vertical 2 × 4's with horizontal 2 × 4's and use V bolts to clamp the shaft housing to the horizontal 2 × 4's.

The next step is to thread the end of the shaft if it doesn't already have threads. Use a ³/₄ × 16 die to cut threads on about 2 inches of the shaft. These threads will be used to connect the power shaft to the wind motor shaft.

The power shaft is a ³/₄-inch rod, long enough to reach from the end of the shaft to the floor. Rod of this type is available in almost any hardware store. Generally 4 feet will be needed. One end of this power rod has to be threaded also. The coupling between the rods can be easily made by drilling and

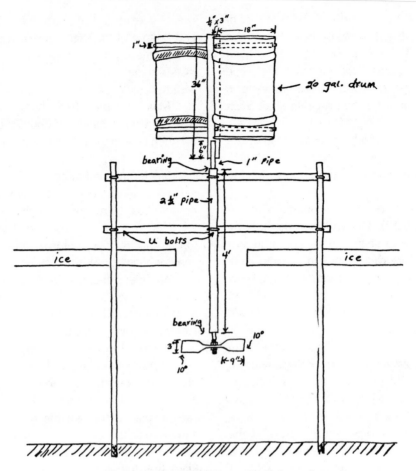

Fig. 6-14. **Wind motor used in fish pond.**

tapping a 2-inch length of 1⅛-inch mild steel hex stock for the ¾ × 16 thread. If this is not desirable, make the connection by sliding a 4-inch section of ¾-inch inside diameter heavy-duty rubber hose over the ends of the shafts. Clamp the hose to the shafts with hose clamp as shown in Figure 6-15.

Now with the power shaft connected to the motor shaft, the next step is to make the lower bearing or steady rest which will keep the end of the shaft from "whipping." This lower bearing has to be made so it is easy to open for removing the shaft.

However, since it is low-speed, a hardwood bearing can be used. Make the bearing by drilling a 1-inch diameter hole in the center of a hardwood block measuring 12 × 6 × 6 inches. Further, drill 2½-inch holes at right angles to the 1-inch hole. Then carefully saw the block in half and fasten one-half to the floor with 8-inch lag screws so that half the 1-inch hole is in line with the bottom of the shaft. When the wind

motor is put in operation, the other half is bolted in place using 1/12 × 10-inch bolts, This will polish itself smooth and be a practically frictionless bearing with a little wear.

Now a pully/flywheel combination can be made up from an automobile tire rim. Generally, it is advisable to use the largest rim that can be found, since the larger the diameter of the pulley the more satisfactory it will be when driving a generator or alternator.

The first step in making this pulley is to cut off one rim flange. This will have to be done with a cutting torch, but very probably your friendly salvage dealer can do it for you when you buy the rim from him. Grind off any rough burrs left after the cutting operation.

Next make up the bracket for mounting the rim to the shaft. Do this by selecting an 8-inch section of ½ × 2-inch strap iron. Drill 2½-inch holes in the section 6 inches apart. Further, drill $2^5/_{16}$-inch holes $^3/_4$ inches on either side of the centerline. Next have a blacksmith heat and twist this section so a butterfly shape is produced with its end sections at right angles to the center. Acquire a $1^1/_2$-inch-wide $^5/_{16}$ U bolt, nuts, and washers (see Fig. 6-15).

Mount the rim to the shaft by bolting the bracket to the rim. Then place the power shaft through the center of the rim and fasten it to the bracket with the U bolt. Be sure the cut-off section of the rim is facing up. If the wheel is off center, slightly slot a $1^1/_2$-inch hole in the bracket and bend the bracket so that the rim can be moved to a true center position (see Fig. 6-15).

The rim can be used for driving a V belt by bolting another belt inside out to the center of the rim to form one side of a pulley. The bottom rim flange will then form the opposite surface. A more expensive way of driving a V belt with a rim is to bolt or weld a

V pulley to the rim. Very little welding is necessary to hold this pulley; in fact, heavy-duty solder will be satisfactory.

When the pulleys are in place, the alternators or generators can be positioned and belts purchased or made up that will fit them. Remember direction of rotation can be changed with a belt by crossing it between the driver pulley and the driven pulley. Moreover, a vertical drive can be changed to a horizontal drive by twisting the belt.

Once the flywheel is in place, a rubbing block can be attached to the floor that will serve as a governor and brake. Slot a section of 2 × 8 as shown in Figure 6-15. Place washers over the bolt on the top surface of the 2 × 8 and use a wing nut to adjust it (see Fig. 6-15).

To have constant current available with a wind-driven generator, it is necessary to store the current in batteries. Batteries, of course, not only store current

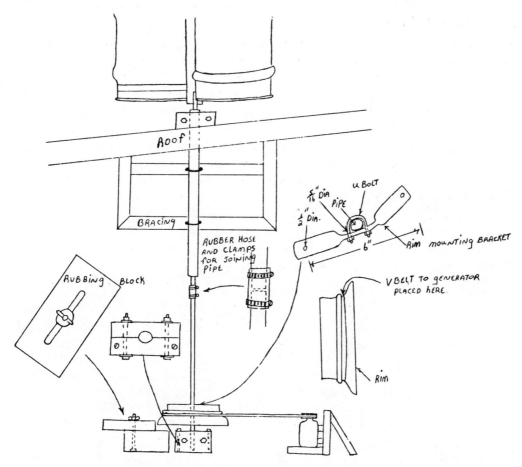

Fig. 6-15.   High-torque wind motor used in workshop.

but smooth it out, which allows appliances and tools to utilize it. The best batteries for this type of use are the nickle cadmium or airplane batteries. Nickle cadmium batteries are superior to lead acid batteries because they won't accept an overcharge and they remain efficient in cold weather. Generally, they last much longer also. However, they are much more expensive. If lead acid automotive batteries are used, a voltage regulator must be wired into the charging circuit to prevent overcharging the batteries and to prevent them from discharging when no current is being produced. Sometimes it's desirable to change the 12-volt DC current produced by an automotive-type alternator or generator to 110 volts AC. This can be done by wiring an inverter into the circuit. Inverters are widely used on campers and are sold by most mail order houses as well as many retail hardware outlets.

Electricity isn't the only energy that can be produced by this wind motor. It will function very well to turn the pump of an air compressor or to pump water. Also in hot weather the shaft can be fitted with a fan and it will help cool the shop. Many more applications for this wind motor are possible, such as turning grinders, lathes, drill presses, and small grain grinders.

PART II

The Best of **THE BACKYARD BUILDING BOOK II**

Chapter 7

A Solar Heated Guest House or Hideaway

The greatest impression I ever made on my children came about many years ago because of solar energy. We began a long, grueling trip at four o'clock in the morning, and by four o'clock that afternoon we all were tired from driving, our nervous systems almost completely short circuited by traffic and heat. The kids were so hungry they complained constantly.

With great relief we saw a deserted roadside park and turned in. Mom quickly prepared some hamburger while the children and I gathered dead branches to use in the grill provided at the park. All went well until we were ready to light the fire and realized that we didn't have a single match left. By now we were reduced to a level of frustration that bordered on hysteria. However, just as we were about to load everything up and get back on the road, I remembered something I had read

recently about starting a fire with a flashlight and the sun. A swift search of the baggage located the large battery operated lantern that we used as a camp light. I removed the lens with a screwdriver, turned the bulb out of its socket, and polished the reflector with my handkerchief until it was shining. Next, with a great show of confidence that I didn't feel, I twisted a piece of facial tissue into the bulb socket and told the kids to hold a piece of newspaper ready to catch the tissue when it started burning.

I pointed the reflector directly at the afternoon sun and within the space of three breaths the tissue started smoking. Suddenly a tiny orange flame appeared on the side of the tissue. I plucked the tissue from the reflector, started the newspaper burning, and transferred the fire to our grill. A few minutes later I sat down to grilled hamburgers amid the worshipful eyes of my kids. "Gee Dad, you can do anything," said my ten-year-old son. "How can you know all that stuff Dad?" agreed his five-year-old sister. The glow of those words was remembered a long time after the heat from the fire went out.

A glance at the history of utilizing solar energy indicates that Archimedes was the first man to develop solar energy on a useful scale. In 212 B.C. he designed a system of mirrors that focused the sun's rays to set fire to an attacking Roman fleet.

People continued to dabble with solar energy over the ages, but the first practical home use of solar energy in the United States came in the 1920's as Californians began installing solar water heaters. Years later, in 1938, the Massachusetts Institute of Technology designed a solar heated house. Since that date about one solar house a year was built in this country until about 1960, and the advent of the space age.

The developments of sun power in the space age, still further intensified by the energy situation in the 1970's, have fanned the interest in solar energy to a fever pitch. Solar heated buildings and houses are being built in almost every state, and it is a rare university or laboratory that doesn't have some solar heating program underway.

Here in Wisconsin we have the experimental Arlington House at the Solar Research Center on the University of Wisconsin campus. The Arlington House utilizes a plate collector with pebble storage and air as an exchange medium. Air is circulated across a roof unit which consists of black plates contained in a box covered with glass. Sunlight heats the plates, which in turn heat the air moving across them. The warm air is then blown into the basement where it is circulated through a large bin of pebbles. The pebbles extract the heat from the air and store it. When the sun isn't shining the flow of air is reversed through the pebbles. Since they are warmer than the air, the air extracts heat from the rocks. The warm air is then circulated through the house like the air from a warm air furnace.

This method is one of the three most practical ways to utilize solar energy for home heating. The other two are the water storage system and the direct heating and storage system, such as heating a wall or floor.

The water storage system is similar to the pebble system, but it uses water as the heat exchange medium and a large water tank as a storage vessel. Coils of tubing (painted black) are mounted on the roof in a sealed box, which is covered with plastic or glass to admit the sun's rays. The coils are connected by a system of pipes to a large water storage tank usually located in the basement of the house. An electric pump circulates the water from the storage tank through the collector on the roof where the sun heats the water in the tubing. The warm water then is returned to the storage tank, and is circulated throughout the house to heat it.

The liquid system is the most efficient in terms of picking up heat and storing it for a long time. However, it has some drawbacks, since the water is subject to freezing in cold climates. The water must be mixed with antifreeze such as ethylene glycol, which is expensive. Further, most of the systems now in use have a tendency to leak, which destroys the effectiveness of the system as well as damages the structure.

Both air and water systems are expensive. The guest house which we have designed uses the third solar heating principle, that of a solid surface which collects the heat from the sun and radiates it directly from its mass.

We have settled on a black concrete wall, one foot thick as the collector. The partitions in the blocks will be filled with concrete (as the wall is built) to increase the mass of the wall and, therefore, its ability to retain heat. Concrete blocks were decided on as a practical matter. A stone and concrete wall would have a greater mass, but you would need forms to build it. We felt the backyard builder could do the job faster and easier with concrete blocks. We mention the solid wall in case the builder would rather do the job that way.

To be effective, this structure must receive

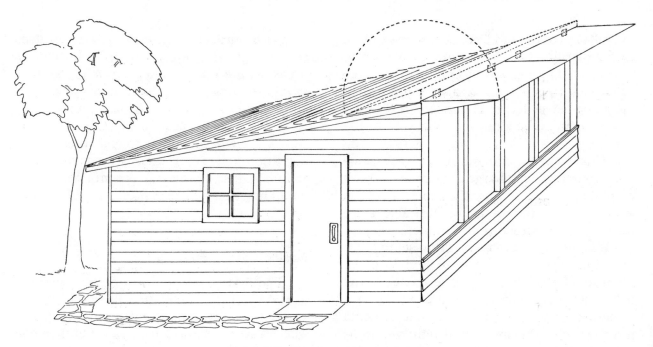

Fig. 1-1 A solar heated guest house.

Fig. 1-2 Solar wall in the guest house.

the full rays of the sun from about nine o'clock in the morning to at least three o'clock in the afternoon. If neighboring buildings or large coniferous trees would shade the south wall of the guest house during this time period in the winter months, building the solar wall in the guest house would be a waste of time. You could, of course, build the house with some other source of heat. Large deciduous trees are no problem because they shed their leaves in winter. They might even be desirable since they shade the structure in summer.

It is interesting to note that in some areas attempts are being made to legislate the amount of sunlight which a home in the urban areas is entitled to, and building a structure or planting a tree where it could interfere with this amount of light would be prohibited. As the years go by such legislation will undoubtedly be worked out and included in most building regulations.

Once you've decided to build the solar wall, you must make sure the subsoil is stable enough to support the weight of the wall without much shifting or settling. The stability of the subsoil can be determined by dig-

ging to a depth of four feet, which is how deep the solar wall footing should be buried. In areas where earthquakes are a problem, a special footing should be designed. Local or state building codes are a good source of information about this. The footing shown in figure 1-3 will be stable enough under most conditions. Heaving due to frost should be minimized, since the wall is contained within a building that will be at least partially heated by the sun.

Staking Out the Building

The first step toward your guest house is to stake out the excavation lines and do the excavating. Start by collecting a dozen wooden stakes about 1 foot long. Sharpen one end of each stake. To stake out the building, you will need a hammer, a 100-foot string, a carpenter's square, a bubble level and a 100-foot measuring tape.

Now determine where you want the excavation lines by using an existing building, street or property line for an orientation point. For example, if you want your guest house to sit 20 feet inside your east property line, measure off 20 feet from the east property line along both the north and south property lines and mark the locations by driving stakes. Next, find the center of this line by tieing a string between the stakes and measuring to find the center of the string. Finally, measure off 8 feet in each direction from the center and mark this 16-foot length with stakes. The line established by these stakes will form the east excavation line for your solar guest house.

With one line of the building established, you can project the north and south lines by using the carpenter's square and a string. Tie the string to the stakes marking the east wall and have a helper hold the square so that the blade of the square lies along that line. Next, tie a second string to the northern stake of that line and adjust the string until it is 16 feet long and at right angles to the east line. Stake and tie this string, and repeat the procedure to find the south building line.

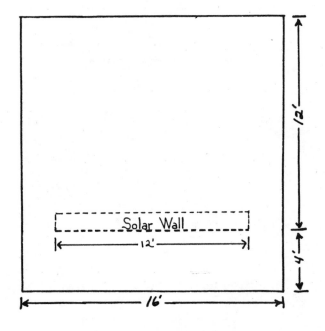

Fig. 1-3 Staking out the excavation.

When the stakes which mark the corners of the west line are driven, just connect the stakes by string to establish the west line. At this stage the layout will probably have to be adjusted slightly to square it up. Do this by measuring diagonally from the corners and adjusting the stakes until the diagonals are even.

Be sure to tie a string around all the stakes to form an outline for the building. Then stand inside the outline as if you were standing on the floor of the building and decide if, indeed, that is where you want the building to be. Some factors could be in error which will not be obvious until you do this.

You are now ready to begin excavating. The trench for the wall foundation should be 1 foot wide and 2½ feet deep. The solar wall excavation should be 4 feet deep, or down to solid subsoil. It will have to be about 2 feet wide to accommodate the 2-foot-wide footing for the wall, and 12 feet long.

Footings

The first step in building is to mix up the concrete and pour the footings. The mix can be the traditional one-two-three mix composed of one part Portland cement, two parts sand and three parts gravel. Add just enough water to make the mix pour; excessive water weakens concrete. Also, steel reinforcing should be added to the concrete footings. You can use concrete reinforcing rods, chicken wire, or even scrap metal from the junk yard. The equivalent of two ⅝-inch diameter concrete reinforcing rods should be added to the solar wall footing. The footings should be allowed to cure for three days before block laying is started. In hot weather be sure to shade the concrete by keeping it covered with a damp cloth as it cures. See figure 1-4.

Block Laying

After the footings have cured properly, begin laying the blocks. Use 8x8x16-inch ce-ment blocks for the outer wall footings, and 12x8x16-inch cement blocks for the solar wall footing. Bags of dry-mixed mortar are available for block laying, which is easier and cheaper to use than mixing your own. You will also need a trowel, carpenter's level, chalk line and a pair of gloves.

Start by laying the corner blocks, which have one flat end. The flat end is, of course, laid to the outside. Set the first blocks on a full width of mortar about 1 inch thick. Level this first block and square it with the footings very well, since this first block determines the line for the rest. Place a corner block at each corner. By the time you finish, the mortar should have stiffened enough to permit placing a chalk line between the first and second blocks. Use this as a guide to lay the first course, or row, of blocks.

Lay the mortar bead 1 inch thick and 8 inches wide. The ends of the blocks should be buttered with a similar bead of mortar. Push the blocks together and level them so that the joint is ⅜ inch thick. The actual size of each block is 7⅝x7⅝x8⅝, but the working size of 8x8x16 allows for a ⅜-inch mortar joint. Be sure to level the blocks in both directions, and keep the joints the same thickness. After the first course is laid, build up each corner two courses at a time, making sure the blocks are level. Alternate the corner blocks from one wall to the other in each course in order to stagger the vertical joints. Then fill in the walls between the corners, lining up the blocks with the first course.

Half blocks are available for filling in places where full blocks cannot be used. Blocks can also be cut to size by scoring them with a chisel, or you can use an electric saw with a masonry blade to cut blocks.

The outer walls should be built two courses above grade (see fig. 1-4). This will provide a crawl space under the floor joists to insulate the floor and install the water pipes and electric lines. An access opening 2 feet wide should be left through the top two courses of the northern wall footing.

Anchor bolts must be placed in the top

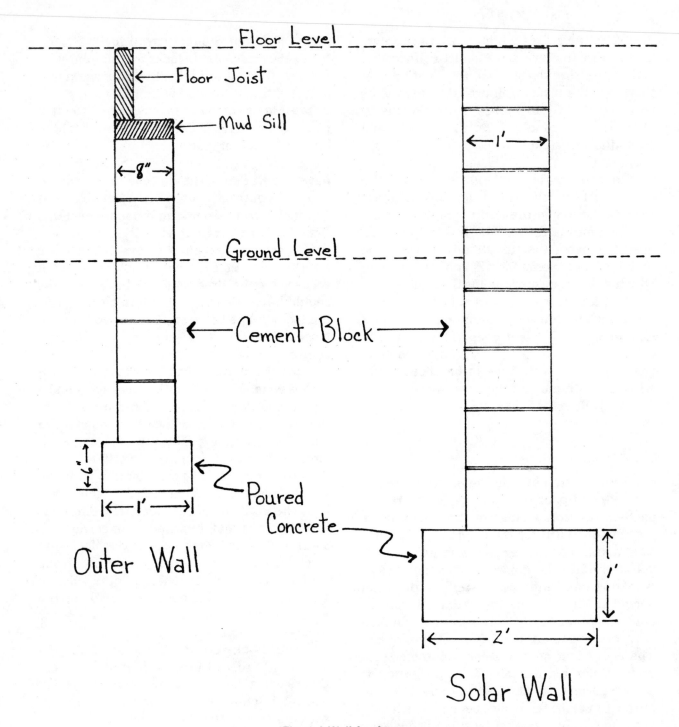

Fig. 1-4 Wall footings.

row of blocks to bolt the mud sill to the wall (see fig. 1-5). They are usually ½x6-inch carriage head bolts set in wet concrete poured into the spaces in the blocks. An alternative is to spike the mud sill to the blocks by filling the

holes with concrete and driving the nails into the concrete after it has hardened to the "green" stage. This practice will not pass the building codes in many places, although for this building it would probably be satisfactory.

The Solar Wall

The solar wall can be built up at this time, or it can be postponed until the walls of the building are in place. It is much more convenient to build it at this time. However, in areas of frequent high winds, some danger does exist that the wall will be blown over if the entire wall is constructed before the concrete in the blocks hardens sufficiently.

The solar wall is 12 courses above the floor level, or 8 feet high. It is 12 feet wide, or the equivalent of nine 16-inch blocks (see fig. 1-6). Note that two 6-inch openings are left at the base of the wall, and two complete blocks are left out near the top of the wall. These openings will allow the air to circulate freely, warming as it passes through the wall. The 6-inch openings are created by cutting 3 inches off the ends of adjacent blocks. Do not position mortar joints above these openings, or the wall will be weakened. The openings at the top won't affect the wall's strength. The openings can be framed with sheet metal or wood, or ventilation screens can be put over them.

Fill each block with gravel and concrete as the wall is built up. Extreme care should be taken to build the wall vertically. Check it frequently with a level. Any tendency to lean one way or the other will cause structural problems from the start.

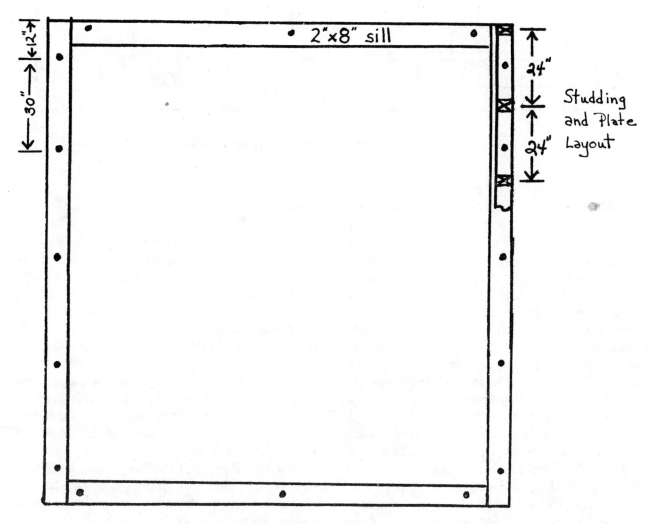

Fig. 1-5 Location for sill anchor bolts.

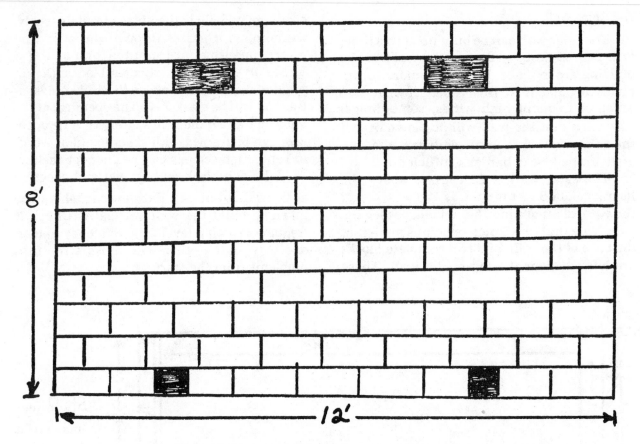

Fig. 1-6 Solar wall showing placement of air spaces.

When the solar wall is done, the framing for the structure can commence. All studding will be 2x6's spaced on 24-inch centers. This type is used because of the greater thickness of insulation that can be used with 2x6 framing. Also, less heat is lost through the walls when fewer solid wooden members extend from the inside to the outside of the wall. Tests have shown that 2x4 framing on 16-inch centers will conduct about five percent more heat than 2x6 framing on 2-foot centers.

The choice of insulation is up to you, but at this writing the most logical choice would seem to be the fiberglass rolls with a vapor barrier. Be sure to use the thickness made for 2x6 framing, and place the vapor barrier facing inward. This will deliver an R factor of 22.4. An R factor of 20 is the minimum that should be used with solar heated homes. More about insulation later.

Foundation Framing

The first framing member to install is the 2x8 mud sill, commonly called a sill. It is bolted or nailed to the wall footings, and will support the floor joists. First, cut the sills for all the walls. You will need two 16-foot members and two 15-foot, 1-inch pieces. Find the location for the anchor bolts by laying the sill alongside the bolts, and project their locations onto the sill with a try square or carpenter's square. An unorthodox but faster way is to remove the nuts from the bolts, lay the sill on the top of them, and tap the sill with a hammer so that the ends of the bolts form impressions in the wood. Then drill the holes. Use a slightly larger drill then the diameter of the bolt to make up for any unevenness in the pattern. After the sills are drilled and ready to put in place, it is advisable to paint the bottom surface with creosote or some other wood preservative.

Before the sills are bolted down, flood the top surface of the wall with wet concrete (grout.) This will insure a level bed for the sill when the bolts are tightened down. Wet the top surface of the blocks thoroughly, and prepare the grout by mixing equal parts of screened sand and cement. Add water until the mixture will pour, and flood the top surface of the blocks with it. Then put the sills in place and tighten the nuts down on the bolts. Scrape off the excess cement and use it on the next wall. Check with a level and pound down any humps in the sill. The sills should be toe nailed

together at the corners to prevent the ends of the boards from lifting.

The sills should be allowed to set overnight before nailing the floor joists to them, so that the grout has time to harden. Nevertheless, the floor joist layout can be done at this time (see fig. 1-7). A carpenter's square and pencil is all you need for the layout. The tongue of the square is 16 inches long, which is exactly the spacing of the joists. Therefore, lay the square on top of the corner of the south and east walls with the tongue lying along the eastern wall. Make marks on the south wall against each side of the body of the square, marking the placement of the first joist. Also

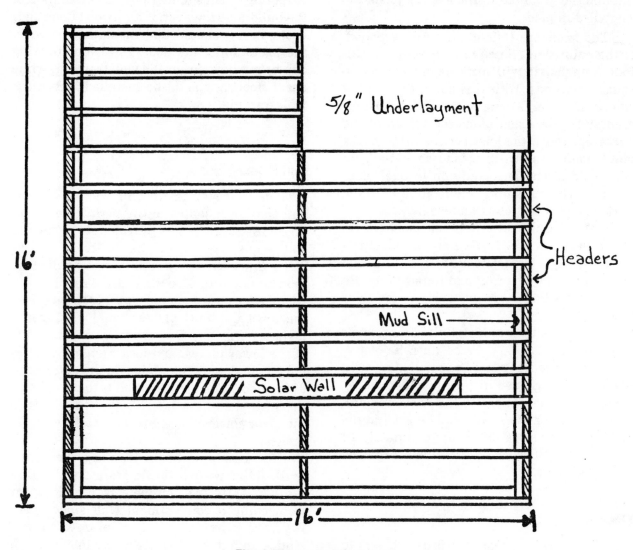

Fig. 1-7 Layout of floor joists.

mark the point where the end of the tongue falls to locate the second joist. Turn the square over and place the end of the tongue at the end of the sill on the east wall. The body of the square is now in position to mark the placement of the second joist. Marking against each side of the body permits placing the joist between the marks and eliminates the possibility of error. Continue to mark for the joists along the east wall, then return to the south wall and mark along the west wall for the joists. An extra joist will have to be installed next to the solar wall (see fig. 1-7). Don't bother marking it on the sill; it can be placed by sighting along the solar wall. When the joist locations are laid out and the grout has hardened, the joists can be nailed in place.

The joists are 16-foot, knot-free redwood, or the equivalent. Since lumber comes in 16-foot lengths, it will only be necessary to square the ends. With this done, the nailing can commence. Be sure to sight each joist for a possible curve and place the crown of the curve up. Place the joist between the marks and toenail it to the sill using two 8d nails on each side of the joist and one in each end. Drive all the nails until the head is partially buried so that the job is more rigid.

Install all the joists, and check them for any unevenness. If high joists are found, chisel under them; if low joists are found, raise the ends with shim material and renail them. Be sure to install a joist at each side of the solar wall.

The next step is to install the bridging, or headers (see fig. 1-7). Since no rim joist is used, solid headers must be installed. A solid row of bridging must also be installed in the center of the floor to stiffen the joists and provide a base for the subfloor. The bridging is cut from 2x10 stock and is approximately 14 inches long. However, it is prudent to measure each space.

Flooring

The flooring is installed in two layers to provide a vapor barrier. The first layer is ⅝-inch underlayment, which can be plywood or particle board. Nail it to the joists using 8d coated nails. Then lay the heaviest builders plastic you can find on the subfloor. Sweep the floor clean before you lay down the plastic, and fasten it with tacks or staples.

The top layer of flooring can also be ⅝-inch plywood or particle board. Be sure to alternate the direction of installation so the joints are not all in the same place. Nail the second layer of flooring to the joists where possible with 8d coated nails, and use #6 rings shank nails to fasten the top layer to the bottom layer when a joist can't be reached.

The floor should be covered with thick carpeting or rugs to increase the insulation of the building. However, if hardwood flooring is desired, you should add insulation between the joists under the floor. Hardwood flooring can be put down after the wall framing, while sheet flooring should be installed before the wall framing.

Wall Framing

The first step in framing the walls is to nail the lower plates to the perimeter of the floor. The lower plates provide a base for the wall studs, and should be cut from 16-foot 2x6's. Since the east and west walls will overlap the north and south walls, the east and west lower plates should be 16 feet long, and the north and south plates should be 15 feet, 1 inch (see fig. 1-9). Be sure to square the ends of the lower plates, and locate them by snapping a chalk line ½ inch inside the outer edge of the floor. The extra ½ inch is to provide for the wall sheathing later. Spike the plates to the floor joists using one 16d nail every 32 inches.

You can now begin framing the south wall. This wall is built from 2x6 milled lumber, as is the complete frame. It is far from being a conventional wall since openings are provided for the solar windows. Notice on figure 1-8 that the two inside rough openings are slightly larger than the two out-

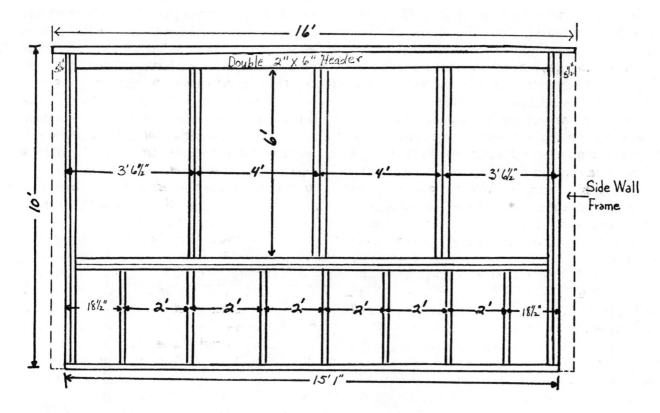

Fig. 1-8 South wall frame.

side window spaces. These spaces can be adjusted to fit the available glass if glass isn't cut to order for this project. Rough openings can be decreased readily by installing additional stud or finish board.

The wall frame is fabricated on the ground and raised into position as a unit. The studding in the south wall should be sturdier than normal because of its large window area. To compensate for this, 2x6 studs are used back-to-back, forming 4x6 studs (see fig. 1-8). Begin by selecting one 16-foot 2x6 and four 10-foot 2x6's. Square the ends of the 16-foot piece; it will form the wall's upper plate. Then cut the 10-foot pieces to 9 feet, 9 inches. These will form the 4x6's, or double studs, at the ends of the upper plate.

Lay the upper plate about 11 feet from the edge of the wall, and position it so the smoothest side is up for pencil marks. Measure in 6¼ inches from each end of the plate to find the center lines for the outside studs. Make a mark completely across the width of

the plate. Spike one 9-foot, 9-inch stud in place over each center line, but be sure to square the studs with the plate before you nail them. Use a minimum of two 16d spikes driven through the top plate into the ends of the studs. Next spike the inside studs in place to form a 4x6 stud at the end of the frame. Spike the two studs together.

When this is done select four more 16-foot 2x6's and cut them to 14 feet, 7 inches. Turn one pair on edge and spike them in place directly under the top plate to form the header above the windows. They will be toe nailed to the studding with four 8d nails each, and they will also be nailed together.

Use the remaining two 14-foot, 7-inch pieces to form the bottom window plate as shown in figure 1-8. When this is done the double studs forming the rough frame for the windows can be spiked in place. They are 6 feet long. The studding under the window is single and on 2-foot centers. These studs are approximately 36½ inches long, but careful measurements of the opening should be taken before any sawing is done.

Once the south wall is completed, it can be put into place. Try to have about four people available for this job. Set the wall on the bottom plate in the correct place. If the ends of the studs were squared off accurately, it will stand by itself. However, at least one person should steady it while another toe nails the studs to the bottom plate, using six 8d nails on the bottom of each stud. When all the studs have been toe nailed the wall should be braced from the top plate to the floor and to the outside (with pieces of lumber that can be reused.) It can then be left standing while the other walls are being built.

The other walls can be fabricated one at a time on the floor of the building and raised into position. The only frame which will have to be carried is the south wall. Build the south wall first followed by the north, and finally the east and west walls. Study figures 1-10 and 1-11 to construct the north, east and west walls. Omit the door frame for the east wall.

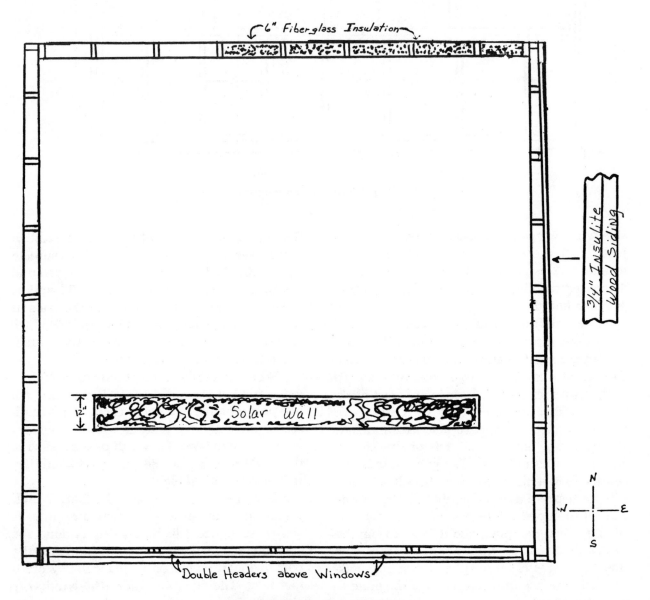

Fig. 1-9 Studding and sheathing.

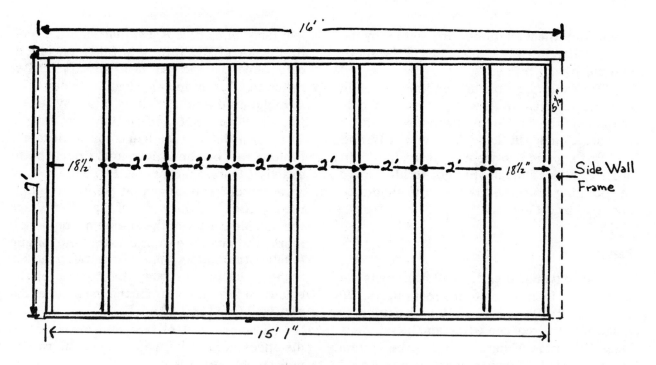

Fig. 1-10 North wall frame.

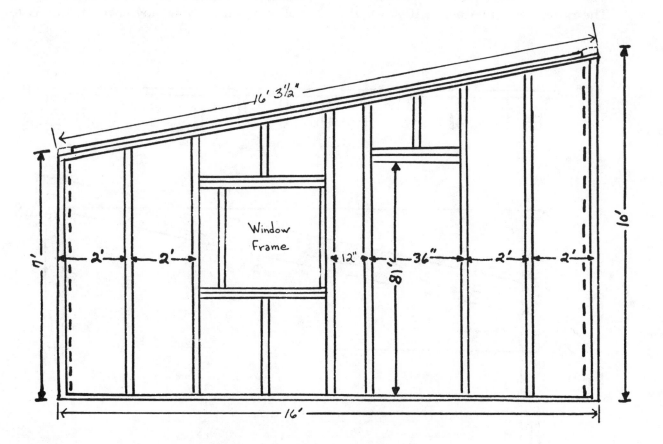

Fig. 1-11 Frame for east and west walls.

Notice that the wall frames tie together by the 5½-inch overlap of the top plates of the south and north wall frames.

The exact sizes of the window frames in the east and west walls will be determined by the sizes of the double-hung windows that you choose. Check the local lumber yards and building suppliers to see what is available. In order to allow enough sunlight to illuminate the building properly, the windows should be about 36 by 36 inches.

Rafters

The next step after the wall framing is the cutting and installation of the roof rafters. We have used 2x10's spaced on 16-inch centers to make sure the roof can withstand heavy snow loads. In areas of light snowfall the rafters can be spaced 24 inches apart, which would increase the insulating value of the roof.

The rafters are cut from 2x10 stock, 18 feet long. Since this is a simple slanting roof, the layout of the rafters is fairly uncomplicated. Because the rafters are alike, a master rafter can be cut and checked, and then used to make up the other rafters. Start by selecting an 18-foot 2x10 and cutting it to 17 feet, 11 inches. Decide which end you want to use for the tail of the rafter and find a point exactly 1 foot from that end. Place the body of a carpenter's square at that point and measure 3 inches into the width of the rafter. Place the outside corner of the square at the 3-inch mark, and pivot the square so that the tongue touches the bottom edge of the rafter at 5½ inches. Outline the body and tongue of the square to form the seat for the top plate of the rear wall (see fig. 1-12).

Now take a steel tape and measure the distances across the walls where the rafters will sit. Measure it to within ¼ inch of the actual distance by making sure the tape is pulled tight. As you may suspect, this is to

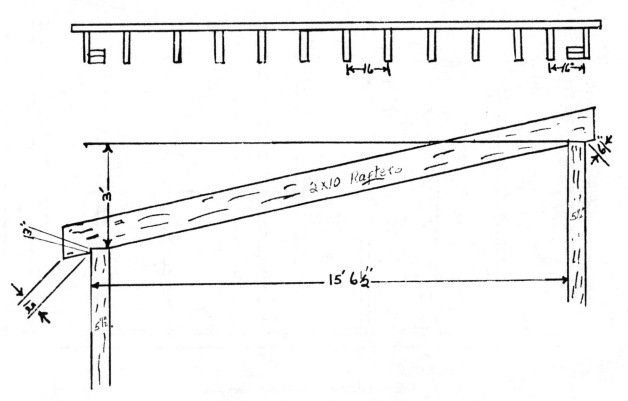

Fig. 1-12 Rafter spacing and detail.

make sure the run of the rafter will fit the building. At this stage it is very easy to be in error as much as 2 inches.

Project this length (which should be near 15 feet, 8 inches) onto the rafter by measuring from the first mark towards the other end of the rafter. Make a good pencil mark there, take out the square and repeat the dimensions shown at the tail of the rafter. This, of course, measures the seat for the front wall plate.

The only remaining cuts are at the ends of the rafters. These two cuts are called the "tail cut" and the "top end cut," and are easily located by using a square to project the horizontal cuts for the wall seats. The overhang is 12 inches in the rear and 6 inches in the front. When all the lines are drawn in, carefully make the cuts. A good sharp crosscut hand saw works well for this.

The master rafter should be checked for fit in several places along the roof. If all is well, proceed to mark off and saw out the desired number of rafters by laying the master rafter on another 18-foot 2x10 and marking the outline.

Toe nail the rafters to the front and rear plates with two 16d nails on each side of the rafter, or drive a single rafter spike through the rafter and into the plate.

When the rafters are in place, the roof sheathing can be installed. Use ⅝-inch exterior grade plywood or the equivalent. Make sure the joints are located over rafters, and nail every 6 inches with 8d coated nails. As soon as the sheathing is finished, the roofing should be added to avoid rain damage. First lay down #60 builders felt, then use composition or roll roofing. The heavier the roofing the greater the insulating value.

The wall sheathing can be installed next. Insulating sheathing such as Celotex will give added insulating value; however, plywood or 1-inch lumber will also be satisfactory. Cover the sheathing with heavy building felt before installing the siding. The siding can be either horizontal or vertical, but I have a personal preference for board and batten siding. What-

ever siding is used should be judged for its insulating value.

Once the wall sheathing and siding are in place, the door framing can commence. Door framing is a complex undertaking that requires special tools such as routers. Perhaps the most expedient way to handle this is to purchase the ready-made door and door frames, which are available at most lumber yards and hardware stores. Pre-hung doors can be set in place in the rough opening, wedged level and nailed in place. Even professional carpenters use them when possible. A storm door should be used with this structure, and adding an entry way would improve the insulating value of the structure immensely, especially in the coldest climates.

You should use the very best weather-tight windows available. Fixed or insulated glass is superior to double-hung windows, even when storm windows are used. The solar windows in the south wall are the areas of greatest potential heat loss. They are also the greatest expense if new glass must be used. Many times glass installers, building contractors, or wreckers have used glass that can be cut to size. The thicker the glass the better insulating value it will have. The solar windows should be made up of two or three sheets of fixed glass with at least ½ inch of air space between the panes.

Equally important is the method of mounting the glass in the window frames. Good results can be obtained by cutting the glass to size and mounting it in the rough opening by using ¾-inch furring strips all around, inside and outside. Mastic should also be used to create a draft-proof seal. Any glass retailer will have full information on how to install the glass so that it won't admit any cold. The disadvantage is that the windows cannot be opened.

After the windows are in place, a method of reducing the heat loss through the window when the sun isn't shining is very important. The heat loss through the glass when the sun isn't shining can be nearly as great as the heating benefits derived from the solar wall.

One of the most economical ways to insulate the window is to install insulated drapes. They are available commercially or you can make your own, especially if a seamstress is interested in the project. To do this, sew insulating material such as fiberfill or beads of styrofoam between layers of drapery material. A 4-inch thickness of fiberfill sandwiched between two layers of the densest material available should give good results.

Just as important as the drapery is some method of sealing the drapes at the top and bottom of the window. It should not be possible for room air to flow across the window, since this would cause the glass to cool the room air.

Our solar window curtains are designed with an overhang at the top of the window and a lip at the bottom for tucking in the bottom of the draperies. A means of fastening the drapes together at the center should also be provided.

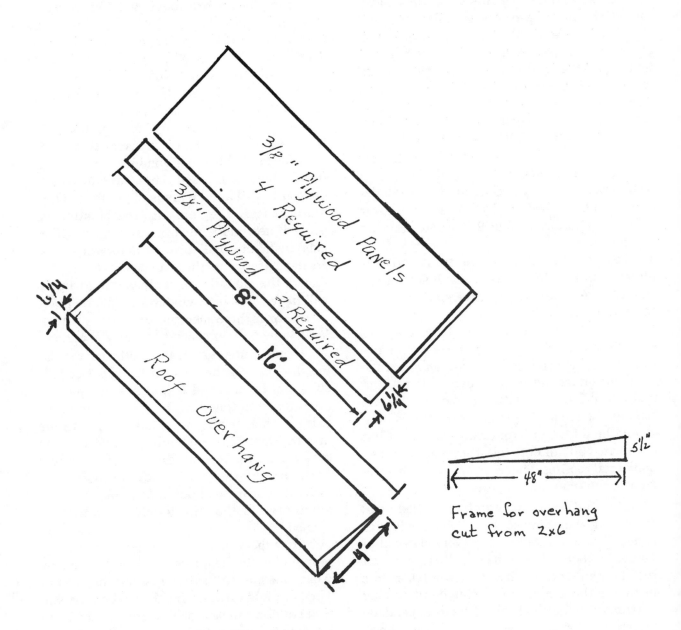

Fig. 1-13 Roof overhang.

We used snaps, which are available at fabric shops and drapery outlets.

Panels made of foam are even better than insulated drapes to counteract heat leakage through the windows. The panels are made so they can be removed from the windows during the day. If attractive pictures or designs are printed on the panels, they can be hung from the inside surface of the solar wall when not in use. The panels could also be made into shutters that fit on the outside. They could be hinged from the bottom and painted white inside to form a natural reflector.

Roof Overhang

The roof overhang is hinged so that it may be swung back over the roof to allow the sun to shine on the solar wall in the winter. During the summer, the overhang will provide shade. The shade will allow the solar windows to be used in the summer for viewing and illuminating the inside of the building.

Build the overhang by selecting two knot-free 2x6's, 8 feet long. Saw ten wedge-shaped frames from the pieces as shown in figure 1-13. Next select five sheets of ⅜-inch exterior grade plywood to cover the wedge-shaped frames. Cut two 6½-inch by 8-foot panels from one of the sheets to cover the back of the overhang. Nail the other four sheets to the frames, forming two 4x8-foot sections. Cover both the top and bottom with roll roofing and install 4-inch butt hinges on each section. If the overhang doesn't slant properly when it is in place, small wedges can be placed at the hinged joint to adjust the slant of the overhang.

Insulating The Ceiling

The ceiling should be insulated with 10-inch fiberglass insulation. If this thickness is not available, use a layer of 6-inch insulation with a layer of 4-inch insulation placed right over it. An alternative would be to have insulation blown in after the ceiling was finished.

Whatever you use should have an R factor of 25. Fiberglass insulation has an R factor of 19 if used as a 6-inch blanket. Additional resistance can be formed by using an insulating ceiling such as fiberboard tiles.

Some supplementary heat should be provided, such as a wood burning stove. Add running water, lighting and the other amenities of life as you see fit. Good Luck.

MATERIAL LIST FOR SOLAR HEATED GUEST HOUSE

Foundation
1. Concrete, 12 cubic yards.
2. 230 8x8x16-inch concrete blocks, 180 12x8x16-inch concrete blocks, three bags of Sakcrete.
3. Sixty-four feet of 2x8 for mud sills.
4. Sixteen ½x6-inch carriage bolts for anchor bolts.

Floor
1. Fourteen 16-foot 2x10's for floor joists, 48 feet of 2x10 lumber for header joists.
2. Twelve 4x8 sheets of ⅝-inch plywood or particle board.

South Wall
1. Four 10-foot 2x6's.
2. Three 12-foot 2x6's.
3. Six 16-foot 2x6's.
4. Four 8-foot 2x6's.
5. Two 39-by-72-inch glass panes, and two 45-by-72-inch glass panes.
6. Furring strips and Mastic as needed.

North Wall
1. Nine 8-foot 2x6's.
2. Three 16-foot 2x6's.

West and East Wall
1. Twelve 10-foot 2x6's.
2. Fourteen 8-foot 2x6's.
3. Six 16-foot 2x6's.

Double Hung Window
1. Approximately 36 by 36 inches.

Roof
1. Thirteen 18-foot 2x10's.
2. Ten 4x8 sheets of ⅝-inch plywood.
3. 350 square feet of #60 builders felt and 350 square feet of roll roofing or composition shingles.

Wall Sheathing
1. Eight sheets of ¾-inch Insulite or Celotex for wall sheathing.
2. 250 square feet of #60 builders felt.
3. One 34x80-inch door and frame. Also storm door to fit outside frame.

Overhang
1. Five sheets of ⅜-inch plywood.

2. One 8-foot 2x6.
3. Four 4-inch hinges.

Interior
1. Solar curtains from available material.
2. Insulation equivalent to 10 inches in ceiling and 6 inches in walls.
3. Paneling of high density fiberboard.
4. Flooring: thick felt pad covered with thick carpet.

Chapter 8

Low-Cost Storage Buildings

CHALET STORAGE BUILDING

It is a pretty safe assumption that every home could use another outbuilding. In these days of renewed interest in burning wood, a shed to store wood is a wise investment. During summer months the shed might be used for storing the snowmobile, skis, snowshoes, snow blower or anything else that won't be needed until next winter.

Also, many families find they are accumulating more odds and ends, tools, furniture, furnishings or building material than they have space for. Indeed, before we built a storage building we couldn't even get our pickup in the garage because of all the accumulated junk.

Retail outlets, of course, do a brisk business in small sheet metal buildings, but they contrast sharply with trees and other natural materials in many landscape ideas. If you can hold a hammer in one hand and know what a saw is used for, you don't have to buy a ready-made building. This chapter outlines three simple, economical storehouses that will fit in well with most homestead schemes.

The first project, a chalet design, has been carefully worked out for the amateur builder so that he doesn't even have to use a carpenter's square. In fact, the only tools which should be necessary are a hand or electric saw and a hammer.

Notice that the chalet has a sloping sidewall, making the upper level wider than the lower. This creates a space for hanging ladders, tools, or even a small boat along the sidewalls while still maintaining plenty of floor and head space for a work shop or storage area. The unconventionally high ceiling also provides space for a loft or shelves. Seldom-

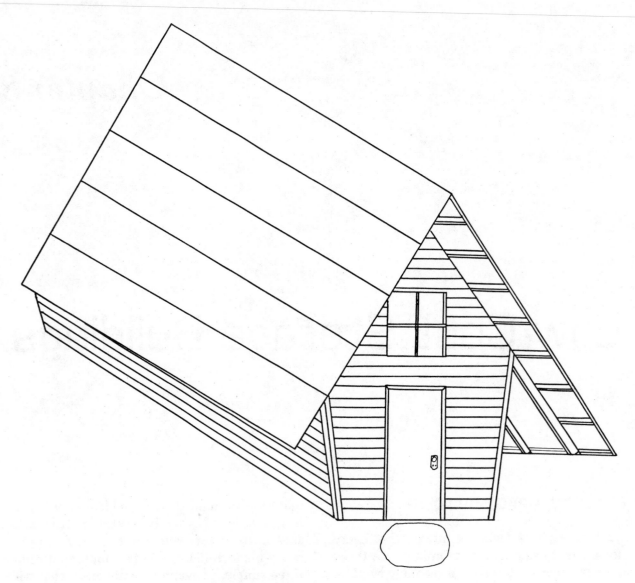

Fig. 5-1 Chalet storage building.

used items can be hung high above the floor. A large window in each end admits plenty of light, so it shouldn't be necessary to wire the building for electric lights.

The very first condition to consider in building the chalet is exactly where you want it located. The site will have to be level, or special provisions will have to be made for leveling the foundation. Since the chalet is fairly tall, consider if it will block light to buildings such as the dwelling. Finally, stop to think about the normal avenues of traffic which it

might interfere with, such as taking out the garbage, or other household tasks that take place daily.

Since the building is not heavy, only a minimal foundation will be needed. It can be made up of pillars constructed from concrete blocks. The building foundation will be 8 by 12 feet. Use stakes and a string to lay out the perimeter of the building. When you have the perimeter established, measure diagonally from corner to corner; the diagonals should be equal for the perimeter to be square. Then proceed to place a stake every 2 feet along both sidewalls. This will mark the location for the 14 pillars that are used for the sill support.

Dig a hole at each stake location for the pillars. The holes will have to be 12 inches deep and at least 16 inches long so that a 8x16-inch block can be placed in them. Align the holes with the length of the block extending along the sidewalls. See figure 5-2.

When all of the holes have been dug, build the pillars by putting one block in the hole and mixing up enough concrete to fill the spaces in the block. Then place another block on top of the first and fill its spaces with concrete too. Before the concrete hardens make a sill pad for the top of each pillar by cutting 14 16-inch pieces of 2x8. Drive six 16d nails through each pad so that when the pad is placed on a block two nails extend into the wet concrete in each of the three spaces. To make the nails hold bet-

ter bend their ends slightly. Do this for each pillar and then let the foundation stand for about four days to let the concrete harden.

When it is time to start building again study figure 5-2 and then square the ends of four 12-foot 2x6's. Spike the 2x6's together to form two 4x6's. Lay them out on the sill pads as shown on the drawing and toe nail them to the pads with 16d nails, using four nails to each side.

Next cut seven 2x6's into 7-foot, 6-inch lengths. Place them between the 4x6's and toe nail them in place with 16d nails. The floor framing is then complete, and it can be covered with ⅝-inch or heavier plywood or underlayment. There is no need to use a double layer of flooring in a storage building.

After the flooring is complete the framing for the side walls can be started. The rest of the frame, including the rafters, is formed from

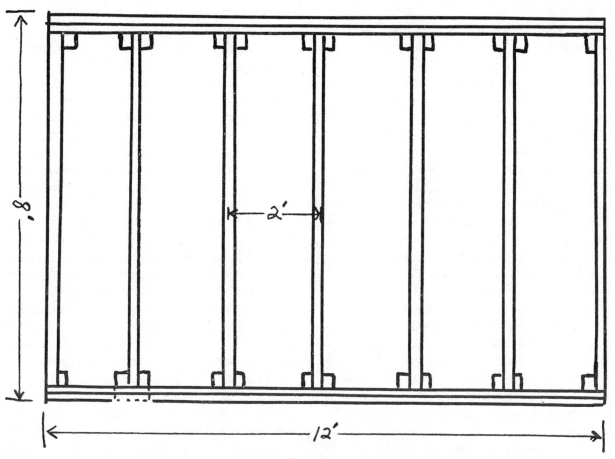

Fig. 5-2 Floor framing.

2x4's for economy. The most difficult part is laying out the studding. Since it is not exactly vertical, both the heel and plate ends have to be cut at angles.

Professional carpenters would do this with a square, but for us amateurs there is an easier way. First lay out two 7-foot, 6-inch 2x4's on the floor. Separate the 2x4's a distance of 8 feet and use a third board to butt both ends against so they are on the same plane. Go to the opposite end and separate the ends of the boards by 10 feet. This, of course, is the position that the studs will finally be in when they are cut and nailed in place. Measure from the outside edge both at the bottom and the top. Now, use a board at least 10 feet long as a straight edge and lay it across the ends of the studs. Align the outside top edge of each stud with the edge of the straight edge. This will leave a triangular piece extending beyong the edge of the straight edge. Just make a pencil mark where the straight edge crosses the studding. At the opposite end, which will be the floor, project the straight edge across the inside ends of the studs. Mark this with a pencil also. Now saw off the pencil marks and you have two studs marked. Use them to cut the remaining 12 studs.

When you have the studs all cut to size, nail a single plate across the bottom end of the studs and a single plate across the top end to form the side wall framing. There will, of course, be seven studs for each of the two side walls. Use two 10d nails to drive through the plate into the end of each stud. Notice that unlike a conventional wall there is no overhang necessary to tie into the end walls.

When you have the side walls framed, get a helper and set them in place on the floor. Nail through the bottom plate into the floor joists with 16d nails to secure the frame. Further, brace each wall with an 8-foot 2x4 so that it doesn't topple over from the wind or its own weight before it is tied into the end walls. When this is done you can proceed to frame in the ends.

The end walls are also framed from 2x4 lumber. Notice on figure 5-3 that both ends are framed the same way, except that the front end has a double header of 2x4 material spiked in place to form a door frame. The window framing, which is "upstairs," can't be installed until the rafters are put in place.

Start the end wall framing by selecting a 10-foot 2x4 to use as a top plate. The easiest way to mark this, and at the same time to compensate for any errors in building up to this point, is to cut the plate to 9 feet, 6 inches and square the ends off. This will form the longest dimension for the plate which will be at its top end. To find the shortest dimension for the plate, simply hold the plate up where it will actually fit and use the edge of the vertical stud to draw a pencil mark along the plate. This will result in a triangle being drawn off at each end. Saw this off and the plate should fit the opening.

Toe nail the plate to the two side walls and then complete framing the front wall by installling two upright studs on center 30¾ inches from the outside of the side walls (see fig. 5-3). Nail a double header 6 feet, 8 inches above the floor to complete the door frame. The rear wall framing is done the same as the front, but no double header is installed between the two center studs. When the end walls are framed in place the rafters can be made up and nailed in place. We have elected to omit the ridge board in this building both to make it more economical and to make it easier to put the rafters in place. When no ridge board is used the rafters are nailed together on the ground. Two men then carry the pair of rafters to the roof and set them in place across the side walls. It is necessary to brace the first pair temporarily until they can be nailed to the second pair.

The rafters are also made from 2x4 stock. This is more than adequate because a roof this steep will not hold snow and create a snow load. As with any roof framing, a pattern rafter can be made up which will be used to mark all of the rest. For this problem we would normally use a carpenter's square and figure the rise per feet. However, as promised at the beginning of the description we are going to build this building without a square. To do this, lay

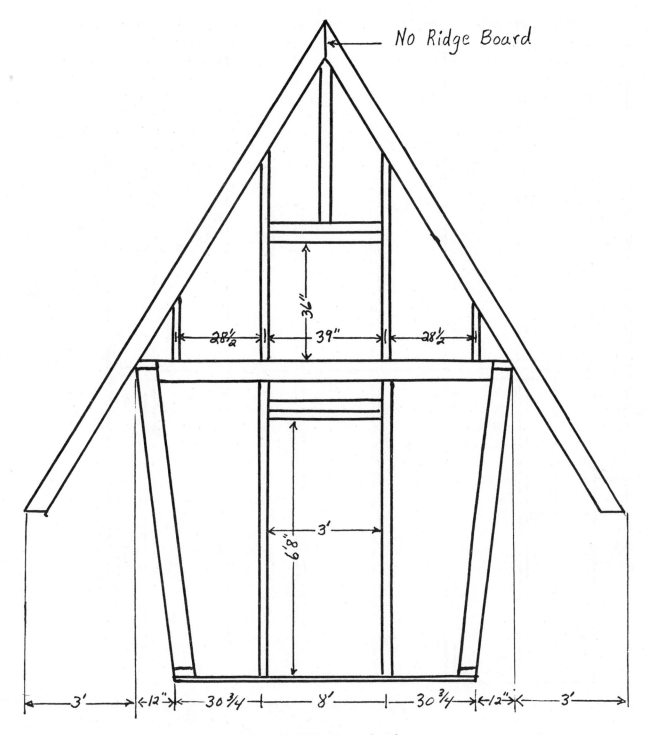

Fig. 5-3 Front and rear framing.

out two straight 16-foot 2x4's on a level surface, forming a triangle of the pieces with the
base of the triangle 16 feet wide. This will be as
measured from the outside of the rafters. At

the top lay one over the other to form an apex
with the corners of the pieces aligned. This will
be exactly the dimensions that you want the
finished rafters to be when they are ready to

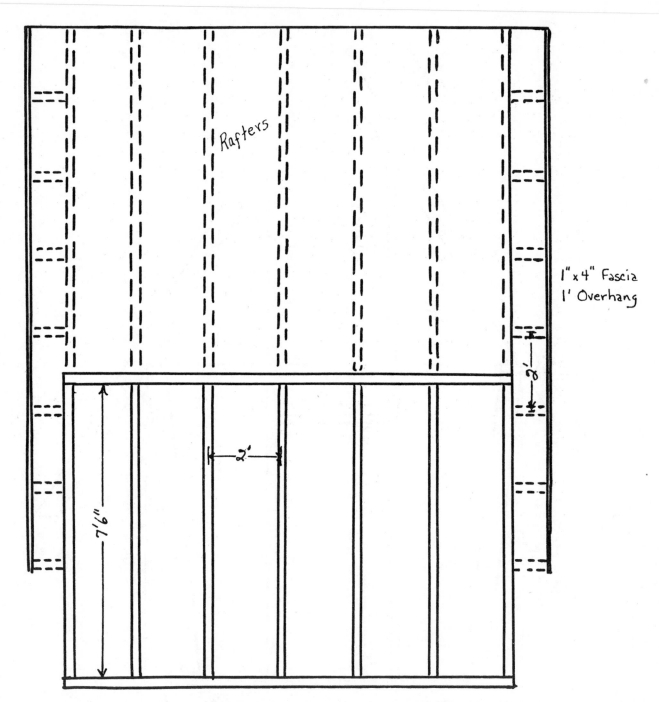

Fig. 5-4 Side wall framing and rafter spacing.

put on the roof. To find the cut line at the apex of the triangle go back to the base and find half the distance between the pieces which will be 8 feet. Drive a peg such as a screw driver exactly at that point and tie a line to the shank of the screw driver. Now take the other end of the string and walk up to the apex of the triangle. Carefully lift the top rafter off and set it aside. Pull the string tight from the screw driver to the top outside edge of the rafter. Notice that where it crosses the rafter it marks off a triangle. Mark this piece with a pencil and cut it off. Be careful cutting it because you are going to use that piece as a jig to mark the opposite rafter for cutting. Complicated as this procedure sounds it only takes about five minutes, whereas a carpenter might spend a half hour just figuring the rise per foot and the correct cut.

With both cuts made to join the rafters at the top we still have to make the seat cut where the rafter sits on the wall top plate. Finding this is easy also. Temporarily, but accurately, place the cut ends at the apex of the rafters together and nail them with a single nail. Make sure the base is separated by exactly 16 feet.

Next, find the point at which the triangle is 10 feet, 7 inches wide. Be sure to measure from the apex so that you have the marks an equal distance down from the peak on each rafter. Once this point is found, mark it clear across the rafters. Measure off an inch of this mark, and with a square piece of board project the triangular piece which will be removed to allow the rafters to sit on the top wall plate. When this is marked, cut it out. Do this for both rafters to complete the first pair. You will need seven pairs of rafters in all.

When they are finished set them in place one by one and spike through the rafters into the top plate with rafter spikes to hold them in place. The first pair will have to be braced while the rest are being installed. After the second pair is put in place, they can be steadied by nailing boards from one to the other.

When this is done the roof sheathing can be installed. Use ½-inch plywood or 1-inch lumber sheathing. When the roof sheathing is finished, put the roofing in place as the next step to protect the framing from rain and other adverse weather. The most economical roofing will be roll roofing, but asphalt shingles or even wooden shingles will be satisfactory also.

Since roofing comes with instructions we don't need to go into that. However, when the roofing is complete the "upstairs" end framing can be finished. The upstairs end framing is made from 2x4 stock also, and both ends are

the same. The dimensions are shown in figure 5-3.

The next step is to install the siding. The type can, of course, be your choice. It is not necessary to use sheathing under the siding unless you are going to use the building for an animal shelter or for some other use that requires the interior to retain heat.

After the siding is finished, hang the windows and doors and the building is ready to use. If possible, try to get prehung doors and windows since they can be fitted in the rough openings and nailed in place. Very often used doors and windows can be found that will be perfectly satisfactory for this type of building.

MATERIAL LIST FOR CHALET STORAGE BUILDING

1. Twenty-eight 8x8x16-inch concrete blocks, two bags Sakcrete.
2. Four 12-foot 2x6's.
3. Seven 8-foot 2x6's.
4. Two pounds 16d nails.
5. Three 4x8 sheets exterior grade plywood.
6. Twenty-five 8-foot 2x4's.
7. Fourteen 16-foot 2x4's.
8. Two 10-foot 2x4's.
9. Thirteen 4x8 sheets ½-inch exterior grade plywood.
10. 400 square feet of roll roofing. Five pounds ⅝-inch galvanized roofing nails.
11. One 3-foot by 6-foot, 8-inch exterior door. One 39 by 36-inch window. Alter rough openings if needed to fit locally available windows.
12. Ten pounds 10d common nails as needed. Five pounds 8d nails for flooring. Two pounds 16d nails for floor joists and sills.

THE FAMILY BANK

The family bank is the second of our storage buildings. As befits a bank it has few frills and is solid and practical. It can be built in a few evenings' work at very little cost if you watch for sales on 2x4's.

Start out by making the foundation. Check to make sure the building isn't being built in a location that will interfere with the normal lifestyle as explained in the previous storage building project; then stake it off. The outside

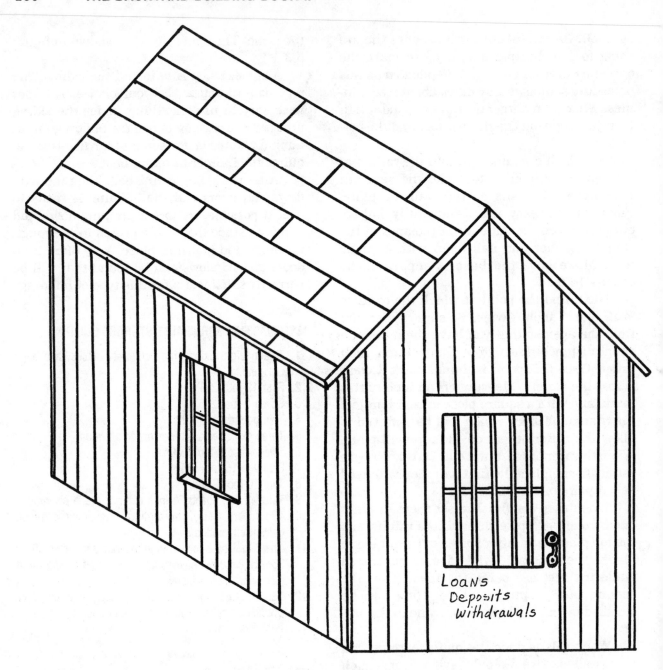

Fig. 5-5 The family bank.

dimensions are 8 by 10 feet. Stretch a line around the stakes and proceed to locate the foundation points. For this project practically any foundation will be acceptable. We have used a piling foundation composed of 12-inch lengths of fence posts set 10 inches into the ground. Use posts with a diameter of 4 inches or more. Three 6-foot posts will make the entire

foundation. Just saw the posts into 1-foot lengths and space them every 2 feet around the perimeter of the building. This will locate a post under each stud. Saw the posts straight and dig the holes carefully so that the posts are level and ready to accept the lower plate of the wall when it is done.

With the foundation completed and leveled

off you can proceed to build the frames for the end walls and side walls. Start with the end wall with the door (see fig. 5-7). First find a level area to work on near the building site, or build one with scrap lumber. Select eight 8-foot 2x4's and saw six of them to 7 feet, 6 inches. These will be the studs. Check the remaining two pieces to make sure they are exactly 8 feet long. These will become the top and bottom plates. Square the ends if necessary. Then nail the 7-foot, 6-inch studs between the top and bottom plates using two 10d nails to both ends of every stud. Space the studding as shown in figure 5-7. Notice that for the front wall the 46½-inch rough opening is

left for the door. The studding is doubled on either side of the door. The rear wall is constructed the same as the front, but only 7 studs will be needed since there is no door or double studding.

When both end wall frames are finished they can be set in place on the foundation. These walls are light enough for one person to handle them, however, it will be much more expedient with two. Set the walls up and nail them to the foundation posts using four 16d nails to each post. Brace each wall as it is done so the wind doesn't blow it over while you are framing the side walls.

The side wall framing will proceed best if

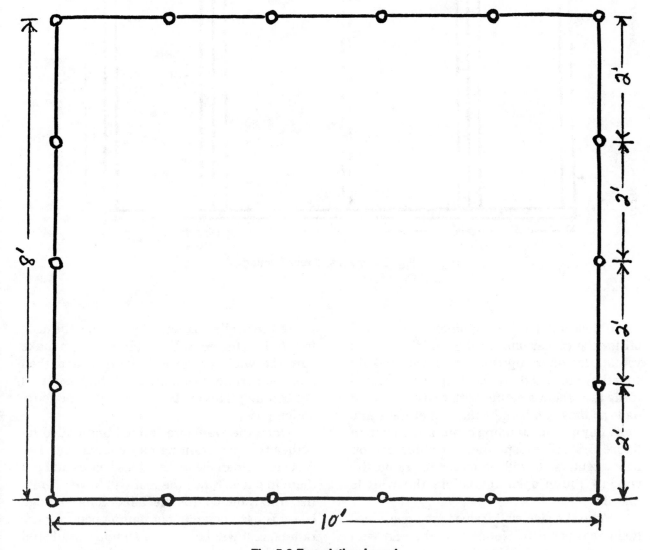

Fig. 5-6 Foundation layout.

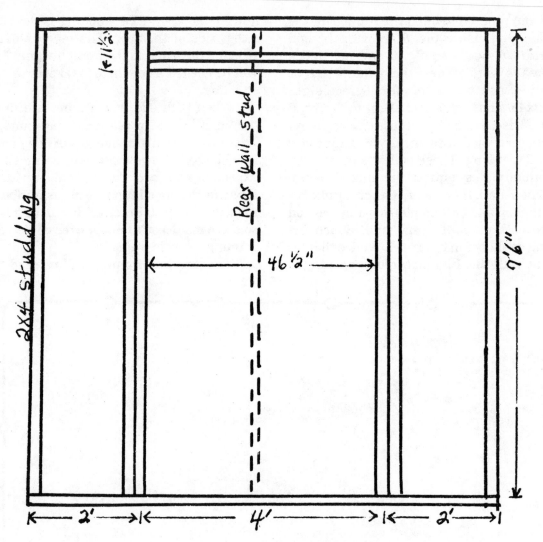

Fig. 5-7 Front and rear framing.

the 10-foot top and bottom plates are marked off for the center lines of the studding before you start. Square up the two plates, making sure they are exactly 10 feet long. Then temporarily tack them together with two or three 8d nails so they can both be marked at the same time. Lay out the studding centers as shown in figure 5-8. All except the end studs are on 2-foot centers. It will be easier to frame the window rough openings before the wall is raised.

When the side wall frames are done, raise them into position. Notice that the end wall frames fit inside the side frames. This is used to tie the walls together by nailing the side frames into the ends. Use a plumb bob to make sure the walls are exactly vertical and then nail the corners together. Don't forget to nail the bottom plates of the side walls to the foundation posts.

Once the walls are framed and nailed together the roof framing can commence. The first step is to make up the ridge boards and put them in place. Since the roof will have a 2-foot rise, the ridge boards are 2 feet long. A ridge board is used as an upper nailing point for the rafters, and will be used as an upper wall stud when the sheathing is installed. Cut a 2-foot length of 2x4 and nail it in place exactly on the center line of the end of the building. Do this at both ends; then proceed with the roof framing.

The first step is to make up a rafter. As with all projects, a pattern rafter is made up and the remaining rafters are made from it. To make the pattern rafter select a good straight 12-foot 2x6. Lay it on a saw horse and cut it into two 6-foot lengths. Use one piece for the rafter. If the edges aren't smooth plane one edge until it is. Then lay it on the saw horse so the smooth edge is away from you and mark a 1½-inch line along the edge from one end to the other to form a measuring line. This is shown in figure 5-9 as a dotted line. Place a carpenter's square on the 2x6 so that the 12-inch mark on the blade of the square is on the measuring line. Lay it on the measuring line as near to one end as you can get it. Then pivot the square so the 6-inch mark on the tongue of the square is also on the measuring line. Use a

hard pencil to mark where the edges of the square cross the board. Then move the square towards the center of the piece until the 12-inch mark on the blade just touches the point where the line drawn at the edge of the blade crosses the measuring line. Again pivot the square until the 6-inch mark on the tongue is exactly over the center line. Again mark off the piece at the edges of the square. Repeat this procedure four times to find the run of the rafter. The last mark you make can be used to saw out the seat notch for the wall plate. The first mark will be used to saw out the correct angle for the ridge board. However, since no allowance is made for the ridge board's width, an additional ¾ inch must be removed from the rafter to make the final length of the rafter correct. Find this actual cutting line by projecting a line along the end of the rafter ¾ inch closer to the center than the lines drawn along the edge of the square would indicate.

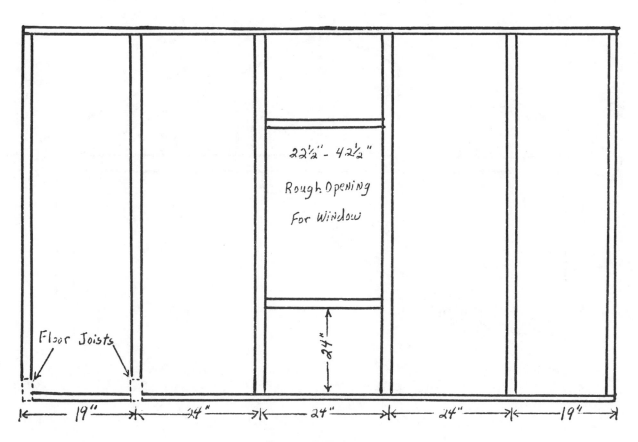

22½"- 42½"

Rough Opening

For Window

24"

Floor Joists

19"   24"   24"   24"   19"

Fig. 5-8 Side frame.

When the lines are all done carefully cut the rafter and put it in place to see if it fits correctly. If it doesn't chisel or plane away material until it does. Shims must be installed to make up for area where the rafter doesn't fit because of too much material being removed. When the pattern rafter is correctly fitted, it can be used to mark off the remaining rafters. Do this by laying the rafter on top of another piece and drawing around it. Then saw off the unwanted material.

Nail the rafters to the ridge boards and to the upper wall plates by toe nailing with two 10d nails to each side of a rafter. When they are up, install the roof sheathing and the roofing so the building will be protected from the rain. Use 4x8 sheets of ⅝-inch exterior plywood for the roof. Either roll roofing or shingles will be satisfactory for the roof.

The next step after the roof will be framing the floor and putting down the flooring. The floor joists are made from 2x6-inch lumber. They will be cut 89 inches long and toe nailed exactly parallel with the wall studs. The lower edges of the joists will be even with the bottom edges of the lower wall plates. You will need six joists. Toe nail with three 10d nails on each side of each joist.

When the floor joists are in place, lay the flooring on top of them and nail it in place. You will need three sheets of ⅝-inch particle board or the equivalent for flooring.

With this done you can install the siding and the windows and doors. No wall sheathing need be used unless you care to heat the building. It is best to use pre-hung doors and windows. They are installed by simply setting them in the rough openings, leveling them and

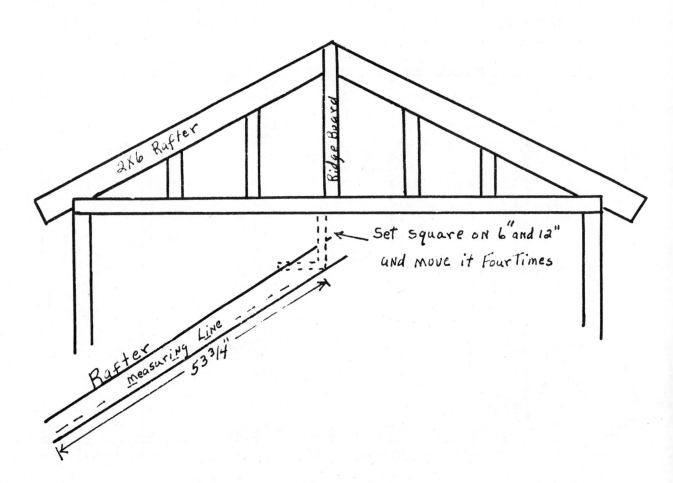

Fig. 5-9 Rafters.

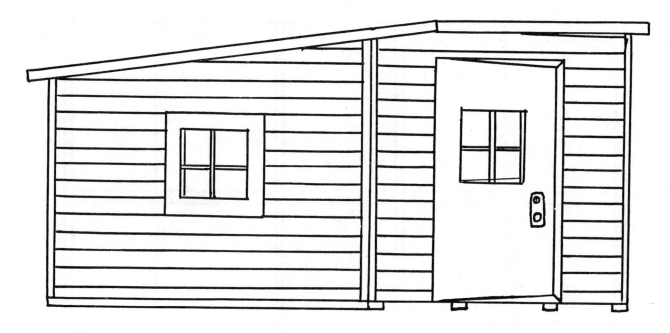

Fig. 5-10 The shanty.

nailing them in place. The windows can be fitted with bars made of ¼-inch dowels for a realistic bank-like touch.

MATERIAL LIST FOR THE FAMILY BANK

1. Three 6-foot fence posts, minimum 4-inch diameter.
2. Thirty 8-foot 2x4's.
3. Four 10-foot 2x4's.
4. Six 12-foot 2x6's.
5. Six 8-foot 2x6's.
6. Three 4x8 sheets of ⅝-inch particle board for floor.
7. Four 4x8 sheets of ⅝-inch exterior grade plywood or equivalent.
8. 120 square feet of roll roofing or shingles.
9. 288 square feet of siding.
10. Nails and fasteners as needed.
11. Two windows, one door with hardware.

THE IRISH SHANTY

The last project in this chapter and probably the easiest to construct is the shanty. Like the others it will blend in with most landscapes, but unlike the others it is portable. It sits on four foundation "skids" or purlines on the top of the ground. It is probably the most inexpensive storage building in this chapter.

The four foundation skids consist of two 4x6's and two 4x4's. They should be treated with a wood preservative, since they will be sitting on the ground. You can, of course, place blocks under the skids to level the building.

The first step is to lay out the skids with the two 4x6's 8 feet apart, but parallel with each other. Between the two 4x6's place the 4x4's as shown in figure 5-11. If these are all fairly level you can proceed; if not, level the skids with scrap pieces of lumber or bricks.

That completes the foundation for this building and you can now add the floor joists. You will need six 8-foot 2x8's for the floor joists. They are spaced on 24-inch centers across the width of the foundation. Be sure the 2x8's are all 8 feet long and check the ends to make sure they are square. Then nail them in place on the skids using two 16d nails to both sides of every joist on each skid. There is no need to add rim joists across the ends of these floor joists unless you wish. If you plan on moving the building often, rim joists will make it sturdier.

When the floor joists are installed the flooring can be nailed down. Use ⅝-inch exterior grade plywood smooth on one side, or particle

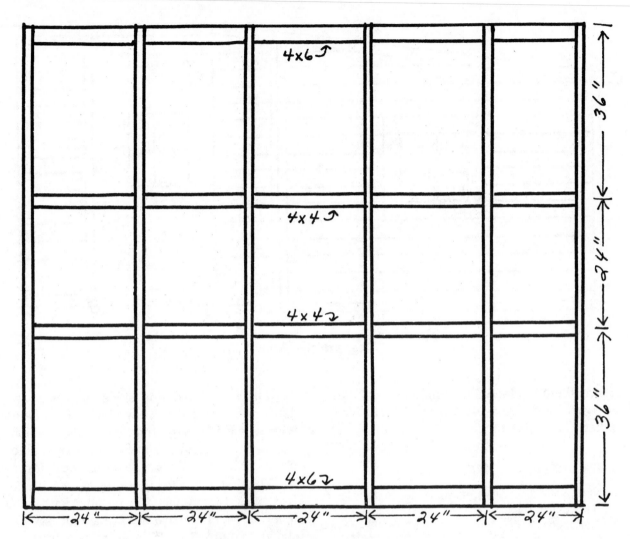

Fig. 5-11 Foundation and floor joists.

board (commonly called underlayment) for the floor. You will need two ⅝-inch sheets. Nail the flooring every 4 inches along the edges and every 6 inches on the intermediate joists.

In this building it is necessary to build the end walls first. After the end walls are done, they are propped in place and the roof rafters are cut and put up. Only then is the framing for the sides added, since the rafters become the side wall plates.

The front and rear walls are constructed the same except for a 46½-inch opening in the front wall for the door. A large door is desirable in a storage building because bulky objects are always being brought in or out. If yours will be used for a special purpose, such as a children's playhouse, the door can be made to suit your needs. No opening for a window is needed in the rear wall because the side windows and the window in the door will take care of the lighting problems.

To build the front wall, saw six 2x4's into 7-foot, 7½-inch lengths for the studding. Next square three 8-foot 2x4's to exactly 8 feet for the plates. To mark for the stud locations on both the upper and lower plates, lay the plates together with ends exactly even and mark both at the same time. This will insure that the studs will be vertical when they are put in place. Then nail the plates across the ends of

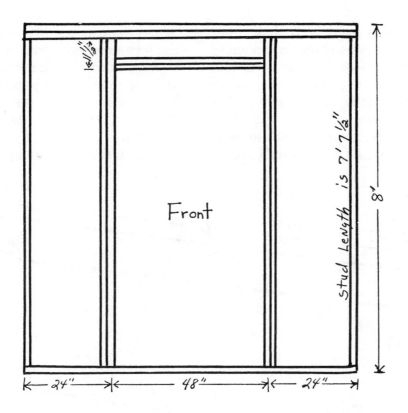

Front

Stud Length is 7' 7½"

8"

24"   48"   24"

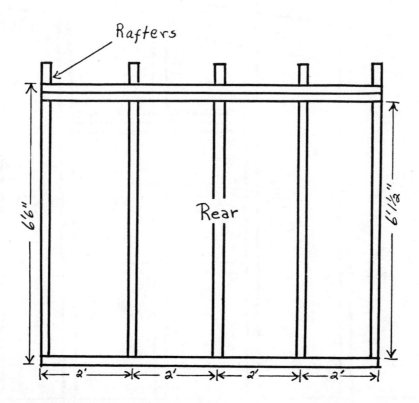

Rafters

Rear

6'9"

6'1½"

2'   2'   2'   2'

Fig. 5-12 Framing for end walls.

the studs as shown in figure 5-12. Notice that the two studs on the sides of the door opening are doubled and the top plate is doubled. The double studs are nailed to the plates and to each other. The double top plates are nailed to the studs and to each other.

When this is done check the walls to see if they are square by laying a carpenter's square across the corners. If they are out of square, use a hammer and block to pound on the walls to square them up. Get some help to stand the walls up in the proper position and nail them in place. Be sure to nail the walls down at each floor joist, toe nailing through the plate into the joist.

When the walls are up, the rafters can be

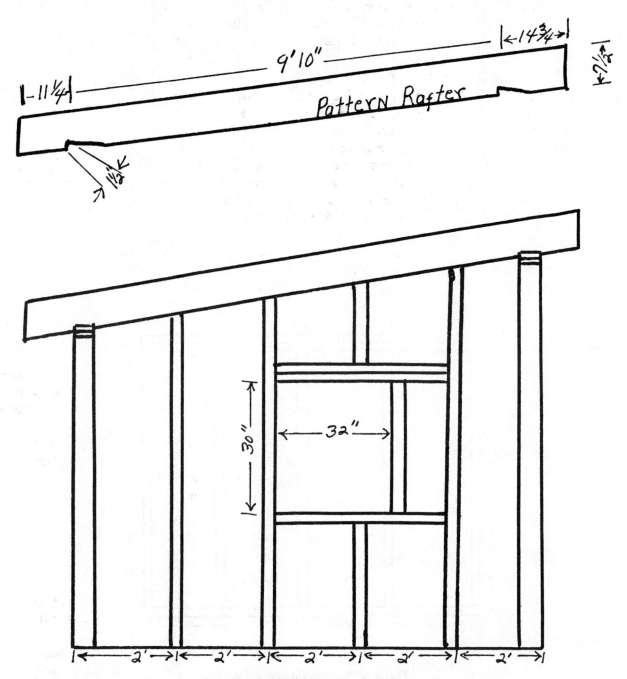

Fig. 5-13 Rafter pattern and side studding.

cut and installed. Making the pattern rafter for this type of roof, called a shed roof, is very uncomplicated. Select a 12-foot 2x8 and square the ends. Then check your walls again to make sure they are square and vertical. Set the 2x8 on top of the walls so the part extending over the outside of each wall (which will be the eaves) is exactly 11¼ inches long. Use a straight edge or a carpenter's square to project a pencil line on the rafter parallel to the outside edge of the rear corner stud and the front corner stud. When this is done take the rafter down, lay it on the saw horse and mark off a triangle 1½ inches deep as shown in figure 5-13. These cuts are made so the rafter rests on the wall plate. When the cuts are made check to see if the rafter fits in several places. If it does, make the other rafters from it and nail them in place. Nail the rafters by toe nailing two 10d nails on each side of the rafter both front and rear.

When the rafters are all in place the side wall studding can be cut and put in place. Notice that a 30-by-32-inch window opening is provided in each side wall. Each stud must be custom measured because of the slope of the roof. First cut the lower wall plate and nail it in place. Then measure each stud individually and nail it in place.

When the side wall framing is done, the sheathing for the roof can be nailed on and the roofing applied. The roof sheathing should be made from 1-inch sheathing lumber or ⅝-inch plywood. Use a layer of 15-pound felt under roll roofing or composition asphalt shingles for the roof.

No wall sheathing need be applied, as the siding can be nailed directly to the studding. The windows and doors can be purchased locally. Give some thought to obtaining used doors and windows, or seconds which are sometimes available from large lumber yards.

MATERIAL LIST FOR THE IRISH SHANTY

1. Two 10-foot 4x4's, two 10-foot 4x6's for skids.
2. Six 8-foot 2x8's for floor joists.
3. Three sheets of ⅝-inch particle board for flooring.
4. Twenty-five 8-foot 2x4's for studding.
5. Five 12-foot 2x8's for rafters.
6. Three 4x8 sheets of ⅝-inch exterior plywood for roof sheathing.
7. Ninety-six square feet of roll roofing or shingles.
8. 288 square feet of siding.
9. Two windows, one door with hardware.
10. Nails and fasteners as needed.

Chapter 9

Pole Furniture

Madison and Jane Lower were three days north of Prairie du Chien, Wisconsin, when they saw what they were looking for: a towering hardwood bluff overlooking the Mississippi River. Madison leaned a little harder into the sweep oar which pushed the homemade flatboat into the easy current of the river and with Jane's help the craft with all of their belongings moved into the sand beach.

When the pioneers had splashed ashore and tied up to a convenient maple tree they decided to go exploring. Hand in hand they climbed the bluff babbling excitedly over the grape vines, heavily laden nut trees and the great patches of blackberry canes which seemed to be all around them. Once on top of the bluff, however, they were welcomed by an even more appealing sight. A yard-wide spring bubbled out of a limestone ledge and formed a

boulder-strewn, clear creek that created its own waterfall as it finally tumbled over the bluff into the Big Muddy.

Surrounding the spring was a 2-acre clearing that had been caused by a lightning fire almost three years before. Nature had healed the scars with prairie grass and wild flowers and the result was a convenient homesite, complete with pasture for a cow and land for a garden. "It will save us two years' work," Madison told his wife, pointing to the clearing. "Just to clear an acre takes a year and here are two by act of providence."

Madison and Jane built their cabin and raised sturdy children on this homesite, and their progeny spread across the entire Kickapoo Valley in the next 150 years. During their lifetime Jane was scalped by Indians (not killed), and their cabin and household belong-

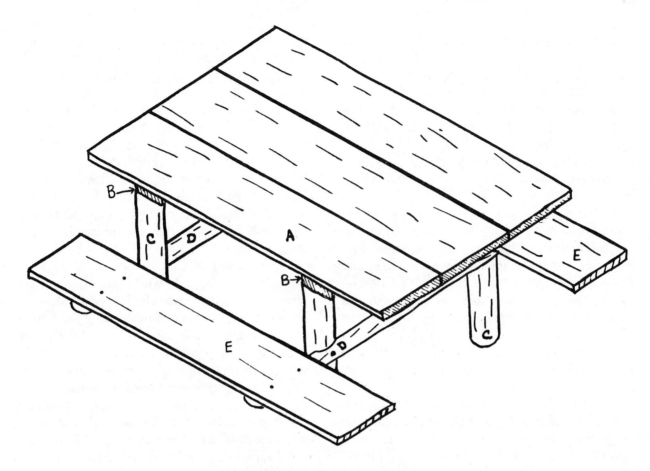

Fig. 4-1 Pine plank table.

ings were burned and completely lost twice. However, apparently with no loss of confidence they built and prospered once again.

The furniture that they hewed from the forest surrounding their homestead was sturdy and massive and intended to be handed down for generations. I have attempted to create replicas of their belongings from such pieces as are left. It is easy to see why the Lower Family withstood the ravages of the frontier if their spirit was as sturdy as their building projects. Possibly a century of normal indoor use could be expected from any of the pieces.

Pine Plank Table

The first project in this chapter and hopefully the least complicated is the pine plank table. Rugged enough to use outdoors, in a vacation cabin, in a screen house or on a patio, it also can be built so that it will make an appealing kitchen or dining room table in a home.

The planks are designated 2x12x8-foot pine. A total of five will be required, three for the table top and two for seats. The actual width of 2x12 planks after planing is 11½ inches. If such planks are not available in your locality or are prohibitively high priced, they can be hand sawn with a chain saw, especially if you have one of the lumber-making devices made especially for that purpose. In fact, the entire table can be made from one tree. Planks sawn with a chain saw need not be planed, but they would have to be sanded to be smooth.

For a picnic or patio table the planks only have to be squared on the ends and planed to remove all the rough or feathery edges. However, if the table is to be used as indoor furniture the edges of the planks can be glued together. To do this, first lay the planks out on a level surface such as a garage or patio floor. If no level surface this large can be found, form a platform by placing 2x4's or other boards on the ground wherever space is available. Make sure they are level by checking both lengthwise and crosswise with a bubble level. The platform can be adjusted by placing shims under the boards. The table top should be supported in at least three places by the platform.

Slide all the table top planks together and scribe a cross mark across them all so they can repeatedly be returned to exactly the same location. Further, note any areas where the edges will not fit tightly together. Mark these with pencil or chalk and sand or plane off the high spots. Keep at it until the planks will fit so well together that no light can be seen between them.

If you dislike this portion of the work it can usually be "farmed" out to a custom cabinet shop or maybe even to a neighbor who has a planer, edger or sander. Make sure he knows you are going to glue the edges together so he doesn't carelessly allow the joints to become soiled or contaminated, which would weaken the glue joint.

When the planks are well fitted together borrow or rent (if you don't own) three glueing clamps which will open up far enough to clamp the width of the table top. These clamps are expensive and it certainly wouldn't pay to buy them for just one glueing job. Further, there is no need to buy them since clamps which will work just as well can be improvised.

First, find three 2x4's that are at least 4 feet long. (The 2x4's used for the platform will serve very well.) Place them so that one is in the center of the width of the table top and the other two are located about 1 foot from each end. Next saw six 6-inch sections from another 2x4 and nail these short lengths to the 4-foot sections on either side of the table top leaving at least ½ inch clearance.

Then form six wooden wedges by sawing scrap pieces of 2x4 stock. The wedges should be about 6 inches long with a 1½-inch base. Finally, place the wedges between the blocks and the table top and tap them in place to see if they will tighten the planks together properly.

If everything appears to be working well up to this point carefully tap the wedges back out again and apply the glue to the joints between the planks. Many good glues are available, but we have had the best luck with casein glue made especially for use when pressure will be applied to the joint. It is also waterproof.

Use plenty of glue and brush it on so no bubbles are trapped. Work quickly once the glue is applied, although this product is designed to allow some time for the piece to be clamped. Place the table top in the clamps, making sure it is aligned correctly, and tap the wedges in place to apply pressure to the joint. Tap each wedge evenly until it "stops." At this point tremendous pressure will be applied to the glued joints and a fine bond should result, which will be as strong as the parent wood.

The work should not be disturbed for at least 12 hours after the glueing is finished. Then it can be removed from the clamps and the excess glue planed or sanded away. The entire surface can be sanded very smooth. After sanding care should be exercised not to damage the top as the rest of the work proceeds.

Of course, if the table is to be used for a picnic table the joints do not have to be glued. In some cases, depending on the opinion of the builder, a space between the planks may be desirable.

The next step in developing the plank table is to form the cleats (B) under the table, which hold the planks together. They are just sections of 2x8-inch lumber sawed into 34½-inch lengths. Two are required. Use an electric or hand drill to drill all the pilot holes for the screws which hold the cleat to the table top and also the eight holes for attaching the cleats to the table legs.

The pattern for the holes is shown on figure 4-2. Make sure that the holes near the out-

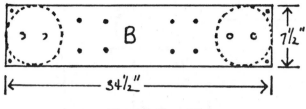

Fig. 4-2 Cleat (B).

side edges do not fall under the area that will be covered by the legs. Twenty-four 2½-inch, #14 screws are used. The screws which attach the cleats to the table top need not be countersunk, since they will not be visible. The hole diameter should be nearly as large as the screw shank, so an ⅛-inch diameter drill can be used. The eight holes for the lag screws are drilled with a ¼-inch diameter drill. A ¾-inch countersinking hole must be drilled for the lag screw head, on the side which will be against the table top.

When the holes are drilled the cleats can be set aside until the four table legs (C) are shaped. This table uses four natural round legs, 6 to 8 inches in diameter. The wood for the legs can be cedar, poplar, pine or hardwood, with pine being the easiest to finish and stain so that it matches the top. Probably the most expedient way to obtain the legs is to visit a lumber or garden store and purchase two fence posts, which usually come in 8-foot lengths. All that is necessary to form the table legs is to cut them into the proper 30-inch lengths, and drill two ⁵/₃₂-inch holes into one end of each leg using the previously drilled holes in the cleat as a guide. Then sand all the legs smooth.

If you cut the legs from green trees, the logs should be cut and peeled about six months ahead of the construction time. Logs cut in the winter will check and crack much less than spring- or summer-cut logs because very little moisture is present in the wood.

Attach the legs to the table top by first fastening the cleats to the table legs. Do this by screwing ¼x2½-inch lag screws through the cleat and into the legs. Next, lay the table top on a suitable platform with the bottom facing up. Position the cleats (and legs) so they are located 10 inches from each end. Then turn the 2½-inch wood screws through the cleats and into the table top.

To fasten the seats to the table, fit the seat platform pieces (D) to the table legs by measuring off 14½ inches on each table leg. Make a pencil mark at this point. Then take a compass and project the width of the platform piece on each table leg for a reference point. Finally, clamp or tie both platform pieces in the proper position against the table legs and again use the compass to project approximately one-fourth of the diameter of the legs on the platform pieces. Then remove the pieces and use a drawknife or rasp to form the notch for the table leg. Finally, clamp it in place and drill a ⁵/₁₆-inch hole through the platform piece and leg, and install a ⁵/₁₆-inch carriage bolt in each hole, with the head outside. The diameter of the leg will determine the length of the carriage bolt. Slide a flat washer and nut on the inside end and tighten the bolt so the head is drawn flush against the leg.

To fasten the seats (E) to the platform, use two 3-inch wood screws on each end. The screws should be countersunk slightly, but do not leave any rough edges that could cause splinters.

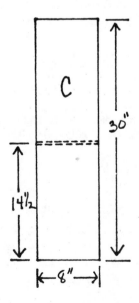

Fig. 4-3 Table leg (C).

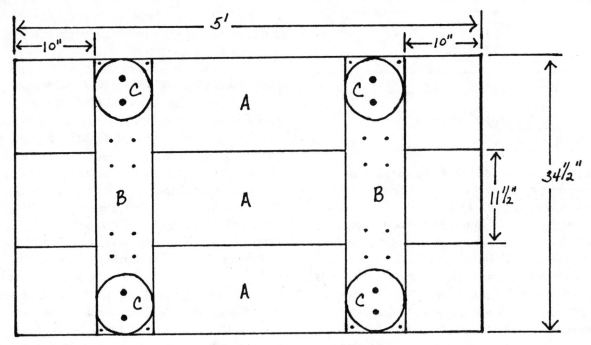

Fig. 4-4 Layout of cleats and legs.

To complete, be sure to sand all edges smooth before applying the finish. If different woods are used for the legs and top, they will react differently to stains and become different colors.

Many people finish the projects in this chapter in natural color by just applying clear varnish. The resulting light colored furniture will help brighten up a dark room.

MATERIAL LIST FOR PINE PLANK TABLE

1. Five 2x12-inch planks 5 feet long.
2. One 2x8-inch plank 6 feet long.
3. Two 4-inch diameter poles 54 inches long.
4. Four 8-inch diameter poles 30 inches long.

QUEENSIZE HOMESTEAD BED

The second project in this chapter is the Queensize Homestead Bed. It is large enough and sturdy enough to suit almost any sleeper, and it should be used in a large bedroom. The plans can be scaled down for the full or twin size also.

Since the entire frame is made from poles, the first step is to find and finish the poles so they can be used for the bed frame. The poles can usually be purchased locally. If a woodlot is available and you can cut your own, peel the bark away and dry them, ideally under a roof so that shrinkage will be minimized. They should dry from six months to a year. Poplar is

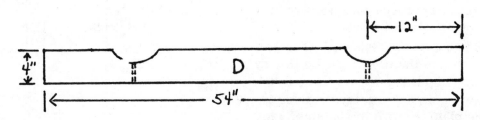

Fig. 4-5 Seat platform (D).

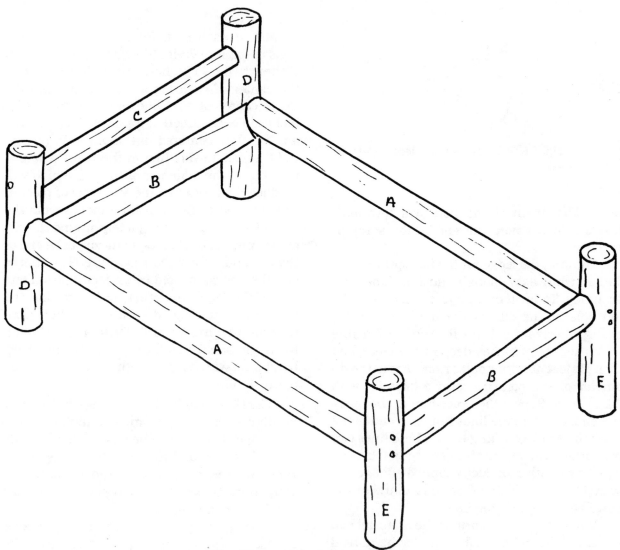

Fig. 4-6 Queensize homestead bed.

a fine wood to use, and it dries to a fraction of its green weight without loss of strength. Most hardwoods would be too heavy, in fact, until they dried out.

At any rate, when you are ready to start building, first cut the side members, which are 80 inches long. (Full and twin sizes are 75 inches.) Each of the two side members has two holes drilled in each end and also has a ledge for the bed spring cut along its side. The holes will be 4 inches apart, exactly on the vertical centerline of the log and perpendicular to the spring ledge. They are 5/16 inch in diameter and set 3 inches deep if 12-inch lag screws are

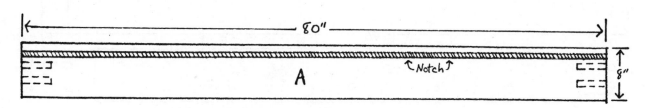

Fig. 4-7 Side pieces (A).

Fig. 4-8 End view of side piece.

used. The depth of the hole will terminate about 1 inch before the end of the screw is reached.

Forming the ledge for the bed spring foundation, while easy enough, must be done with accuracy. To lay it out, project a line from the top hole at the end of the piece to a point exactly horizontal from it. Mark off a line which will be 2 inches deep in the piece and then project at right angles from that to the diameter of the piece to form a "notch" with 2-inch legs. Repeat the procedure at the opposite end. Connect the lines from one end to the other to form the cutting lines. These lines can be marked with a long straight edge such as an 8-foot 2x4 with a perfectly formed edge, or by stretching a chalkline from one mark to the other and snapping the line.

When the mark is formed the material can be sawed out with a table saw or hand-held electric circular saw. It would be difficult, but not impossible, to saw it out with a hand saw, and it could be planed out with a groove plane, or chiseled out with a well-sharpened wood chisel. The two side members (A) can then be set aside.

The foot and head sections (B) are a little more difficult since a rectangle must be formed at each end. First, cut the two sections of log into 76-inch lengths. (Full size: 70 inches; twin: 55 inches.) Next, draw a line at the center of each log at each end. Find the exact center of this line and measure off 3 inches in each direction from the line, forming a 6-inch line centered in the piece. Project at right angles to this line to the point where it runs out at the diameter of the log, which will produce a pattern like the end view of piece B (fig. 4-9). Next, find a point 8 inches from the end and draw a line completely around the circumference of the log. Go to the opposite end of the log and repeat the procedure. The marks can then be connected by projecting from one end of the log to the other, to insure that the rectangles are aligned with each other. Connecting the marks will form a 4-by-6-inch rectangle at each end. Cut it out with a sharp hand saw with coarse teeth, if available. See figure 4-10.

Carefully study the drawings before proceeding with the legs. Saw out all four legs to the proper length. The headboard legs (D) are 36 inches long and the foot board legs are 32 inches. Square the ends and remove any roughness by sanding before you make the notches for the headboard piece and the footboard cross section. Notice that no notch is necessary for the ends of the side piece. In-

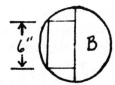

Fig. 4-9 End view of head and foot pieces.

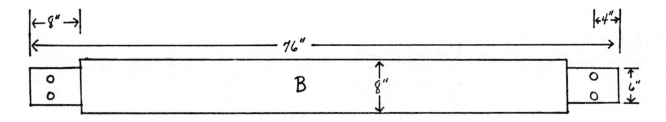

Fig. 4-10 Head and foot pieces (B).

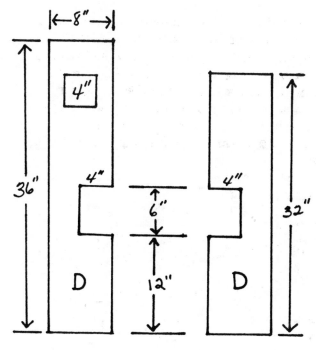

Fig. 4-11 Legs (D).

stead, it is butted against the rectangular section of the foot and head pieces (B).

Making the notches in the legs might seem worrisome at first glance. However, it can be handily done by first drawing a line across both ends of the leg pieces exactly in the center to establish the diameters. Then project from one end to the other of the log along the log to establish a centerline to work from. Establish both a horizontal centerline and a vertical centerline.

Next, cut out a piece of heavy paper in the shape of a rectangle which measures 6 by 8 inches. Lay this paper on the piece (D) (12 inches from the end) so the 8-inch dimension of the paper is aligned with two centerlines. Draw around the paper and you have formed the outline for the 4-by-6-inch notch shown on figure 4-11.

Once the notch is laid out, take a hand saw and carefully saw down to the centerline in several places. Chip out the material between the saw cuts with a sharp wood chisel. The marked off area at the top of the head pieces is just a flat area for a secure fastening for the end of the head board

Drill the holes for the side pieces (B) by laying the side piece into the notch and using the holes already drilled in it as a jig. It should insure a perfect alignment for the bolt holes. For this reason no spacing is given for the holes on the drawing. It is expected they will be centered on the squared off area of the head and foot pieces. Finally, the holes can be drilled in the ends of the side pieces after the squared off area of the end pieces is used to drill the holes in the legs. Naturally all parts must be held in the final assembled position before the holes are drilled.

When the holes are drilled for the assembly the frame can be assembled except for the head board (C). Use $5/16$x12-inch lag screws. Be sure they are turned in tightly so no movement of the bed is possible. After the rest of the frame is assembled the head board (62 inches long) can be tapped into place and a single hole drilled through the leg into the ends of the head board. When that is done the bed is assembled and can be finished as desired. If poplar wood is used it should be varnished immediately, since it could turn a rather dingy gray if it is allowed to age too long.

MATERIAL LIST FOR QUEENSIZE HOMESTEAD BED

1. Six 8-inch by 8-foot logs.
2. One 4-inch by 6-foot log.
3. Eight 12x⅜-inch lag screws.

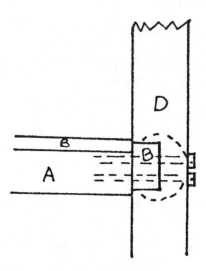

Fig. 4-12 Joint of side and foot pieces to leg.

Fig. 4-13 Log couch and chair.

LOG COUCH

The next project in this chapter is a log couch. As with the other projects start by selecting the wood and peeling it if necessary. Fence posts, which are usually available locally, will be ideal, especially if they are peeled cedar or pine.

The first step is to cut the seat pieces (A) to size, which is 80 inches. When this is done, form the 6-inch square 1 inch deep at the end of each piece. Do this by finding opposite centerlines on the circumference of each piece. Then correct the centerlines from one end of the log to the other to insure that the squared

Fig. 4-14 Seat pieces (A).

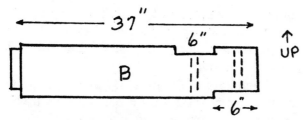

Fig. 4-15 Side seat pieces (B).

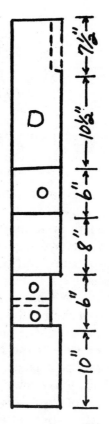

Fig. 4-17 Back legs (D).

sections will be directly opposite each other. One way to handle unsymetrical pieces so the ends are marked in the same vertical plane is to suspend the log over two chairs or a similar platform so the ends project from the chairs. Take a plumb bob and find the line which will be exactly vertical on each piece. Once the vertical line is found a right angle projection will find the horizontal lines. Finally if the lines at each end of the log are connected a working mark is produced. To lay out the 6-inch square at each end just measure 3 inches in all directions from the center and connect the marks.

Saw out the marks, and the square at each end is the result. Notice that this square is only 1 inch deep. When the parts are fitted together it may be necessary to shave the corners at each end to fit it into the legs. Lay the pieces aside.

The pieces marked B on the drawings are not complicated to make, but they require careful marking and fitting. Initially, of course, they should be cut to size, which is 37 inches overall. Then sand away all slivers and burrs which would make working on them difficult.

Next, form the 6-inch square on one end in the same way as the squares were formed on

piece A. Decide which surface of the squared-off end is going to be "up" in the finished product and mark it. Then rotate the piece so "up" is down and lay out the surface which will mate with the vertical part (F). The unwanted material can be removed with a hand saw by making a notch 1 inch deep and 6 inches wide, depending on the diameter of part F.

Next, use the hand saw to form the 6-inch notch at the top of the piece. Finally, rest the flat area on a level surface and drill the hole shown on the drawing which will be used for fastening part B to part E.

Shaping part D, which slightly resembles a totem pole, is done by first laying out all of the cuts so they will be in the right plane to each other. Part D is the rear "legs" of the

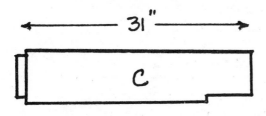

Fig. 4-16 Armrests (C).

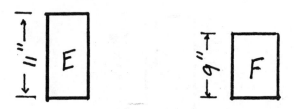

Fig. 4-18 Front leg and armrest support.

couch and almost every other part is connected to it. There are two part D's.

Its overall length is 48 inches and as before cut each of the two legs to the proper length before proceeding with the rest of the shaping. First, shape the flat areas at the top, which receives the 2x8 back rest. This will orient the piece, and each of the other cuts can be made in relation to it. The next cut will be made in the same side of the log as the top notch; it is the rear seat piece notch. Notice that it is located 32 inches down from the top.

As a point of interest, always measure from the same point, such as the same end, when laying out a series of cuts, since if the projections are made from one cut to the other any error in measuring one will be projected to the others, perhaps ruining the piece.

When this second notch is sawed out the flats for the side rest and arm rest pieces can be shaped. They are directly opposite the two already made, and in fact, the lower cut is made directly opposite the notch for the lower back rest, as can be noted on the drawing. The top notch is located at 18½ inches from the top. All notches are dimensioned as 6 inches; however, it is expected they will be custom-made to fit the end of the parts already formed. One of the charms of home-built furniture and espe-

cially log furniture is that it looks like it has been handmade and logs and notches "slightly out of whack" add interest to the finished product—we hope.

When both of the parts D have been made up, the rest of the couch is easy. Finish up by cutting two parts E and two parts F. Sand smooth and finish as before.

Assemble the log couch by laying out parts D on a level surface. Then attach parts B and C to D and finally parts E and F. Do this for both ends, stand them up and complete the project by attaching parts A and I. It requires two people to make this assembly easy.

When the frame is together the material which will support the cushions can be put in place. A good material to use is the jute webbing made expressly for the purpose. Webbing is available from most upholstery and furniture outlets. Sears and Montgomery Ward also sell it. A special tool called a webbing stretcher must be used to install the webbing correctly. They are also sold wherever webbing is sold or they often can be rented.

This size couch will require 30 yards of webbing. It is installed in a special pattern so that the strips are woven together. The ends are fastened to the couch frame with tacks. Full instructions for installing the webbing is included in the webbing and usually with the webbing stretcher; however, we will review it in case it is not available to a prospective builder.

Use 3½-inch jute webbing. Starting at the center of the seat, tack a strip of webbing to the front, leaving a 2-inch flap. Lay the flap over the joint and tack it again, staggering the tacks so they don't split the wood. Then pull the strip over the back frame. Attach the web-

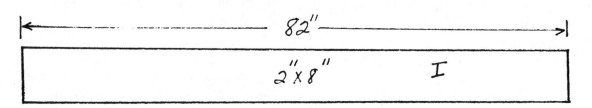

Fig. 4-19 Backrest (I).

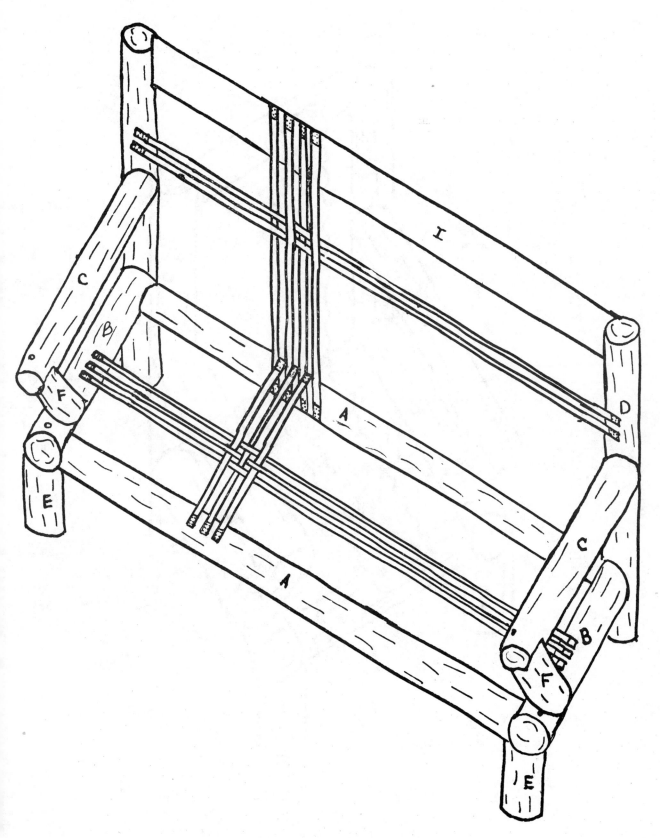

Fig. 4-20 The log couch.

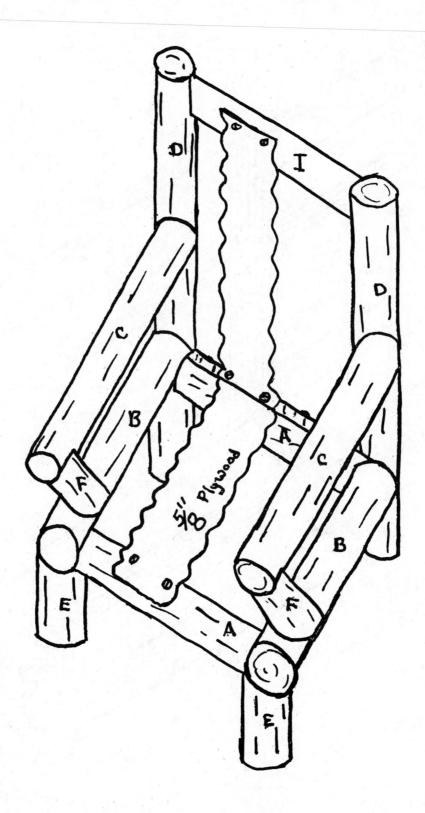

Fig. 4-21 Tree trunk chair.

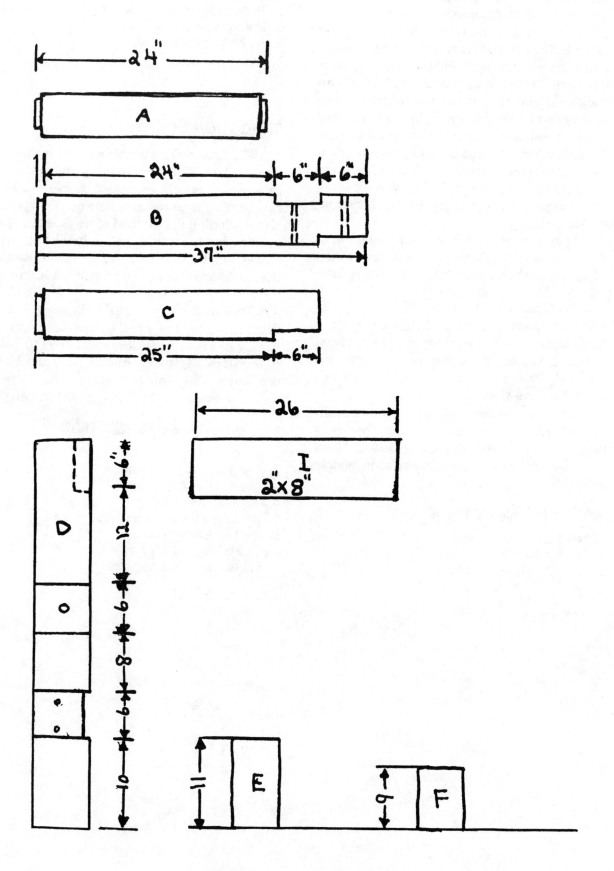

Fig. 4-22 Pieces for construction of chair.

bing stretcher and tighten the strip so that it feels tight when thumped.

Tack it on the rear frame with two or three tacks to hold it and then cut it off leaving a 2-inch flap again. As before, lay the flap over the tacks already in place and install an additional four to five tacks, staggering them so they don't split the wood. Proceed to install strips of webbing 4 inches apart until the entire seat is covered in a front to rear direction. Next, start near the center and install strips of webbing from a side to side direction weaving these strips over and under the previously installed webbing.

When this is done install the webbing on the back rest stretching it from bottom to top initially and then proceeding to stretch it from side to side.

If it is not desirable to install webbing, the same purpose can be fulfilled by nailing hardwood strips to the frame in place of the webbing, or the frame can be covered with plywood. Use ⅝-inch interior grade plywood, sanded on one side.

Cushions are available from many suppliers, including the large mail order houses or they can be handmade, using 6-inch foam plastic or filler. Covering material is widely available.

MATERIAL LIST FOR LOG COUCH

1. Two 8-inch by 8-foot posts.
2. Two 8-inch by 6-foot posts.
3. Two 4-inch by 6-foot posts.
4. One 8-foot, 2x8-inch plank
5. Thirty yards 3½-inch jute webbing.
6. One box upholstery tacks.
7. Six 2½-inch wood screws.

TREE TRUNK CHAIR

The final project in this chapter is the Tree Trunk Chair. The chair is fabricated about the same as the couch, except, of course, the back rest and seat parts are shorter. Everything else, including the method of weaving the jute backing is the same. It will only take 10 yards of webbing for the chair. If plywood is used for the cushion rests an extra strip of hardwood must be added to part A.

This about completes building the pole furniture. Total cost of all four of these projects are far less than what it costs to buy one piece in the store. Moreover, just as Jane and Madison Lower did, you can hand them to your children when you're through with them.

MATERIAL LIST FOR TREE TRUNK CHAIR

1. One 8-inch by 8-foot post.
2. Four 8-inch by 6-foot posts.
3. Two 4-inch by 6-foot posts.
4. One 4-foot 2x8 plank.
5. 10 yards, 3½-inch jute webbing.
6. One box upholstery tacks.
7. Six 2½-inch #14 wood screws.
8. Fourteen ¼x10-inch lag screws.

Chapter 10

The Screened Trail Shelter

Several years ago my wife and daughter and I took a backpacking trip to Isle Royale, an island in Lake Superior that is preserved in a wilderness state. Isle Royale is the home of 1300 moose and a considerable pack of wolves that live by preying on the moose.

It is an unique relationship because no hunting or trapping is allowed and the moose and wolves are more or less confined to the island. Some of the authorities of Isle Royale say that this is the greatest density of wolves and moose per square mile in the world. We didn't see any wolves on the island, but we did see the carcass of a calf moose that was killed only hours before. Moose were a different story. When we were camped at Washington Creek Campground we saw moose every morning and evening, and on damp or overcast days they frolicked in the waters of the creek all day.

Two events that happened at Washington Creek stick in our minds. About three o'clock in the morning of the first night we were camped there we were awakened by a sound that resembled a freight train scraping along a tunnel wall. Worse, the floor and sides of the sturdy shelter we were camped in were trembling in time to the sounds. What was it? Earthquake, tornado, our sleep-fogged minds couldn't decide. Finally I found the flashlight and directed its beam towards the sound. The light revealed two huge, round glowing eyes and an ugly, hairy face. Moving the light slightly allowed me to identify the apparition as a bull moose, scarcely 18 inches away scratching a fly-bitten shoulder on the corner of our trail shelter. He didn't pay any attention to our flashlight or our voices, and to tell the truth, we were afraid to move too much.

We had probably watched him for five to ten minutes when my wife decided to light a cigarette to quiet her shaking hands. That was the end of the episode, because when the match flared and the smell of cigarette smoke reached the animal he bolted straight ahead through the 6-foot-deep water of the river and beyond. When he reached the other shore we could hear him crashing deep into the forest.

Nor was that the only adventure we were to have on our stay at that particular campground. About mid-morning on the day we were to leave the sky suddenly darkened and a wind and rain storm assailed us. The wind was so

strong it collapsed several of the backpacking tents in the nearby campground and sent the occupants scurrying about for protection. We shouted to several of the campers to come inside and share our shelter with us, and soon we had upwards of ten guests.

The storm lasted for about an hour and we engaged in lively conversation while our sturdy, well-made structure kept us warm and dry.

This remained in our minds when we reluctantly left the unspoiled Isle Royale, and we lost no time when we got home in designing a shelter as near to it as we could. It is as we expected,

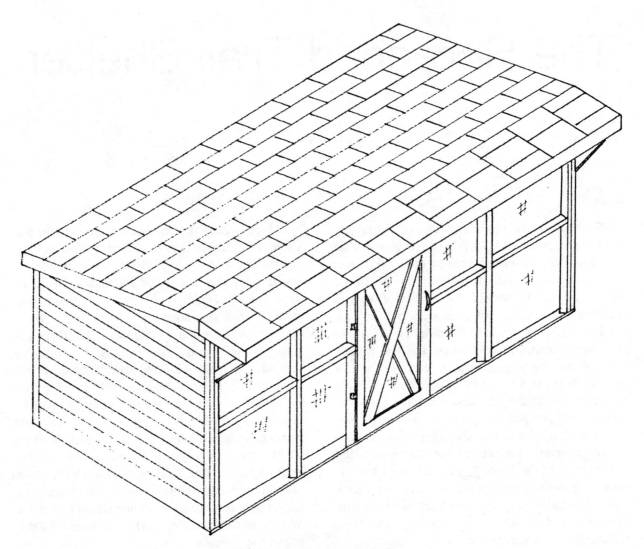

Fig. 12-1 Screened trail shelter.

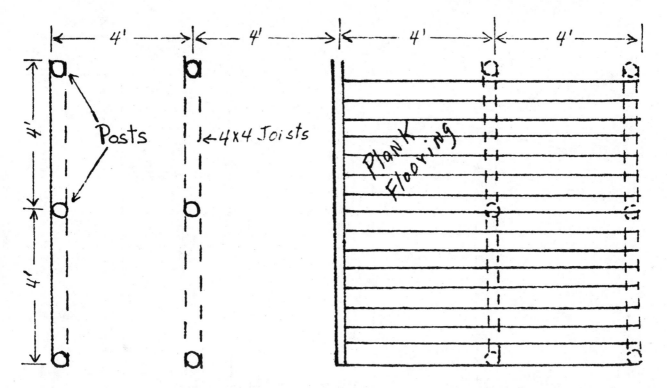

Fig. 12-2 Foundation and floor.

a very helpful addition to our wooded setting here in northern Wisconsin, and we wouldn't care to get along without it.

As in all other projects, start the building by laying out the foundation. A point to remember if you build in an urban location is to line the shelter up with the lot lines or existing building lines. If you build in a rural area all you have to remember is to align it with a magnetic compass so it will face true to the four directions. Generally the screened shelter will be used most in the summer and it will be desirable to keep it as cool as possible. Therefore, it should face north if this can be done without sacrificing a particularly scenic view.

Lay out the outline for the building by using a magnetic compass to find the north-south line. Use stakes to designate this. In a building where no excavation lines have to be established, the only stakes that are necessary are the corner stakes and a stake for each post location. Stake out the post locations as shown in figure 12-2.

There are many ways to designate the loca-

tion for these posts, but we have found one of the most expedient ways is to simply use small pieces of tape placed along the perimeter string. Find these locations by measuring along the string from the corner stake. If the foundation perimeter was correctly squared by measuring diagonally from corner to corner, the posts should be located directly across from each other. This can be checked by measuring from each location to the opposite diagonal location. For instance, if you want to check the first two posts directly north of the proposed south wall, you would measure from the southeast corner stake to the piece of tape directly northwest of it as a first measurement. Then you would measure from the southwest corner to the piece of tape directly northeast of it as a second measurement. If the two lengths don't agree, they are to be adjusted until they do.

When the post locations are established, use a post-hole digger to excavate for the posts. Dig each hole down to solid subsoil. If the soil is unusually loose or wet, set the posts in cement by filling the holes about ⅓ full of cement before

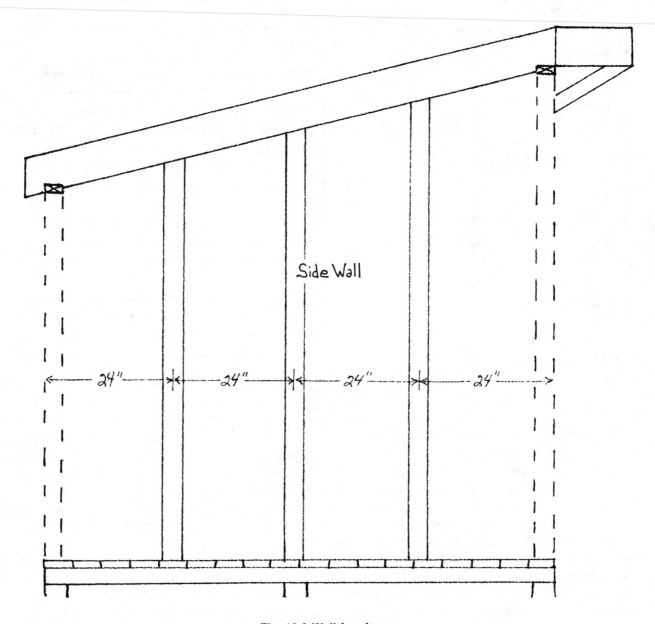

Fig. 12-3 Wall framing.

placing the posts. Dig each hole only large enough for a post and tamp the dirt around it very well.

The next step is to place the 4x4 girders across the posts to form the foundation for the floor. To do this correctly, choose one set of posts and designate them as "grade." Naturally the grade posts should be level. Cut the grade posts to form a level horizontal about 2 inches above the soil. This is the minimum clearance under the building necessary to allow air circu-

lation, which will prevent the flooring from rotting.

After the grade posts are cut to the desired height, place a 4x4 girder across them and use a carpenters level to make sure that everything is level. Then spike the girder to the posts with 16d spikes toe nailed from the sides of the girder into the posts. Use four spikes to each post. Continue leveling the posts and spiking the girders in place until all five are located. Then nail the plank flooring in place at right angles to

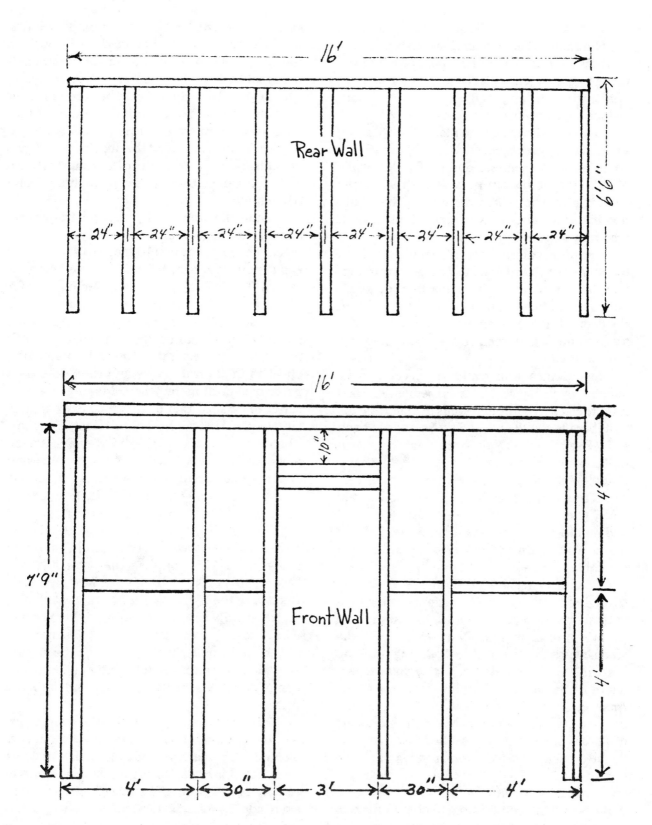

Fig. 12-3 Wall framing *(cont.)*

the girders as shown in figure 12-2. Plank flooring eliminates the need for floor joists. However, some savings in material could be gained by using 2x8 floor joists placed on 16-inch centers across the girders, and then covered with ⅝-inch plywood or particle board.

When the flooring is in place, the studding for the walls can be placed. Study figure 12-3 to fix in mind the general outline for the walls. Notice that no bottom plate is used since the studding can be nailed directly to the plank flooring. If the alternative flooring is used then, a bottom plate will have to be used also.

Cut nine 2x4's to 6 feet, 4½ inches to form the studs for the rear wall. Lay out an imaginary bottom plate on the plank floor by snapping a chalk line 3½ inches inside the edge of the floor. Mark off for each stud location with a square and pencil, then repeat these steps for the front wall.

Installing a wall frame in pieces can be done in several ways, but an expedient method is to stand each of the end studs in place and toe nail them to the floor. Use four 8d nails to each stud. Use a level to plumb the studs and then nail a short temporary brace to hold them. Complete this step for the two center studs also. Then select the two 8-foot 2x4's for the top plate, place them across the tops of the studs and nail them to the studs to form the skeleton for the wall. Use a 16-foot 2x4 for the top plate if available.

Be sure as you nail the top plate to each stud that it is exactly plumb. Check for plumb with a carpenter's level placed on the thickness and the width of each stud. Nail the plate to the studs by driving two 16d nails through the top into the end of the studding. Notice that the rear wall does not use a double plate at the top as the front wall does. The studs for the front wall are doubled at the corners because of the increased distance between the studs. The top plate is also doubled because of the increased load at each upright.

Start constructing the front wall by sawing and placing the corner studs. Toe nail each in the proper place, then use a carpenter's level to make sure they are plumb. Install the two center studs which will form the rough opening for the door. Plumb and brace these also. Then nail a 16-foot 2x4 across the tops of the studs. If a 16-foot 2x4 is not available, it will be necessary to install a "cripple" stud between the door headers and the plate, with the center of that stud 8 feet from either corner.

Toe nail each stud at the floor level with two 8d nails. Nail the top plate to the studs with two 16d nails driven through the plate into the end of each stud.

When the front and rear wall framing is completed, the roof rafters can be cut and put in place. The roof requires 10-foot 2x8's; however, each is cut to 8 feet, 6 inches before being installed. The 18-inch pieces left over are used for an overhang. It will be easier to make up the rafters first, cut them to size and put them all in place before installing the overhang. As with most roofs a pattern rafter should be made first, checked in several places and then used as a pattern for cutting the others. Making a pattern rafter for a shed roof of this type is extremely simple. Cut a straight 2x8 to 8 feet, 6 inches. Then place it on the roof so that the edge is even with the front plate. Use a straight edge and pencil to mark on the rafter where it rests on the plates. Then project a line 1½ inches deep at each plate mark on the rafter. Connect the depth of this line to the opposite plate mark to form a triangle. Saw this triangle out as shown in figure 12-4 to complete the pattern rafter. Use a plane or knife to remove any unneeded wood. Try the pattern rafter in several places, and then make up the remaining eight rafters to complete this part of the project. Toenail the rafters to the plates using two 10d nails to each side of each rafter, or use rafter nails driven completely through the rafters and into the plates.

The next step is to make the overhangs. Square the ends of the 18-inch pieces and saw out a 3-inch triangle from the inside ends as shown in figure 12-4. Toe nail the overhangs to the front face of the rafter with three 8d nails to each side. Bracing is provided by nailing a 1x8 "scab" on each side of the joint. The overhang is braced against snow loads by four 2x4 braces

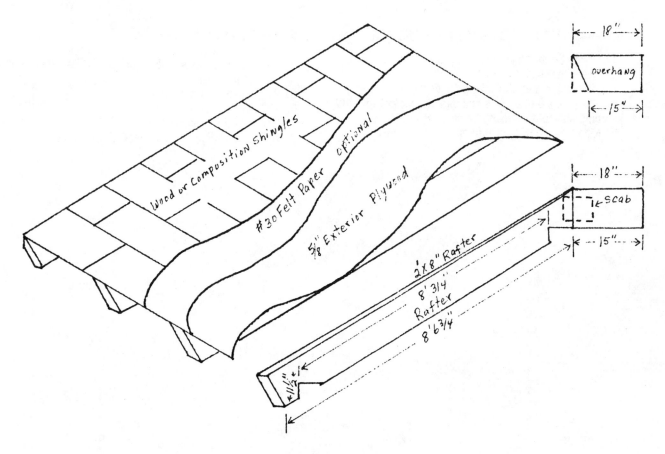

Fig. 12-4 Rafters and roof.

which extend from the overhang to the front wall. Complete the framing by installing the side wall studs as shown in figure 12-3.

When the framing is done, the roof sheathing can be applied. Use ⅝-inch exterior grade plywood or the equivalent. Cover the plywood directly with composition shingles. No felt paper underlayment is needed because insulation is not a factor. If available, wood shingles will blend in with the forest surroundings better than the asphalt shingles. However, they could increase the cost considerably.

Almost any type of commercial siding can be used. You can use sheets of plywood or even 1-inch boards butted against each other. We have used commercial wood 8-inch lap siding. The siding is nailed directly to the studding since no sheathing is used.

When installing horizontal siding there are

a few points to consider. Start at the bottom and start the first row straight. This is done by snapping a chalk line where the top edge of the first board will fall. Locate the first row low enough so that it encloses all of the framing members. Each succeeding row of 6-inch siding will cover 5 inches of surface. Since it is easy to get siding out of level even with a straight starter row, it is prudent to snap several chalk lines at 5-inch intervals on the studding. This allows for a quick visual check of your progress. Some wood siding is subject to splitting when nailed, so use the smallest diameter nail that will get the job done. Siding designated as 6-inch spruce or pine should be fastened with 8d galvanized nails. The nail heads can be countersunk and the resulting holes filled with plastic wood if desired.

MATERIAL LIST FOR SCREENED TRAIL SHELTER

1. Fifteen 3-foot posts, minimum diameter 4 inches.
2. Five 8-foot 4x4's.
3. 128 square feet of planking for floor.
4. Thirty-nine 8-foot 2x4's and one 16-foot 2x4 for studding and roof overhang brace.
5. Nine 8-foot 2x8's for rafters.
6. Two 8-foot 2x8's for overhang.
7. 187 square feet of ½-inch exterior plywood.
8. 187 square feet of #60 felt paper and 187 square feet of roofing material.
9. 256 square feet of siding.
10. 128 square feet of screen.
11. One 36x80 screen door and hardware.
12. Nails and roofing nails as needed.

Chapter 11

Dog Houses

SOLAR HEATED DOG HOUSE

Not far from our home in northern Wisconsin, an international natural gas pipeline stretches to the south as far as Texas and north to Montreal. It must be a huge pipe since it can be heard humming and gurgling for yards away, even though it is buried deep. The pressure inside the pipe generates considerable heat. In many locations the snow melts over the pipe, showing its exact location. During the coldest part of the winter this bare ground attracts deer, who browse on the exposed vegetation. But it is especially attractive to coyotes who, quick to take advantage of a good thing when they see it, bed down on the warmed ground directly over the line.

Occasionally, when hunting rabbits along the pipeline, we would find a sunny spot, at noon and use the bare ground as a picnic area.

Our beagle would happily gulp his lunch in two bites and flop down on a warm, dry spot to snore loudly while we ate and rested.

We noticed how comfortable he was, and we started thinking about how nice it would be if we could build a dog house for our beagle directly over the pipeline where the ground would be warm all winter. This, of course, wasn't possible so we began scheming a way to imitate the warmed ground in a small area right at home. Since we have many bright sunny days in winter, one of the first ideas that came to mind was a solar heated dog house. After considerable planning and false starts we decided to combine the principle of the heated ground and the mechanics of solar heating into a system which would heat the floor of the house. The dog would be warm and snug in the coldest weather as long as he stayed dry and the wind didn't blow on him. We also incorporated auxiliary heat in case of long spells of sunless weather.

On the other hand, our summers are often very hot. We thought it would be nice if we could somehow air condition the house so that the floor would be cool. A single additional pipe accomplished that. We now have a solar heated, air conditioned house which is economical, uncomplicated, and should give even the most particular dog a sense of well being.

Solar Tank

Start building the solar heated dog house by finding a 55-gallon steel drum with all the plugs in place. They can be purchased for about five to ten dollars at fuel oil dealers, service stations, flea markets or garage sales. You can wash the barrel out by filling it about half full of hot water and detergent, putting the plugs in, and rolling it around the lawn for 15 to 20 minutes. Then with the barrel on its side, the large plug up and the small one down, insert the garden hose in the large hole, turn it on full force and remove the bottom plug. Barrels which contained antifreeze will not have to be rinsed.

When this is done take the barrel to a welding shop and have the fittings for the solar pipes welded in place. We used ⅜-inch NPT fittings for the pump suction line. The suction line (inlet) to the pump is fitted with a "stand pipe" arrangement to prevent it from sucking residue from the bottom of the tank which could plug the lines and foul the pump (see fig. 2-1). The stand pipe consists of a 4x⅜ inch NPT nipple, a ⅜-inch elbow, a 2x⅜-inch NPT nipple and a ⅜-inch NPT coupling. The stand pipe assembly is put in place and welded at the coupling. Be sure to put it in the bottom of the barrel, opposite the plugs.

Directly above that and about 1 inch from the top of the barrel, have the welder install a ¼-inch NPT coupling. At the same horizontal line, but on the opposite side, cut a hole and weld a ¾-inch NPT coupling in place. The first coupling will be the return line for the air conditioning. The second is the return line for the

solar collector. It is important to have the return lines located near the top of the barrel so the draw down, or amount of solution removed from the barrel during operation of the pump, will lower the level below the return lines. Otherwise the fluid wouldn't return to the barrel fast enough to permit efficient operation.

The pipe fittings were used because adapter fittings to change from NPT thread to tubing thread are readily available. However, there is no need to copy these fittings exactly if other types of tubing and fittings are available to you at little cost. Almost any type of line can be used to carry the liquid, including plastic hose and automobile gasoline lines salvaged from a junk yard. You will need about 12 feet of tubing plus the necessary fittings. Plastic lines, of course, require no intermediate fittings since they will turn where necessary and clamp onto termination fittings with hose clamps.

The pump may be the most expensive component to acquire. Although a very small pump can be used, it must have the ability to raise liquid about 6 feet, pump at least two gallons per minute and be wired for 110-volt current. Check with the local heating and refrigeration contractors for any used, small capacity pumps. If a used one isn't available, they can probably order a new one for you. The valve located at the top of the solar collector regulates the output from the pump so that the fluid coming in doesn't exceed the fluid draining out. Too large a capacity pump would be almost impossible to control in this manner without overloading its drive motor. Another pump would have to be used in the drain line to pump the water back in the barrel, increasing the cost considerably.

With these problems solved, the pump can be installed, all the lines and fittings connected to the barrel, and the wiring connected to the pump. Use three-wire cable with underground insulation and waterproof connections. Next, dig the hole for the barrel (which is now a solar storage tank) and lower it in place.

The excavation for the tank should be 3 feet below the level you want the floor of the

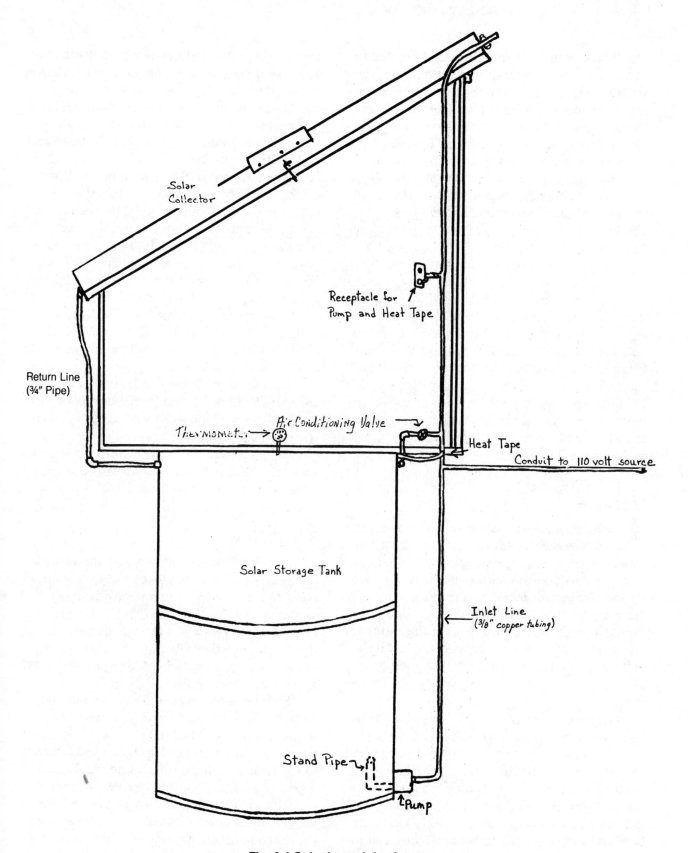

Solar Collector

Return Line
(¾" Pipe)

Receptacle for
Pump and Heat Tape

Thermometer → Air Conditioning Valve

Heat Tape

Conduit to 110 volt source

Solar Storage Tank

Inlet Line
(³⁄₈" copper tubing)

Stand Pipe →

↑Pump

Fig. 2-1 Solar heated dog house.

dog house, and at least 3 feet in diameter to allow room for the pump and fittings. Set the storage tank in place *with the drain line to the south.* Remove the large plug from the top of the tank and fill it with a 25 percent ethylene glycol, 75 percent water solution. This solution is fairly expensive, but you can use the antifreeze from your car's radiator if you decide it is time to change it. Clean it before putting it in the solar tank by straining it through several thicknesses of cheesecloth to remove any line-clogging rust particles.

When all the lines are hooked up and the tank is full of solution, activate the pump to see if it works. To prevent losing the fluid, just run it back into the tank at the top. Check to make sure the draw down is below the return line holes. If everything checks out, fill the space between the tank and the outside diameter of the hole with fiberglass insulation. This insulation will prevent the top layer of earth (which might freeze in winter) from extracting heat from the solar storage tank. You can now start building the dog house.

Dog House

Measure and cut out the two side panels as shown in figure 2-2. Notice that they are made from ½-inch exterior grade plywood. Next cut out two 4-foot, two 3-foot, two 2-foot and two 43-inch lengths of 1½x2-inch framing and nail them to the plywood as shown on the drawing. Nail through the plywood into the lumber using 6d coated nails. Measure and cut out the front and rear pieces, cut the 1½x2-inch framing shown, and nail the plywood to the framing.

Notice that an entrance is provided for in both the rear and front sections. The entrance in the rear, facing south, will be used in winter. The entrance in the front, facing north, will be used in summer. The entrance which isn't in use is closed off. Provide for this by cutting the entrance holes out in a single piece. Use a jig saw and angle the blade about 45 degrees to the center when cutting the holes, which will form a chamfer. The panel can then be fit back

into the hole and held in place with turn buttons. Glue insulation to the panel if insulation is used for the rest of the house.

Nail the side sections to the front and rear sections to form the shell. Use 8d nails for fastening the sections together. The first and second floors, which are identical pieces, can now be measured, cut and nailed in place. However, before proceeding give some thought to whether you are going to insulate the house.

Insulation is recommended (though not mandatory) since it will keep the house warmer in the winter and cooler in the summer. Styrofoam insulation 1½ inches thick will give good results. If your dog chews it, an inside wall or wood paneling will have to be installed over the foam. Use the insulation along the side walls. The upstairs floor can be made from a foam panel.

After insulating the dog house, cut out the roof panel and nail it in place. The square hole cut in the top of the front wall gives access to the upstairs storage section of the house. The cut out panel can be hinged to make a door, and held shut with turn buttons. You are now ready to build the solar collector.

Solar Collector

Cut two 48-inch and two 34½-inch lengths of 1x4 stock. Nail the pieces together with 8d nails so that the 34½-inch length is inside the longer pieces. Next cut two ¾x½-inch pieces 1 foot long, and two 2 feet long. Nail the strips to the frame as shown in figure 2-3, forming a seat for the glass which will cover the frame. Use 6d finishing nails.

Foam insulation should now be installed to insulate the back of the collector from the roof of the dog house. Insulation is also used inside the frame. Cut it to the size shown and fasten it to the frame with ring nails and washers sold especially for nailing this type of insulation.

The collector plate can be made from a copper, aluminum or steel sheet. Steel is the most economical. A piece of aluminum roofing, especially the corrugated type, will work very well. Scrap pieces are available from in-

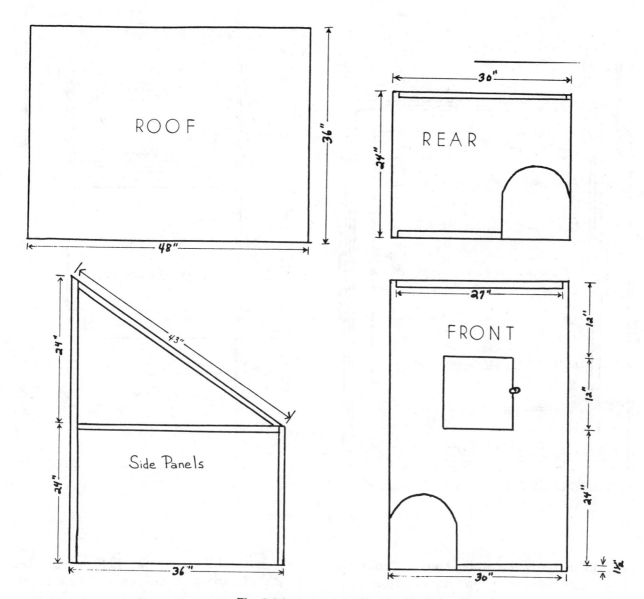

Fig. 2-2 Layout of dog house.

sulation and roofing installers. Strips can also be soldered together to form the correct size with little loss of effectiveness.

Glue the collector plate to the foam backing. It is most important to seal the edges of the plate around the frame so that no antifreeze solution leaks through. Several sealants, including tar and caulking compound will give good results. You will also have to cover the plate with black enamel paint. Wash aluminum with vinegar before applying the paint for best results. If a black or dark panel is available, no paint is necessary. Experiments have shown that the heat collected by a black surface exceeds the heat collected on a dark surface by very little.

Finally make up the distributor tube which will bring water from the storage tank line to the collector. It consists of a shut-off valve, about 4 feet of ⅜-inch copper tubing, one elbow and necessary fittings to plumb into the valve and make the 90-degree bend inside the collector box.

The distributor tube provides a sprinkling

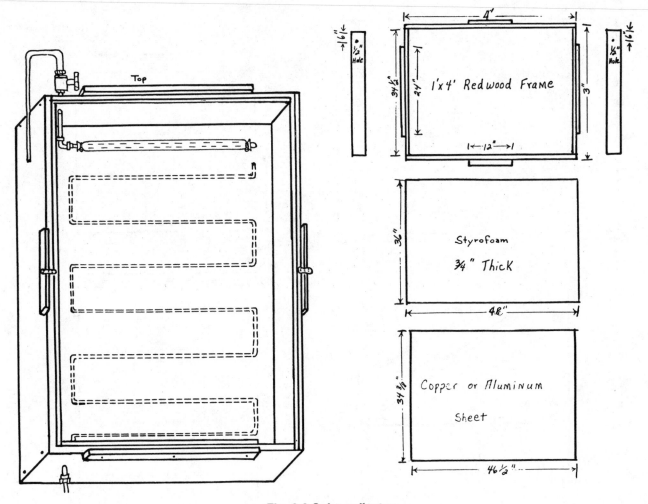

Fig. 2-3 Solar collector.

system to spray the water onto the collector plate. The water runs down the plate and exits through the drain at the bottom, where it returns to the storage tank. The solution leaves the distributor tube through six ⅛-inch holes drilled in the bottom of the copper tubing. To slow down and distribute the water more evenly, the horizontal tube is fitted with a sleeve made by sewing a piece of canvas into a bag that can be slipped over the tube. The flow of water can be further controlled by regulating the valve located above the collector.

The drain at the bottom of the solar collector includes a ¾-inch NPT collar, a ¾x4-inch NPT nipple and coupling, and enough pipe to reach from the nipple to the coupling on the solar storage tank. Install the collar inside the

collector by drilling a 1-inch hole in the correct location for the drain line. Countersink an area around the hole large enough to seat the collar, with the flange down, so that it is slightly recessed into the wood. Fasten the collar in place by coating its recessed surface with sealer and then installing wood screws through the provided holes.

If you live in an exceptionally cold climate, you may have some problems with the glass of the collector fogging up as a result of condensation on the inside of the glass. This will diffuse the sunlight and result in less effective heating of the collector plate. You can correct this by installing a continuous tube between the inlet and the outlet of the collector box, so that no solution is exposed to the air. This tube should be copper and should be installed in a series of loops across the collector plate. It should also be soldered to the plate, and painted black. The broken lines in the solar collector in figure 2-3 indicate the correct position of the tube if used.

Operation

The collector box can now be put in place on the roof of the dog house. Make sure it is secure by installing screen door hooks on all four sides as shown in figure 2-1. With this done, the dog house is ready to be set over the tank. However, before you do this place heat tape (the type used for preventing water pipes from freezing) on the top of the barrel so that it is evenly distributed with the bulb end inside the rim of the barrel. The cord has to be stretched to the outside so it can be plugged into the outlet provided on the side of the dog house. Not mandatory, but a decided convenience, is a thermometer with the sensor bulb placed on top of the barrel under the floor to keep track of the actual temperature of the solar storage tank.

With this done set the dog house over the barrel, connect the lines, including the air conditioning lines, and put the plate of glass over the collector and lock it in place.

The solar heated dog house can be placed in operation by the following steps. First, permanently activate the heat tape by plugging it into the outlet. It has its own thermostat and will not generate heat unless the temperature between the tank and the floor of the dog house drops below 38°F. Second, close the valve for the air conditioning and open the valve at the top of the collector. Third, turn on the switch to start the pump. If all goes well the water from the tank should flow evenly out of the distributor tube at the top of the collector, run down over the collector plate, be heated by the plate and run out of the drain on the bottom. If it collects in a pool on the bottom, slow the flow down by closing the valve slightly. Continue to run the pump for about one hour during sunny weather, which should heat the water in the

tank to about 100°F. The pump can then be shut off, and the water will stay warm for up to 12 hours. However, conditions vary so much that you will have to determine an effective schedule by trial and error.

To cool the floor of the dog house in the summer, just close the valve on the top of the collector and open the air conditioning valve. The pump will circulate the water in the bottom of the barrel (which should be cooled to about 55°F.) to the top where it will impart its refreshing temperature to the floor. The longer you run the pump the cooler the water in the tank should become, until it finally reaches earth temperature. You can then turn off the pump.

What dog wouldn't be happy with his own solar heated, air conditioned home!

MATERIAL LIST FOR SOLAR HEATED DOG HOUSE

1. One 55-gallon barrel with all plugs in place.
2. Tubing, pipes and fittings to connect the components, from whatever is available. Two shut-off valves.
3. One water pump, 110-volt, two GPM or larger.
4. Sixteen feet of 1x4 lumber.
5. Three 4x6 sheets of ½-inch exterior grade plywood.
6. Twenty-five feet of 1½x2-inch stock. This can be formed by rip sawing two 8-foot 2x4's.
7. Three storm window buttons.
8. Three screen door hooks and eyes.
9. Seventeen square feet of ¾-inch Styrofoam insulation.
10. Fifty gallons of 25 percent ethylene glycol, 75 percent water solution.
11. One pound 6d coated nails, one pound 8d common nails.

THE BEAR DEN

It is often hard to improve on nature. Animals know that a burrow in the earth remains warm in winter and cool in summer—a condition that people spend fortunes trying to imitate in their houses above the ground, where they are subject to the whims of the weather.

However, animals such as bears, with no limit to their choice of dens, can pick and choose until they find one that will have a stable, comfortable temperature and remain dry. Dampness from the surrounding earth and moisture from surface water running into the mouth of the den are the greatest handicaps to subterranean living.

At times, an extended thaw during winter has actually melted enough snow to flood bears from their dens. The huge animals have no choice then but to temporarily end their hibernation and roam the forest until they find a drier winter home. Also, a Canadian biologist recorded instances of bears freezing to death because they would den in such poorly drained locations that water would run into their dens.

This, of course, points out that while the earth is a great protector, we must beware of improper building even here. Common sense indicates that a side hill is an almost ideal place to build our Bear Den dog house. The drainage is perfect, so if you have one to use go ahead and dig a hole in the hill, build the house and set it in place. However, most of us aren't so fortunate, so we have to find a way to imitate the actions of a side hill.

The means of doing this are available to most of us at little expense. It's as simple as calling the local contractor and having him bring a 5-yard load of mixed clay soil. This earth, usually called fill dirt, is very economical. Using a hand dirt tamper, you can construct your own hill in less than a day of pleasant activity.

Before you can build the hill you have to nail together the shell of the house, since it will sit snug and warm in the center of the hill. You can place the house anywhere on your lawn, since it will not have to be shaded or built behind a wind break. Moreover, it doesn't have to be oriented to any specific direction, and it will blend in with any setting since it is actually part of the lawn.

The amateur builder will also find the project a delight because it requires no skill and only some very basic tools. The entire structure is built from 2-inch stock. The building is made from 2x6's, and the entrance is made from 2x4's. Use 10d nails, and be sure to select good straight lumber so the edges will fit tightly together. Cut three 10-foot 2x6's into 12

30-inch lengths, and cut a 12-foot 2x4 into four 33-inch lengths for cleats. Lay six 2x6's together on a flat surface, square the ends and nail them together with two cleats to form a side wall (see fig. 2-4). Repeat the procedure to build the other side wall. Now stand the two sides up to form a triangle, with the bottom of the triangle about 3 feet apart. Nail the sides together by driving two 10d nails horizontally through each board at the top. There is no need to chamfer the top since a watertight seal will be formed by roofing paper. However, the sharp edges of the boards should be cut or planed to prevent the pressure of the earth from pushing them through the roofing paper. With this done stand the house on end and measure the opening for the end boards. The purpose of standing it on end is to make it easy to measure for each piece. Although it does waste some lumber, the easiest way to form the entrance hole is to make both ends solid and saw out the opening later. It will actually be 11 inches high since the width of two 2x6's is 11 inches. Be sure to nail the end boards together around the entrance.

With the ends nailed in place and the entrance hole cut out, the bottom can be put in. Since any errors in measuring or nailing are going to cause problems, be sure to measure for the floor boards before you proceed; they should be close to the 33 inches shown on the drawing. A ¼-inch bevel must be cut on both ends of each floor board so that the floor will fit in place. Use 10d nails to nail the floor boards to the sides by nailing through the side boards into the floor.

The entryway can now be built from 2x4's held together with 2x4 cleats. Notice that a 1-inch chamfer is cut from the back of the entryway so that it will fit against the opening on a slight downward angle. This will prevent any moisture from running into the house during a cloud burst. Nail the sides together to form the entryway, then butt it against the entrance with the chamfer at the bottom of the house and nail it in place. The next step is to nail roofing paper all over the house to seal it from

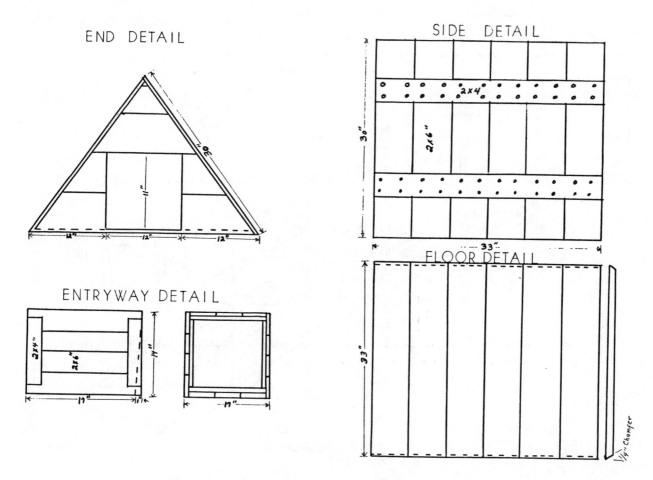

END DETAIL

ENTRYWAY DETAIL

SIDE DETAIL

FLOOR DETAIL

Fig. 2-4 Construction of bear den.

the ground moisture. This means over the roof, the ends and even the bottom. Use galvanized roofing nails.

Now call in the truck with the 5 yards of dirt and have him dump it close to, but not on the spot where you want the house. You will need a shovel, a wheelbarrow and an earth tamper to build the mound. First make a 1-inch thick base area about 5 feet square on the lawn exactly where you want the house to sit. Tamp this down very well. A dirt tamper can be rented, or you can make one by nailing a piece of 2x6 to a handle so it forms a T. Pack the earth well enough so you can walk on it without leaving deep tracks. Then set the house in place so that the front of the entryway is even with one edge of the base. Gradually

shovel and tamp the dirt up around the house until you have it covered to form a mound. Mix organic top soil and grass fertilizer in the top 2 inches, plant grass seed and tamp the soil down. It may be necessary to cover the mound with straw until the grass starts growing. The grass should sprout in three or four days if you soak the seed 24 hours before applying it to the mound. Keep the mound moist until the grass gets a good start.

That about completes building the house, and your dog can start enjoying it. If he is inclined to dig the dirt away you might have to cover it with chicken wire until he forgets this wasteful procedure. Otherwise it shouldn't require any care at all.

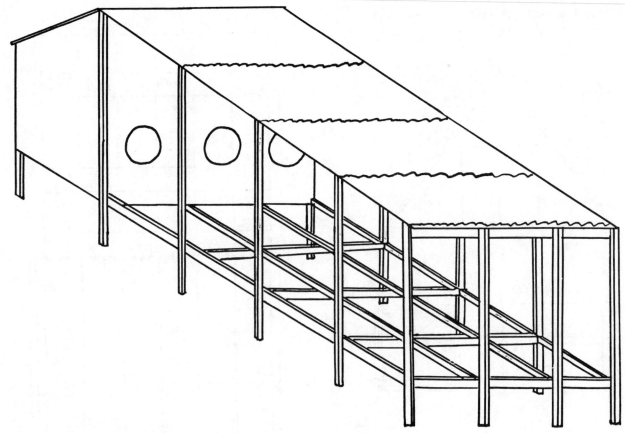

Fig. 2-5 Beagle pen.

MATERIAL LIST FOR THE BEAR DEN DOG HOUSE

1. Five to six yards of fill dirt, one pound of grass seed, five pounds of lawn fertilizer.
2. Three 12-foot 2x6's for floor.
3. Six 8-foot 2x6's for sides and ends.
4. One roll of 90-pound roofing paper.
5. Five pounds 10d nails.

THE BEAGLE PEN

Beagles with their calm nature are very well adapted for living in the pen-like dog house that we call the beagle pen. Wire especially made for dog pens covers the floor of the pen so that droppings and urine fall through the wire where they can be removed once a week or so. The dog pen can be further equipped with self feeders and waterers, making it vitually self-contained except for occa-

sional maintenance and filling the feeder once in a while. However, any dog should be visited at least once a day by his master for at least a few words, and should be exercised as often as possible.

The entire pen is built from 2x4's, ½-inch plywood and wire mesh. First cut out the 16 uprights by sawing eight 8-foot 2x4's in half. Don't worry about the odd lengths that the uprights will finally be sawed into, just make them all 4 feet long. Next, saw six 6-foot 2x4's into 69-inch lengths. They will be the six center cross members. Lay out six pairs of uprights and, using another 2x4 as a guide, nail the cross members to the uprights with 10d nails (see fig. 2-6). Next saw out ten pieces 21 inches long and toe nail them into the uprights to form braces that connect the legs. With this done you should have a good grasp of how to proceed to form the floor. A total of twenty 21-

inch pieces will be needed to build the floor level.

When the floor is finished, the uprights can be marked for their final lengths. Use the second row of uprights in from the end as a pivot point, since they are the only ones that will remain the same. Mark one side at a time, snapping a chalk line from the top of the pivot upright to a point 4 inches below the top of the front upright. This will form a slanting roof line for the pen as shown in figure 2-6. Do this on both sides and then go to the back uprights and snap the line which will form the outline for the roof of the shelter. Finally, snap a chalk line at the proper height across both the front and rear pairs of uprights. This will mark the uprights between the front and rear pairs.

Carefully saw off the unwanted material, and proceed to nail in the 2x4 braces which will form the frame for the roof. The roof is the same as the floor, but the interior 21-inch braces are used only for the roof of the shelter (see fig. 2-6).

Notice that the braces which form the slant for the roof will have to be sawed on a bevel to fit correctly. The quickest, most accurate way to do this is to hold a 22-inch brace in the position that it will be nailed in and mark with a pencil where the saw cuts have to be made.

Once this end of the frame is complete, the ½-inch plywood panels which cover the shelter can be cut out and nailed in place. We have used 9-inch diameter entrance holes set 8 inches from the floor, which is correct for a medium sized beagle. Larger dogs might need a bigger entrance. Any partitions that you decide to use should be nailed in place before the roof panels. This pen can be divided into three runs and house three dogs, kept separated if desired. If they do not need to be kept apart, two entrances should be enough. One doesn't work well because the biggest dog might lie in front of the entrance and keep the others out of the house.

Nail the panels to the frame to form the

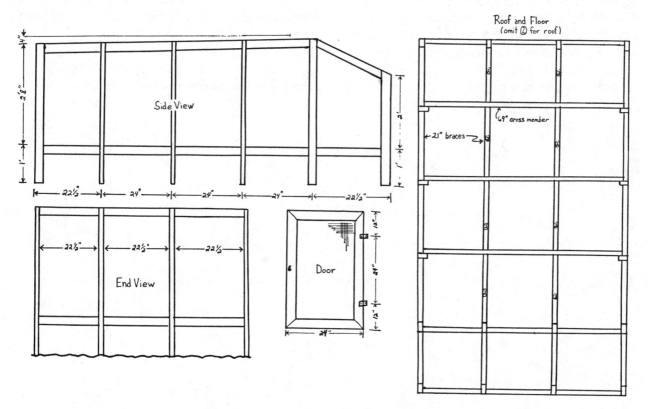

Fig. 2-6 Construction details of pen.

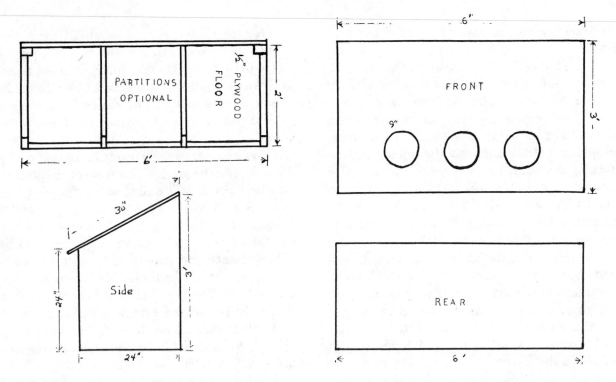

Fig. 2-7 Layout of shelter.

dog shelter and install the roof last. The shelter roof should be covered with roll roofing to shed moisture. The roof on the pen should be metal or plastic commercial roofing panels.

The entire frame can then be covered with welded wire mesh. At least one pen entrance door should be provided in the end opposite the shelter. This door should be large enough for a person to enter the pen, because sooner or later you may have to. A door is shown in figure 2-6.

This pen will work very well as a whelping pen for a bitch and her puppies. The puppies can be left with the mother until buyers come around and take them to their new homes.

Chapter 12

Bird Houses, Bird Baths and Bird Feeders

At one time we lived in a rustic log cabin in northern Wisconsin. We didn't have electricity, so a battery-operated radio was our only entertainment. Because of the remote location the radio reception was very poor. We solved this problem by stringing an aerial wire on the roof. To string the aerial it was necessary to nail wooden poles to either end of the roof. It worked fine, and it produced an unexpected benefit.

Shortly after daybreak on the day after we strung the wire we were awakened by a thunderous rat-tat-tat coming from the roof. At first we thought someone was playing a trick on us by pounding on the roof with a hammer. However, as no one knew where we were that explanation puzzled us also. Quickly, I went outside and looked up. There attached firmly to one of our radio antenna poles was a gigantic

pileated woodpecker, beak flashing furiously as he chiseled out inch-long sections of wood, searching, no doubt, for a buried grub. I shouted at the noisy intruder and he flapped away. However, the next morning at the same time he was back again. Moreover, we were treated to that alarm clock every morning after that and finally came to depend on it. We were even able to shut him off without getting out of bed by rapping the roof underneath him with a bamboo fish pole we kept handy for just that purpose.

The pileated woodpecker is a fascinating creature, but so are all birds. Consider for example that birds are able to grow feathers from flesh. No one on earth can begin to understand the genealogical process that prompts the growth of the amazing pattern of barbs and barbules that make up a feather. Yet each of the 8600 species of birds can grow as many as they like, replacing worn-out members with ease.

Ornithologists do know that an embryonic feather looks exactly like a reptile's scale; and in fact, most birds' feet and legs are covered with reptilian scales.

If birds resemble reptiles, they also are like man in some ways. For instance, they are visually oriented instead of odor oriented as are most mammals. Like man, they dress themselves in bright clothing and one species, the flamingo, even paints itself with bright colors. They also sing to an audience, perform dances, and build houses that are pleasing to the eye, as does man.

All these fine qualities are academic, however, when we consider that many scientists believe that birds are necessary for human life to exist upon this planet. Birds save man and most of the other mammals because they look over every foot of the earth's surface from the highest mountains to the lowest dry land and from the desert to the tropics and the surface of the great oceans for the ubiquitous insects which if allowed to multiply unchecked would soon destroy all living vegetation upon the planet. Yes, anyone trying to decide upon an interesting subject to study could well consider birds. Literally the more you know about them the more interesting they become.

One good way to indulge your interest is to build a bird attractor in the yard or garden. It will offer shelter, food and water to the feathered wonders. You can start by building the houses.

EIGHT-FAMILY PURPLE MARTIN HOUSE

Martins are familiar to many people since they inhabit all of North America and the West Indies. In the wild they nest in natural tree cavities, but they readily take to artificial housing where they always nest in colonies. A colony of martins is a highly desirable addition to the backyard, and it has been estimated that a single pair of martins will eat over 10,000 insects during the ten-day period that they are brooding their young. Since this house will hold eight families it is expected that they will easily keep one backyard insect-free. Additionally, martins are such pleasant birds to watch as they soar gracefully about their hunting that many pleasant hours of bird watching can be spent on a colony of martins, especially by shut-ins and older folk.

Some dos and don'ts will be mentioned before we get to the construction phase. First, don't place a martin house in a tree. It must be set on a pole at least 15 feet above the ground. Further, it should be placed at least 50 feet from the nearest elevated obstruction such as a building. Martins like to circle their home when entering and leaving. Don't substitute metal or thin lumber for the material shown in the drawings. Metal will permit heat to build up in the house and probably kill the young birds. Don't leave any nails protruding into the inside of the house and don't paint the inside. Finally don't place two martin houses close together so the colonies have to compete with each other for food, and be sure to seal the entrance with screen when the martins leave in the fall so English sparrows won't take over the nests.

Construction of the martin house should require only one or two hours. First, saw out the sides and ends from 1x12 stock to the dimensions shown on figure 7-2. Then mark off the entrance holes in the ends and saw them out. Fasten the sides to the ends with #10, 1½-inch wood screws, spaced every 4 inches.

Next, the partitions and floors (from 1x6-inch stock) can be made and put in place. The first floor (bottom) is the only section that is fastened. All the partitions and second floor are "free floating" so that when the bottom is removed for cleaning the partitions and second floor will fall out, allowing them to be cleaned. Bird houses should be cleaned every fall.

Before you put the partitions and floors in place drill two ⅜-inch diameter holes through each partition and through each floor in each compartment to permit venilation and to permit moisture to escape.

Fasten the bottom to the sides with at least

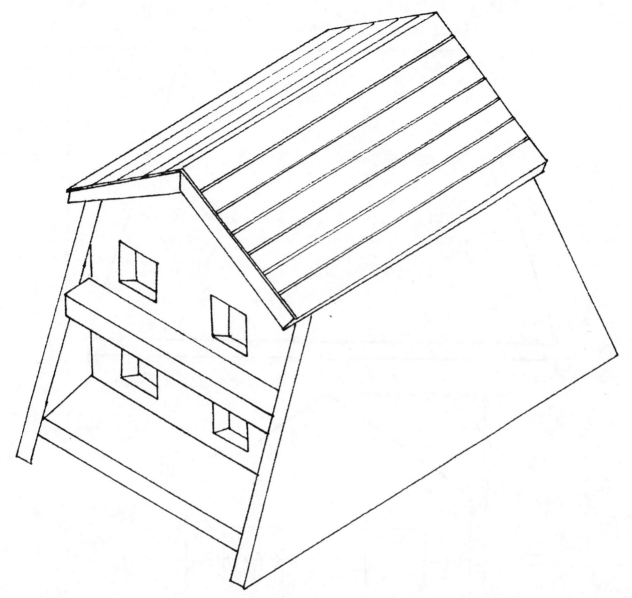

Fig. 7-1 Purple martin house.

three wood screws to each side and two along each end. Finally, add the roof boards, which are made from 1x10-inch stock. The roof boards are sawed to the 14-inch length, and then the edges which will form the peak must be sawed or planed on an angle so the top edges will butt together. The roof is fastened to the ends with #10, 1½-inch wood screws also, three on each end. Finally add the shingles. Asphalt or wood shingles are a good choice.

Be sure to paint the house for appearance and longevity. White is a good color choice as martins apparently find it compatible. Avoid glossy bright reds or greens.

Be sure to put the martin house on a secure platform on a pole that is hinged (like a flagpole) so the house can be taken down for cleaning.

TWO-FAMILY BLUEBIRD HOUSE

Building the bluebird house, which is the next project, will be easy after constructing the

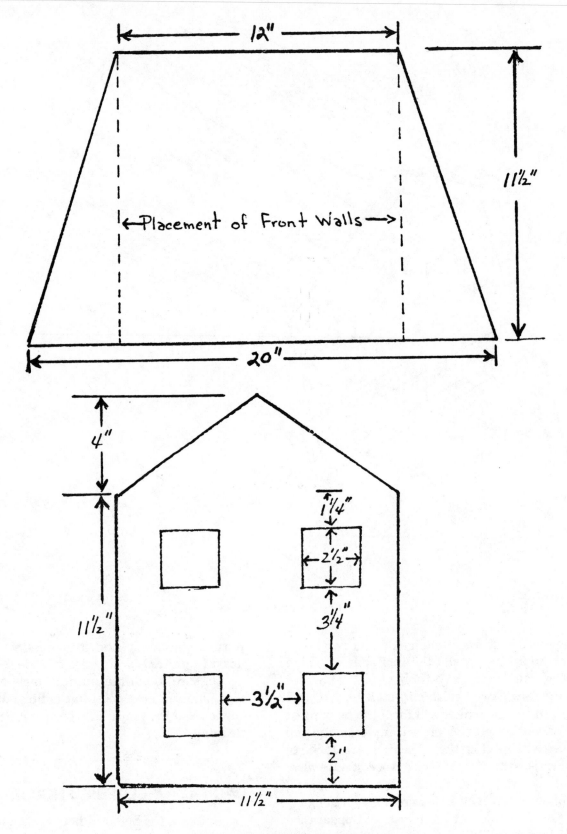

Fig. 7-2 Front and side walls.

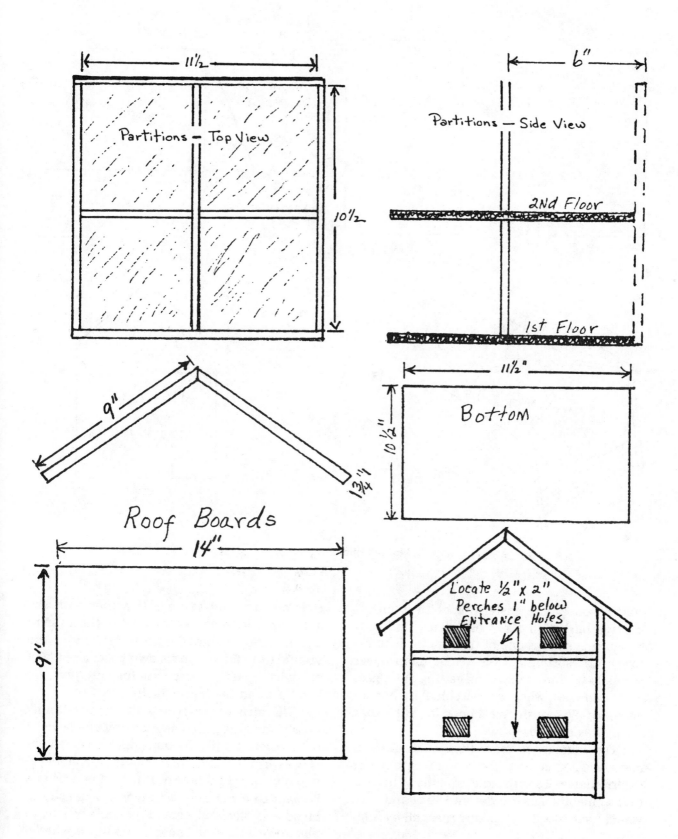

Fig. 7-3 Construction details.

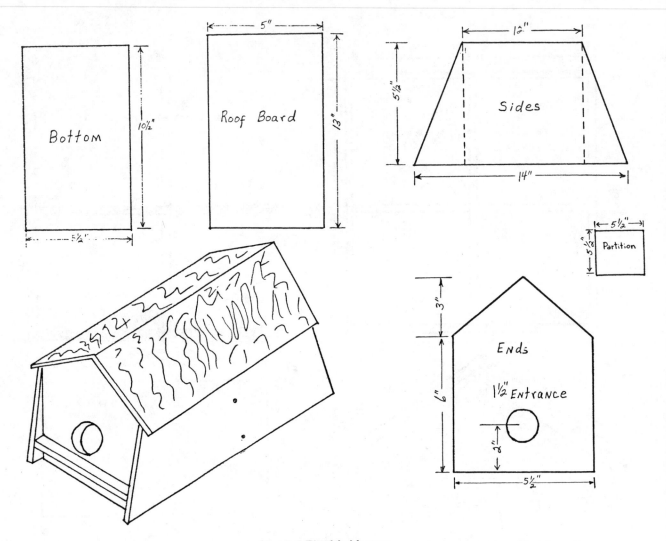

Fig. 7-4 Bluebird house.

martin house. The eastern bluebird is an attractive bird with a sky-blue back and red-brown breast. It is one of the first birds to arrive in the spring, but unlike the robin never seems to be embarrassed by getting caught in a late snowfall; when we see a bluebird here in northern Wisconsin we know for sure that spring has arrived.

The bluebird is more than beautiful. He has a melodious voice and is a fantastic insect exterminator. To equal the amount of insects that a bluebird eats in a day an 180-pound man would have to eat a 10-pound roast all by himself.

Build the bluebird house of ¾-inch wood.

It is cut out and fastened together with the same methods as are given for the martin house. The bluebird house is set low to the ground (3 to 5 feet) on its own post. The top of an existing fence post is a fine location. Be sure to clean the house each year.

This structure can be built as a two-family unit by installing the partition or it can be used by a single family by omitting the partition. However, bluebirds take readily to double occupancy of a bird house. Bluebird houses can be painted a flat gray, green or brown color to blend with the landscape. If possible be sure to place the bluebird house in full-time shade. Lacking full-time shade it should be erected where it will be shaded during the hottest part of the day. This is also true for the wren house which is the next project.

WREN HOUSE

The wren is a well-known, small brown bird with bright eyes and a sharp beak. Properly named the Northern House Wren, this sweet singing bird is most often found around clearings and backyards.

Its very musical voice endears it to most people and unlike most birds it will sing even when the weather is cold and damp and less spirited birds are silent. Contributing to the very musical tones of the wren's song is the

fact that the male and female often sing a duet, with each contributing certain notes to the melody. Many ornithologists believe it is the only bird to practice this delightful behavior.

The wren is highly nest-oriented, and both the male and female build nests. The female nest will be built in a sheltered place such as a bird house and will likely be used for incubating eggs, while the males build a nest just for sleeping. Likewise, when the young birds have left the nest, the female will use it for her nightly slumbers.

Another unusual aspect of wren behavior is the tendency of some species to stay together in family groups with the first generation of

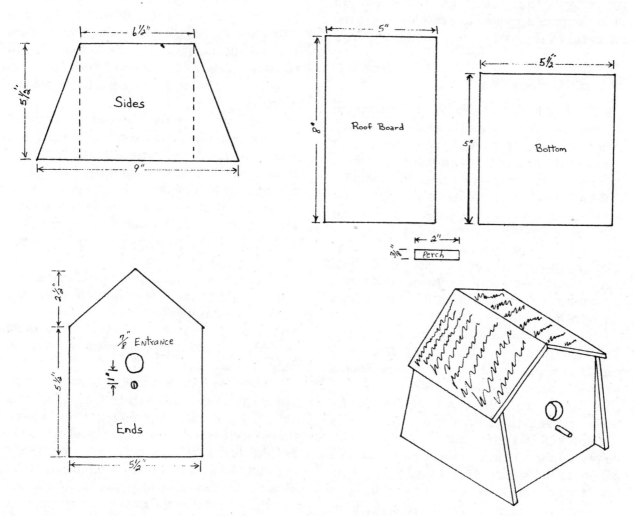

Fig. 7-5 Construction of wren house.

young sometimes helping the parent birds feed the second clutch of chicks.

Backyarders could hardly do more to enhance the pleasure they derive from backyard living than to encourage a family of wrens to move in. The almost non-stop music they deliver will more than pay for the effort extended even if they didn't destroy hundreds of insects every day.

The materials needed for building the wren house can be calculated from figure 7-5. No special tools are needed, and the house is only one room and one story. Be sure to use wood screws for attaching the bottom to the sides so the bottom can be removed for cleaning out the old nest.

Wrens, bluebirds and martins as well as many birds that you might not know are around can be attracted to a certain spot in the backyard by the next project, the bird bath.

THE BIRD BATH

The bird bath is so simple and economical to make that it is within the reach of anyone. Bird baths are important because they offer a safe, convenient location for drinking, which every bird must do several times a day, and for bathing, which many birds do every day. Be sure to place the bird bath where it can be seen from inside the house as you will no doubt derive hours of enjoyment watching your feathered friends cavorting in the water. If possible, locate it away from any concealment so that a prowling cat doesn't make a free lunch from the busy bathers.

Start the construction by locating a suitable container to use for a mold. The mold should be round, about 2 feet in diameter and 1 foot deep. An old wash tub is almost the ideal size. However, if the container you locate doesn't taper to the bottom as a wash tub does you can still use it by lining the inside with heavy paper so that the concrete doesn't adhere to the sides, which would make it almost impossible to remove.

The concrete mixture to use consists of four parts washed mason sand to one part port-

land cement. Add just enough water to make a pliable mix. The concrete should be reinforced with steel also. One of the easiest ways is to simply buy a pound of 8d nails and mix them right up with the concrete.

Do the mixing in a large pail or in a steel wheelbarrow. The project requires less than 2 cubic feet of concrete, which makes it economical to use the premixed product available from lumber yards and other places. Pour the fresh mix into the mold to a depth of 8 inches and then cover the mold with a wet burlap or other shading device so that the sun doesn't shine directly on it and weaken the final product. Watch the hardening process closely however, and when it is set up enough to hold its shape remove the unwanted material to form the cavity as shown in figure 7-6.

Simply carve out the unwanted concrete with a trowel, large knife or even a tablespoon. Discard the unwanted concrete and smooth the sides of the excavation to form a slick surface. Be sure to push any nails back into the concrete.

When you have the excavation completed take a broom handle or wooden dowel about ¾ inch in diameter and push it to the bottom of the tub in the center to open the hole which will be used for piping the water into the bath. Twist the dowel as you insert it. Be sure that no nails are left across the hole at the bottom also. Make certain the concrete is not gripping the dowel, and then simply leave it in the hole until the concrete hardens. To be safe, the concrete should be allowed to harden about five days before it is dumped out of the mold. Even after you remove it from the mold the concrete is very green and care must be taken, as it will chip or crack easily.

When the bath is removed from the mold, insert the pipe in the center hole. This pipe should be ½-inch diameter national pipe thread so it will fit the mister head available for bird baths. Misters are sold by pet shops and other dealers of speciality items. Insert the pipe so the threads will protrude far enough into the cavity that the mister can be screwed on, which requires a minimum of about ½ inch

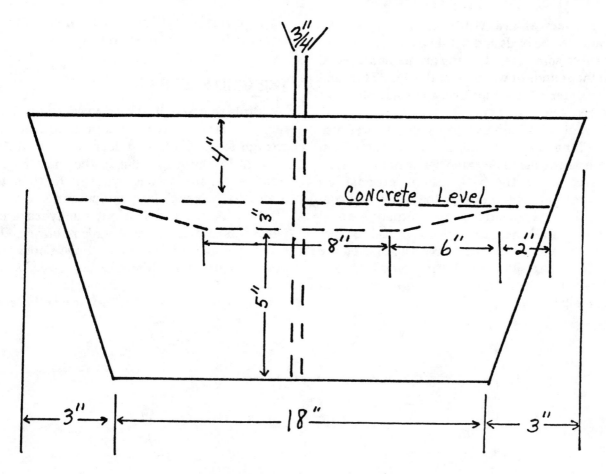

Fig. 7-6 Tub mold for bird bath.

of exposed thread. When this is done, mix up some grout by adding water to pure portland cement until it makes a thick paste. Use this grout to form a water-tight seal around the pipes so that the water from the bath doesn't run down along it. Seal it well because water leaking into this location could lead to ice damage to the bird bath when winter comes.

It is good to let the bird bath set for about two weeks for the concrete to cure so it can be handled with safety. While it is hardening you can be making up a stand. It should be placed at least a foot from the ground with 3 feet being even better.

If you have a stump that you would like to beautify, fine. About all the preparation necessary is to saw the top flat and level and then saw out a V notch so the water pipe can sit under the bath.

As shown, the water pipe will run down the side of the stump and could be buried in the ground between the stump and the water source. An alternative is to use a garden hose and leave it lying on top of the ground where it is available for its customary uses if desired. When the garden hose is connected to the bird bath the faucet is adjusted to a very low flow. The mister is designed to operate on ½ gallon of water per hour, which is less than a dripping faucet might lose.

A stone platform can also be used for supporting the bird bath. In this case it should be built about 3 feet high and 2 feet in diameter. An opening can be left between the stones for the water pipe.

When the bird bath has cured long enough and the stand is done get a helper or two, lift it up and set it in place. Then connect the plumbing. Chances are within an hour it will be found by the birds and within a day it should be used to some extent. Birds are more attracted to the sounds of water than the sight of it, and the water which drips over the side will prove to be a big attraction.

This bird bath can be used in winter also by filling it from a pail. Keep the water from freezing by using an extension cord to get electricity out to the bath. Then purchase an aquarium heater, put it in the water and connect it to the electricity. An alternative would be to use a heat tape such as is used for preventing water pipes from freezing to keep the bath ice free. Birds need water all winter and they will bath on the coldest days if open water is available.

Also very useful during the winter is a bird feeder, which is the next project.

THE BIRD FEEDER

Birds that stay in the northern states during the winter have a tough time finding enough food. If a bird is deprived of food for even a day he might die in the most frigid weather, because food is necessary for them to maintain their high body temperature.

Having fed birds in our backyard and pheasants and other game birds in our woods and fields over the years, we have noticed a few related facts. Although they desire supplemental feeding during the winter, very few of them will become "bums" existing off hand-

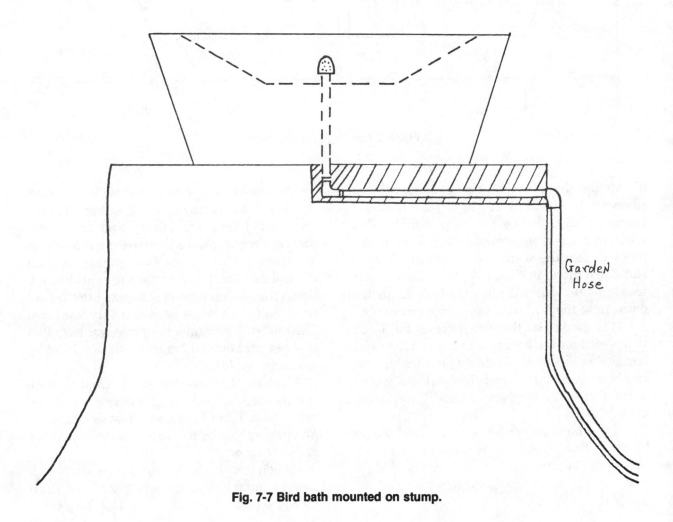

Fig. 7-7 Bird bath mounted on stump.

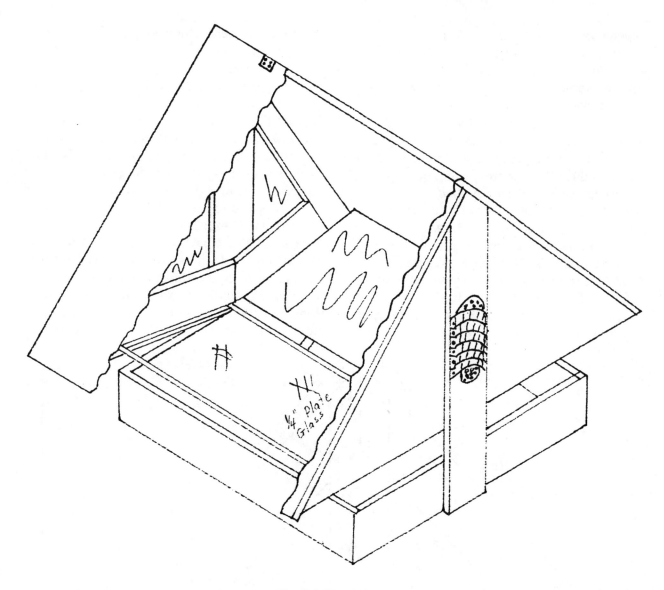

Fig. 7-8 Bird feeder.

outs. Generally they will come to the feeder only when natural food is difficult to find, and they will abandon it as soon as possible. However, since feeding does tend to concentrate the feathered songsters, it is very cruel to start feeding birds and then get tired of it and stop feeding in the middle of the winter.

Feeding birds is sure to deliver two bonuses for people. First, almost every weed seed and insect in proximity to the feeder will be eliminated as the birds look over the area on their way to the feeder. Second, many long winter days will be made more enjoyable by the brilliant colors and graceful movements of the avian diners.

There are two general classes of song birds, and they eat different foods—the insect-eating birds, such as the woodpeckers and brown creepers, and the seed-eating species, such as the sparrows and juncoes. Many of our winter bird friends, such as the chickadees and jay, will dine on both kinds of food, but they seem to prefer protein such as beef suet above any type of seed.

We have found that many of the commercial mixtures sold for feeding birds are overly expensive and contain too many seeds that birds do not like. A good mixture for feeding song birds is 25 percent sunflower seeds, 25 percent hemp, 40 percent millet, and 10 percent cracked corn.

The automatic bird feeder shown will hold enough feed so that you should not need to fill it very often during the winter unless you have a tremendous flock of birds using it. To permit a close check on the contents, one of the slides is made of glass. Long before it gets empty you will notice it and it can be refilled.

It can be used to feed song birds the commercial mixtures of bird feed and it can also be used to feed corn to wild or tame birds, and it can even be used to feed dog food, or whatever is desired by simply adjusting the opening between the slides with a wooden wedge. In addition to seeds, each end of the feeder is equipped with a suet feeder made from a section of wire mesh.

Only the usual tools will be needed for this project, such as a hammer, saw and square. If a protractor is available it also can be utilized.

Start the construction by building two frames as shown in figure 7-9. Use #10, 1½-inch wood screws for fastening the roof frame boards to the upright. The roof brace members are toe nailed to the roof boards with 6d common nails. The 1x1-inch strip is nailed to the brace and roof board with 6d nails also.

When the frames are done, the food tray should be built. As shown in figure 7-10, saw out two 21-inch-long 1x4's and two 22½-inch-long 1x4's. Nail these together as shown with the longer pieces inside the shorter, using 8d

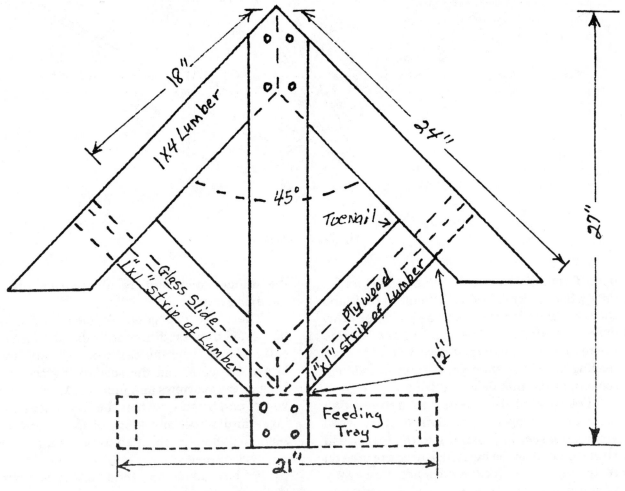

Fig. 7-9 Frame of feeder.

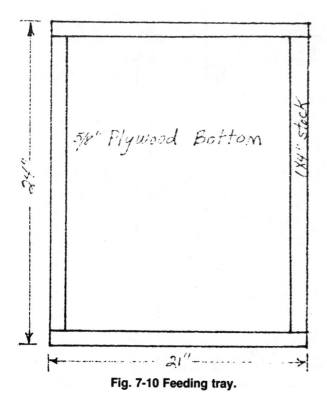

Fig. 7-10 Feeding tray.

common nails. Finally cut out the plywood bottom and nail it to the frame with 6d common nails spaced every 3 inches. When this is done the previously built frames can be fastened to the food tray with #10, 1½-inch wood screws.

The next step is to construct and install the plywood and glass slides, which will automatically feed the seed into the food tray. One slide is made from plywood and is nailed directly to the 1x1-inch strip previously attached to the roof brace. The opposite slide, which can be made from plywood or glass is simply set in place without being nailed. The slide can be moved back and forth to adjust the rate of flow of the food. Gravity prevents the slide from moving out of place and it will also keep the slide against the wood wedge which is placed between the fixed slide and the moveable slide to adjust the opening.

Next, cut out the plywood sections for the roof. One side of the roof is nailed in place, while the other is hinged. The hinged section

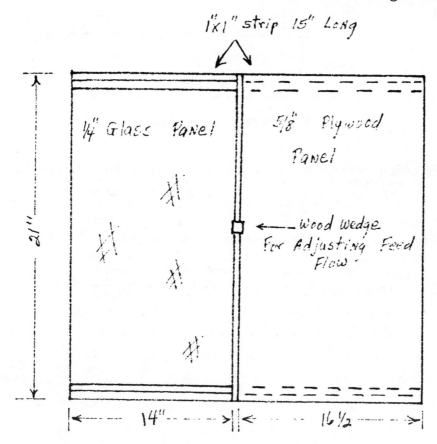

Fig. 7-11 Top view of feeder chute.

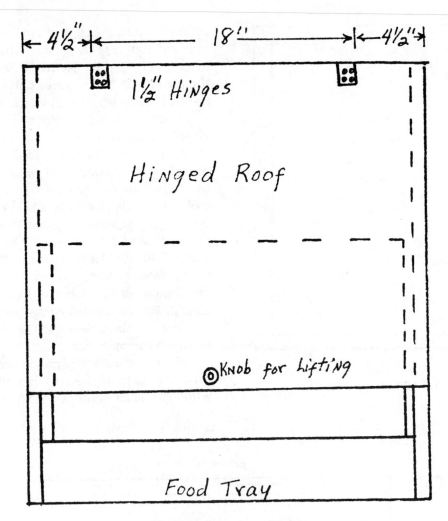

Fig. 7-12 Side view of feeder.

can be opened for adding the feed to the hopper.

The roof should be covered with asphalt shingles or roll roofing, and all bare wood should be painted on the outside. The feeder can be placed close to the ground on wooden cleats for feeding game birds and it can be placed on a picnic table or stump for feeding song birds.

MATERIAL LIST FOR AUTOMATIC FEEDER

1. 20 feet of 1x4 lumber.
2. One 4x8 sheet of exterior plywood.
3. One pane of ¼-inch glass, 14 by 19 inches or to fit. Glass is optional; ½-inch plywood can be substituted.
4. 8 square feet of roofing material.
5. One 8-foot furring strip.
6. Nails, screws and a 5-by-5-inch strip of ⅜-inch wire mesh for suet feeders.

Chapter 13

Lawn Glider and Porch Swing

THE GLIDER

Many years ago I was trying to find out if I would want a career in real estate. Part of my questing was to ride around with a practicing realtor of my acquaintance during business hours. I did not enter the real estate field, but it was interesting to see how people reacted to houses and lawns. I noticed that the variety of houses that are available is almost endless, as is the various tastes of people looking for houses. However, I never saw a couple that didn't react in a positive manner to a large well-kept lawn. A house with this feature might not be long on the market. Add furniture to the lawn and arrange for someone to be relaxing in a porch swing or a lawn glider when the prospects drive by, and a closer look with the chance of a sale is almost assured.

The universal appeal is well founded, be-

cause the smooth, hypnotic quality of the lawn glider is almost the perfect way to relax after a hard day at the office or shop. It takes very little effort to produce motion, and a tired or distraught feeling will disappear like magic as one rocks in comfort in the fresh outdoor air.

The glider that is explained in this chapter will produce that effect, but of course, before we can start rocking we have to build and the first step is to assemble the materials.

Glider Construction

A project of this type can literally be started anywhere, but logically the building would commence by building the frame. First, separate the 8-foot 2x4 legs and make sure they are the same length by sawing if necessary. Before proceeding further lay out and drill a bushing

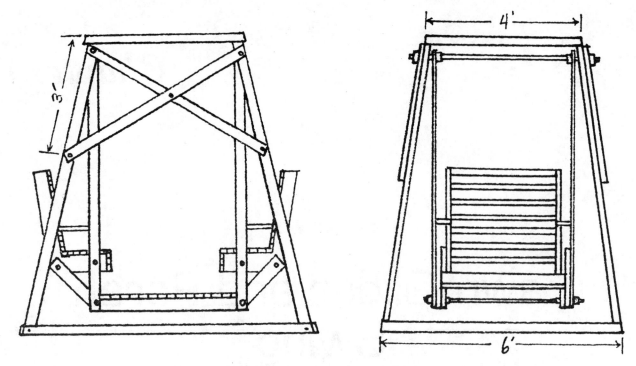

Fig. 8-1 Construction of lawn glider.

hole in each piece. This hole is located 8 inches from the upper end. Notice in figure 8-1 that there are four pivot locations which require bushings. Two of the locations are located at the top of the frame and two at the bottom, at the ends of the foot platform. All of the locations have to be drilled to the correct outside diameter of the bushing. If ⅜ NPT sections are used for bushings, an ¹¹/₁₆-inch drill is correct. If hardened steel bushings are used, they often have a thinner wall and a reduced size drill would be correct.

When all four leg pieces are drilled, proceed by laying out the 1x4 cross braces with the upper ends centered over the bushing holes in the 2x4 legs. Tack each cross brace in place with a 6d nail and then pivot the lower ends to form the correct figure as shown on figure 8-1. Tack the lower ends in place and then drill the bushing holes in the upper ends of the braces to match the holes previously drilled in the legs. The lower brace ends are drilled to ⁵/₁₆-inch diameter. The point where the braces cross is also

drilled to ⁵/₁₆-inch diameter. Use ⁵/₁₆x2-inch carriage bolts to secure these three points. Be sure the round head is placed to the outside.

The next step is to put four ⁷/₁₆x2¾-inch bushings in place at their upper locations. This bushing is placed through the legs and the cross braces. They should fit tightly in the holes. If they don't the bushings should be glued in the holes so they will not turn in the wood when the glider is in use, since any motion at this point would wear the wood away.

When this is done the 6-foot, 9-inch suspension pieces can be added. They also have to be drilled for the bushings (see fig. 8-2). The ¾-inch length bushings are placed in the bores on the suspension pieces after drilling. When this is done the suspension pieces can be hung by placing the upper ⁷/₁₆-inch steel rods in position. Do this by first threading a nut on each end of both rods as far as it will go. Back the nut with a flat washer and then place the ends of the rods through the bushings in the frame. At the outside of the frame a second flat washer is put in

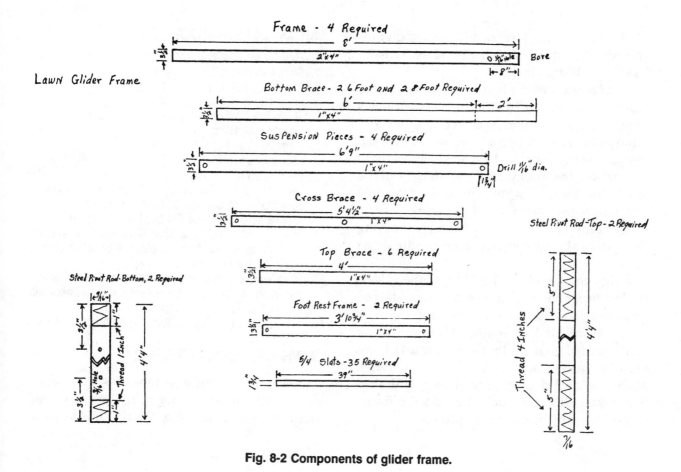

Fig. 8-2 Components of glider frame.

place and then the outside nut is threaded on to a snug (but not tight) position.

Next put the six top and the four lower braces in place and fasten with two #10 wood screws at each location. When this is done the glider frame is fabricated and it can be set upright to wait until the seat and foot rest platforms are made up and put in place.

To build the seats, saw out the backs, sides, braces and arms as shown in figure 8-3. Then assemble the seats by nailing the seat slats in place, using two 6d nails in each end. The arms are fastened with two #10 1½-inch wood screws placed through the seat backs. Later when the seat is put in place on the glider frame the outboard sections of the arms are fastened to the suspension pieces with two of the same screws.

When the seats are finished, lay them aside

and build the foot rest platform. This is a simple procedure which involves cutting out the two foot rest frame pieces and then nailing the 15 slats across them (see fig. 8-2). Again use 6d nails for fastening the slats to the frame.

With all the components made up, place the seats and platform in their correct position on the frames as shown in figure 8-1, and use C clamps to hold them in place while you drill the holes which will be needed.

The lower end of the suspension pieces, the seat brace and the foot rest frame must all be drilled together for the lower bushings. As each location is drilled the bushings can be slid into place. When all four are drilled and the bushings are in place, the lower pivot rods are slid through the bushings and secured in place. Notice that the lower pivot rods are drilled to receive a ³/₁₆x1⅛-inch roll pin on the inboard while the outside is threaded for a $7/16$-inch nut. The inboard flat washer is held in place with the $3/16$x$1\frac{1}{8}$-inch roll pins.

When the lower pivot rods are in place, finish the assembly by drilling $5/16$-inch holes through the suspension piece and seat side and through the seat brace and seat side. Place the designated $5/16$ bolts in place and tighten them to complete the assembly. If the tilt back of the seat is not suitable, adjust it by moving the hole locations in the seat brace. It will also be necessary to remove the #10 wood screws securing the arm to the suspension piece to adjust the tilt.

This completes the building of the glider. Be sure to use a wood sealer on all exposed wood and then paint or varnish it because it will be exposed to all kinds of weather. If desired, a roof can be added to the glider by tacking a 4x4-foot piece of canvas across the top of the frame. Make the roof slightly peaked so it will shed water by nailing a 4-foot 2x4 across the frame before you put the canvas in place.

MATERIAL LIST FOR GLIDER

1. Four 8-foot knot-free 2x4's.
2. Six 8-foot 2x4's.
3. Six 8-foot 1x4's.
4. Eight 4-foot 1x4's.
5. Thirty-five 39-inch 5/4 slats.
6. Eight 3-foot 1x4's.
7. Eight 20-inch 1x4's.
8. Four 20-inch 1x6's.
9. Four $3/16$x$1\frac{1}{8}$ roll pins.
   Twelve $3/8$x$2\frac{1}{2}$-inch carriage bolts, nuts and washers.
   Four $3/8$x2-inch carriage bolts, nuts and washers.
10. Twelve #10, $1\frac{1}{2}$-inch flat head wood screws.
11. Eight $7/16$x$2\frac{3}{4}$-inch and four $7/16$x$3/4$-inch bushings. Sections of $3/8$-inch diameter pipe will be satisfactory if bushings are not available.
12. Four $7/16$x52-inch steel pivot rods threaded and drilled as shown on figure 8-2. It is expected that this work will be done at a machine shop.
13. Six $7/16$-inch nuts and sixteen $7/16$-inch flat washers.

LAWN OR PORCH SWING

One of my earliest memories of my grandmother was of her sitting in the porch swing shelling peas, chatting all the while to a

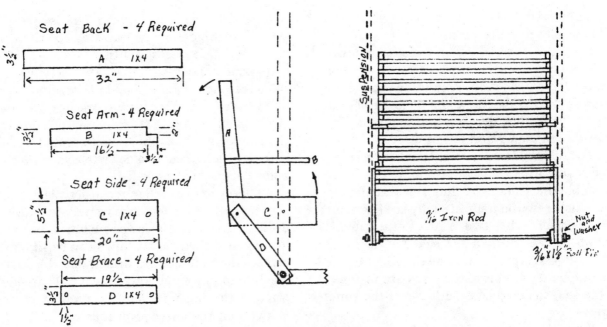

Fig. 8-3 Seat assembly.

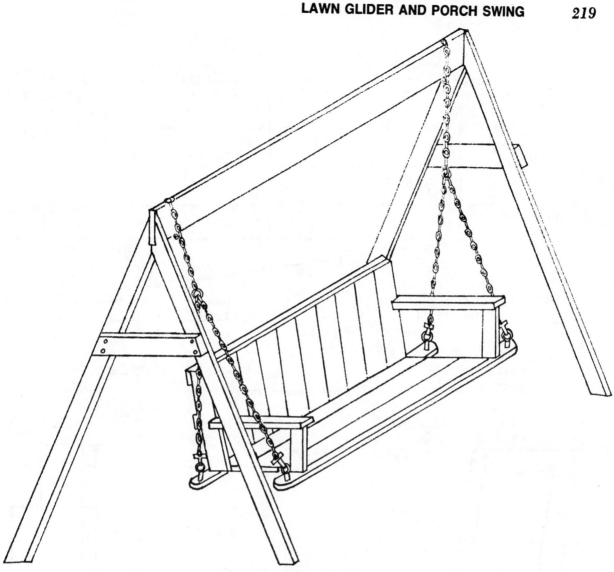

Fig. 8-4 Porch and lawn swing.

neighbor or two. I am sure that she thought of this as a rest between the demands of the household and the farm chores—a snatch of leisure that she richly deserved.

My cousin and I would crank up this porch swing until it would smack against the roof. We finally had to be banished from using it while it still was intact. I never sat in another until I had a place of my own years later.

The lawn swing is worthwhile for anyone, but the youngest and oldest people will appreciate its soothing motion most of all. It is a fine complement to the glider, and is economical and uncomplicated to construct.

Lawn or Porch Swing Construction

The first parts to make up are the 2x4 bed pieces. Use hardwood 2x4's for the bed pieces since they must act as both the frame and suspension points. Saw them off 60 inches long, measure back 1½ inches from each end and drill a ½-inch hole through the end of each as shown in figure 8-5. Next make up the three seat braces shown in figure 8-5 and use 8d finishing nails or #10 3-inch flat head screws to fasten them to the bed pieces to form the seat frame.

Make up the seat back and the arm rest brace and fasten them to the seat frame. Use

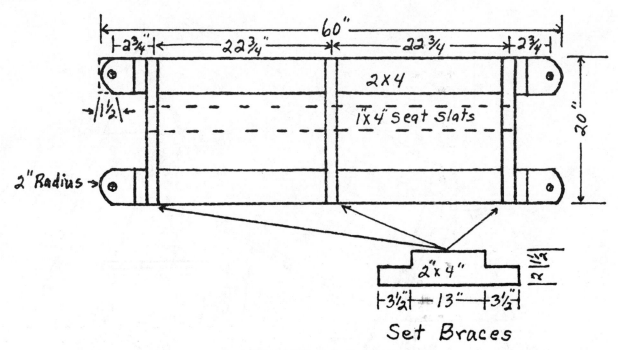

Fig. 8-5 Seat frame.

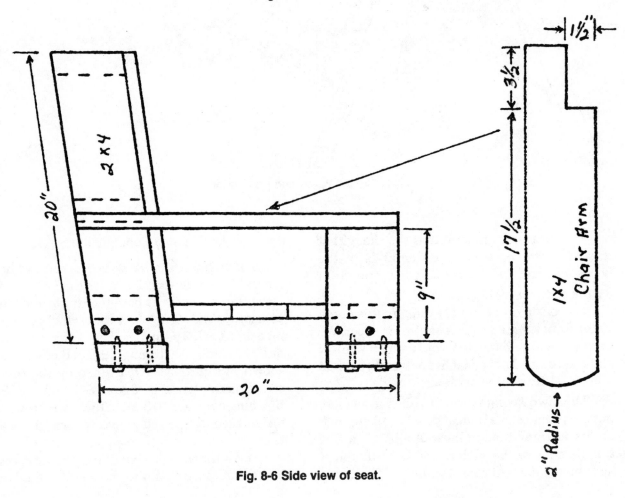

Fig. 8-6 Side view of seat.

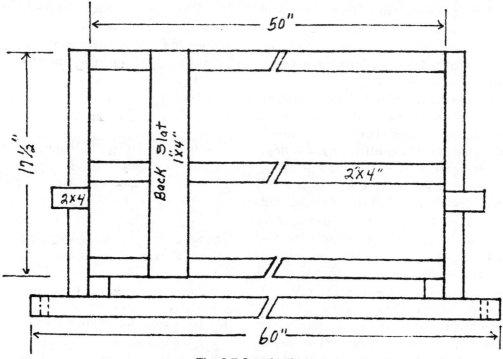

Fig. 8-7 Seat back.

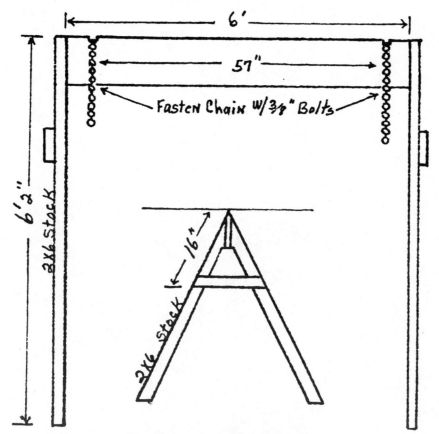

Fig. 8-8 Swing suspension frame.

#10 3-inch flat head screws and fasten the arm and back pieces to both the bed pieces and the seat braces as shown in figure 8-6. This is important because it braces the swing in opposing directions.

At this time the three 50-inch 2x4's that are used to brace the seat back can be made up and installed. Fasten the seat back braces to the seat back pieces with two #10 3-inch flat head wood screws to each joint (see figure 8-7).

Once the frame is built, it can be covered with the 1x4 seat slats. Nail the five 45½-inch 1x4's in place on the seat braces. Then nail the thirteen 18-inch 1x4's to the seat back. Use two 6d coated nails at each joint. The last step can be to cut the seat arms and put them in place. They also are fastened with wood screws.

Be sure to sand all rough edges and cover the wood with at least two coats of a good sealer before you paint it. Any good enamel or outside flat paint will keep it looking good for two to four years.

If you elect to hang the swing on the porch, there is no need to construct the lawn frame shown in figure 8-8. Be sure to hang the swing securely on a framing member of the porch to avoid possible accidents.

MATERIAL LIST FOR LAWN OR PORCH SWING

1. Two 6-foot 2x4's or one 10-foot 2x4.
2. Five 20-foot 2x4's and two 21-foot 2x4's.
3. Three 50-inch 2x4's.
4. Thirteen 18-inch 1x4's.
5. Five 45½-inch 1x4's.
6. Twenty feet of ⅜-inch chain, four 1-inch eye bolts, four chain snaps, 2x⁵/₁₆-inch chain rings.

MATERIAL LIST FOR SWING SUSPENSION FRAME

1. One 8-foot 2x8.
2. Four 8-foot 2x6's.
3. Two 2-foot 2x6's.